JAMES

JAMES MADISON HOOD

Lincoln's Consul to the Court of Siam

George C. Kingston

McFarland & Company, Inc., Publishers
Jefferson, North Carolina, and London

LIBRARY OF CONGRESS CATALOGUING-IN-PUBLICATION DATA

Kingston, George C., 1948–
    James Madison Hood : Lincoln's Consul to the Court
of Siam / George C. Kingston.
      p.   cm.
    Includes bibliographical references and index.

    ISBN 978-0-7864-7194-2
    softcover : acid free paper ∞

    1. Hood, James Madison, 1815–1871.   2. Consuls—United
States—Biography.   3. Lincoln, Abraham, 1809–1865—
Friends and associates.   4. United States—Foreign relations—
Thailand.   5. Thailand—Foreign relations—United States.
6. Legislators—Massachusetts—Biography.   7. Legislators—
Illinois—Biography.   8. Ship captains—Massachusetts—
Somerset—Biography.   9. Shipbuilding—Massachusetts—
Somerset—History—19th century.   10. Businessmen—
United States—Biography.   I. Title.
E415.9.H73K56 2013
973.7092—dc23
[B]   2012051686

BRITISH LIBRARY CATALOGUING DATA ARE AVAILABLE

On the cover: *photograph* James Madison Hood, center, bearded,
wearing a white captain's uniform, surrounded by members of the
Court of Siam and of the American community in Siam (albumen
print by Francis Chit, circa 1867); *background* detail from a general
map of the East Indies, showing the Kingdom of Siam (Library
of Congress)

Manufactured in the United States of America

McFarland & Company, Inc., Publishers
  Box 611, Jefferson, North Carolina 28640
   www.mcfarlandpub.com

To Jean, the love of my life.

Acknowledgments

I first want to thank my wife and editor, Jean Delaney, for her support, encouragement and involvement in the writing of this book. Without her, it would never have been written. I also want to thank Diane Goodwin, the director of the Somerset Historical Museum, who first suggested that I turn the story of Captain Hood into a book, and who generously spent many hours going through both her own museum's collections and those of the Taunton Historical Society.

I especially want to thank Holly Atheridge and her father, Ronald Gilmore, for introducing me to the fascinating James Madison Hood.

I appreciate the generous help provided by Jean Elliott, archivist, at the National Archives Conte Office in Pittsfield, Massachusetts, and the staff at the National Archives in Waltham, Massachusetts; the Sycamore Illinois Historical Society; the Joiner Historical Room at the Sycamore Library; Kenneth M. Grossi and his staff at the Oberlin College Archives in Oberlin, Ohio; the Old Colony Historical Society in Taunton; and, the American Antiquarian Society in Worcester, Massachusetts. Special thanks go to the East Longmeadow Public Library for cheerfully handling my many interlibrary loans.

I also appreciate the support of my writing coach, Sylvia Rosen, and the members of her Friday morning creative writing class.

Table of Contents

Preface

This is a book about a man who flourished as a self-promoting entrepreneur in an era when fortunes were made and lost, seemingly overnight, and an enterprising man could go as far as his abilities and connections could take him. Captain James Madison Hood was a Yankee trader who sailed and built ships, made laws, ran factories, and represented the United States as consul at Bangkok, Siam, half a world away from his hometown of Somerset, Massachusetts. He was far from perfect, but all who knew him were struck by his cheerful, convivial nature, which, combined with his shrewd Yankee insight, saw him through the many peaks and valleys of his life.

I was first introduced to Captain Hood by a descendant of one of his brothers who knew that he was mentioned in *Anna and the King of Siam*,[1] and asked me to find out more about him. In doing so, I met the director of the Somerset Historical Society, who did not know of his consular career but did know of him as a prominent local ship builder. I then discovered his legislative career and decided that his rich, multi-faceted life deserved a fuller treatment.

This book is meant to be a factual biography of James Madison Hood, but because he left no personal papers, I have had to reconstruct his life from newspapers, local records, legal documents, diplomatic correspondence, and the written testimony of those with whom he came into contact. Where I lacked specific information on an event in his life, I have said so and in some cases speculated about probable happenings based on the best information available to me. I accept responsibility for any errors that may have crept into this book.

People in mid-nineteenth century America were no different from people today, but they lived in a very different world. In tracing the career of Captain James Madison Hood, it will be important to bear in mind that time and distance were different dimensions then, that money had a different value, and that personal connections meant everything. Even after the introduction of the telegraph in the first half of the century, news was disseminated primarily by handwritten letters and printed newspapers. Government was smaller and bureaucratic oversight, while present, was simpler and easier to evade. America's diplomatic entanglements abroad were minimal, and her interests in Asia were just beginning. This was the world in which Captain Hood operated.

Because so much of his life was involved with the sea, nautical terms play a significant part in this book. The language of the sea was precise, and to a landsman, somewhat esoteric. In describing the various vessels that played a part in the life of James Madison Hood, I have used the terminology of the nineteenth century. Sea-going vessels were described principally by their rig, that is, the arrangement of their masts and sails, and their size, expressed as tonnage, with perhaps a modifier to describe their hull type. Thus, the *Raven* was a clipper ship of 711 tons.[2] The term clipper refers to her hull, which was narrow and sharp at both ends, while the term ship refers to the fact that she was square rigged and had at least 3 masts, and the tonnage places her at the smaller end of her class.

This terminology was not a mere formality. When a vessel was sighted at sea, her rig and approximate size could be discerned at a great distance. These characteristics, combined with a knowledge of what ships were expected in the area and other details such as the color of the hull and the cut of the sails were often enough to identify it, or at least to narrow the possibilities. At a time when the only means of communication at sea was visual, a report of a "three masted schooner with a white hull" sailing northward off Cape Charles might be the only way an owner or shipper could determine the whereabouts or condition of his vessel.

Tonnage originally referred to the weight of cargo that a vessel was capable of carrying. Since actually measuring the capacity of a given vessel was complicated due to the complex geometry of a hull, simple formulas developed over time. By the era of this book, the tonnage of a vessel was calculated as:

$$\text{Tonnage} = \frac{(\text{length} - (\text{beam} \times 3/5)) \times \text{beam} \times (\text{beam}/2)}{95}$$

The length of a vessel being the distance from the stem to the stern-post on the top deck and the beam the widest point on the top deck. Thus a 10 ton sloop might be 30 feet long and 9 feet wide, while a 1,000 ton ship might be 160 feet long and 38 feet wide.[3]

The problem with this calculation was that it estimated the depth of the hull as being half the beam, which, since ships were taxed according to their tonnage, encouraged merchants to order narrow but deep vessels so as to underestimate their actual capacity, and the formula was changed after the 1850s. However, it is the calculation that was used for almost all the vessels discussed in this book.

In the nineteenth century, there were a wide variety of rigs in use on sailing ships. A square rigged sail was one that hung from a horizontal yard perpendicular to the length of the vessel. A fore-and-aft rigged sail was one that was fastened to a mast and whose base was extended by a boom backwards along the length of the vessel. The most common rigs are defined below.

Brig: a vessel with two square rigged masts.

Bark or Barque: a vessel with three or more masts, the aftermost mast rigged fore-and-aft and all others square rigged.

Barquentine: a vessel with three or more masts, the foremast square rigged and all others rigged fore and aft.

Lighter: a barge used to transport freight or passengers to and from an anchored vessel.

Ship: a vessel with three or more square rigged masts.

Sloop: a vessel with one fore-and-aft rigged mast.

Schooner: a vessel with two or more fore-and-aft rigged masts, the foremast being no taller than any other mast.

There were, of course many variations on these basic rigs, the study of which has been the subject of entire books.

The first commercially successful steamboat is generally acknowledged to be Robert Fulton's *North River Steamboat of Clermont,* which went into service on the Hudson River in 1807.[4] The first sea-going steamer in America, the *Savannah,* was launched in 1819, but sailing ships, which were faster, more reliable, and cheaper to build and operate, continued to dominate the sea lanes up until the Civil War.[5] During the times covered by this book, steamships did continue to spread around the world, especially for shorter voyages or mail packet service, where time was of the essence. When Captain Hood was running his shipyard, he could travel to New York City via Long Island Sound on a regularly scheduled line of steamers.[6] By the time he arrived in Siam, there was regular, though not scheduled, steamship service between Singapore and Bangkok.[7] As far as we know, Captain Hood was never the master of a steamship and he died just as the era of steam navigation on the high seas was getting underway.

Another problem in writing about the mid-nineteenth century is how to convey the value of money. It is always difficult to understand what real value a sum of money represented in former times. In the mid-nineteenth century, the standard of living, even for the affluent, was very different than what it is today. So, to compare the wages of a laborer in 1850, when his rent was minimal and 80 or 90 percent of his income went to the purchase of basic foodstuffs, to those of a laborer in 2010, when rents are relatively much higher and even those earning minimum wage have a standard of living that includes things like cable TV, Internet service, and cell phones, is unrealistic. There are least three accepted methods of comparing the historical value of money. These are wage comparisons, consideration of the sum as a percentage of Gross Domestic Product, and comparison of land or commodity prices. For some baseline numbers, consider that James Hood's salary of $2,000 a year as U.S. consul at Bangkok was equal to that of a major general in the U.S. Army. Today, a major general earns around $170,000 a year, including a housing allowance. One thousand dollars in liquid assets or real estate in 1865 was roughly equivalent to $160,000 today, and even more in 1850 before the inflation caused by the Civil War. Comparisons for this book were made using the calculators developed by Lawrence H. Officer and Samuel H. Williamson of the University of Chicago and provided on their website, MeasuringWorth.com.[8]

The unit of currency in Siam was the tical, equivalent to the modern baht. In the 1860s it was worth about $0.60 in Mexican silver dollars, the accepted international currency in Southeast Asia at that time. A tical was the equivalent of 15 grams of silver.[9]

When quoting from the dispatches of Captain Hood and the diaries of the Rev. Dan Beach Bradley, I retained their grammar, spelling, abbreviations, and punctuation, except where necessary to clarify their meaning, where my additions are placed in square brackets.

1

The U.S. Consul at Bangkok

U.S. consulate
Bangkok, Sept 13, 1865

Sir,

I have the honor to inform you that I arrived at my post of duty yesterday. I immediately called upon his Excellency the Phra Khlang, Minister for Foreign Affairs, presented your despatch to him notifying His Excellency of my appointment as U.S. consul for Siam, also my commission in accordance with your instructions.

His Excellency received me with great cordiality and immediately gave the necessary permission to act as consul, but in relation to the matter of the Exequatur, preferred that I should address his Majesty on the subject and receive it from him. The suggestion of his Excellency on this subject has been attended to.

The inventory containing the list of books, papers, etc. constituting the archives of the consulate and all government property is herewith enclosed. In my next communication I will give the department some facts in relation to this consulate which I trust will receive due attention.

I am Sir,
Your Obedient Servant
J.M. Hood
U.S. consul

Hon F.W. Seward
Assistant Secretary of State
Washington, D.C.[1]

Captain James Madison Hood, the new United States consul at Bangkok, stood on the deck of the Siamese steamer *Chao Phraya* in the relative cool of the early morning of Saturday, September 9, 1865, as it finally crossed the bar of its namesake river and entered the independent Kingdom of Siam, the country now known as Thailand. It was the end of the rainy season, but the hot and steamy voyage up the gulf of Siam from Singapore had done nothing to dampen his enthusiasm. His appointment by President Lincoln to this consulship was the capstone of a long career in business and politics, and Captain Hood was proud to represent his country as the senior, if only, American representative there.

Captain Hood was 50 years old, short, a little over five feet tall, and stout, weighing something more than 200 pounds. On this important morning, he wore his best consular uniform, even if the dark blue, double-breasted jacket did bring forth copious perspiration in the tropical heat. He was determined to make a good first impression, not only on the Siamese government and the representatives of the other Western powers, but also on the American community in Bangkok, of which he intended to assume the leadership.

It had been five long months since Captain Hood and his young wife, Sarah, sailed from New York City on the barquentine *Amaranth*, just days before President Abraham Lincoln was assassinated. Captain Hood had heard the terrible news as the ship sat off Sandy Hook in the lower bay waiting for a fair wind. He could only speculate on what changes to foreign policy would occur under the new administration and hope that Secretary of State William Seward retained his position under the new president, Andrew Johnson. The voyage they were beginning took the Hoods down the middle of the Atlantic Ocean, around Africa and across the Indian Ocean to Singapore, and there would be few chances to get any news until they arrived there. Although the *Amaranth* was a roomy vessel and the Hoods traveled in the first class cabin, the journey was tedious.

In Singapore, the Hoods left the *Amaranth*, which was headed to Hong Kong, and had to wait for the Siamese steamer *Chao Phraya,* which provided regular passenger and mail service to Bangkok. While they waited, they probably stayed with Isaac Stone, the United States consul in that city, giving Captain Hood the opportunity to learn the latest news of the area. Now, Captain Hood was finally in Siam and eager to take up his duties.

Although a United States minister, Townsend Harris, had secured a commercial treaty with Siam giving the United States most favored nation status in 1856,[2] little trade had developed between the two countries. Even that came to a halt with the onset of the Civil War in 1861, when Confederate raiders roamed the seas, seizing and burning Union merchant ships. During that period, the United States was represented by part-time consuls who were, with one exception, either missionaries or traders already resident in the country, and who financed the consulate through the fees that they collected for their services. They carried out their commercial responsibilities when American ships did appear, and adjudicated disputes between American citizens residing in the country, but did little else. Captain Hood was the first full-time salaried United States consul to be sent to Siam, and he felt that he had a mission to re-establish the reputation of the United States as a major power, ready to expand its trade with Asia, now that the financial drain of the war and the threat from Confederate commerce raiders had ended. He felt that it was up to him, personally, to demonstrate that the U.S. must be treated with the dignity and respect given to the other great powers in the area, England and France.

The *Chao Phraya* had anchored some three miles off shore the day before and sent a boat to the Customs House at Paknam, near the mouth of the river, from which a messenger was sent to ask the king's permission for them to ascend to the city. From the anchorage, Captain Hood could see the golden spire that capped the ghostly white pagoda called Phra Samut Chedi, which guarded the river's entrance. Now, on the morning flood tide, the ship proceeded upstream and into the teeming city of Bangkok. The river was lined with densely packed houseboats that sheltered the majority of the city's 400,000 inhabitants. Captain Hood could observe the daily routine of these families as they washed, cooked, and traded among themselves. Behind the houseboats rose the more substantial structures of wood and stone that housed the prosperous Thai and Chinese merchants and the small European community.

We have no accounts of Captain Hood's arrival in the city of Bangkok, but news of him would have been sent from Paknam, and we can speculate that he was met by representatives of the Siamese government and the American community. The arrival of the *Chao Phraya* was always an event that attracted foreign residents of the city, as the steamer was the only regular source of news from the outside world. Among the American merchants who may have been on the dock was the acting vice-consul, George W. Virgin, a trader and longtime Bangkok resident, whom Hood would have looked on with suspicion, knowing that Virgin coveted the consulship for himself and might be happy to see Hood fail.

Group photograph, Siam, ca. 1867. Based on descriptions and a resemblance to his nephew, William P. Hood, one concludes Captain Hood is probably the short, stout man in the white captain's uniform (1). The young Siamese man near the center is Prince Chulalongkorn (2), and Dr. Dan Beach Bradley is the man with the full beard behind the prince (3). The other individuals are unknown (albumin print by Francis Chit, also known as Luang Akani Naruemitr, Siam, ca. 1867, owned by G. Kingston).

With Virgin may have been John Hassett Chandler, an ex-missionary and mechanic turned merchant, who also had vested interests in the operation of the consulate. In a separate group may have been some of the leading members of the protestant missions, including the Rev. Dr. Dan Beach Bradley, who was the publisher of the local English language newspaper, the *Recorder*. Also present may have been the British consul, Thomas George Knox, and a member of the French delegation, the French consul, M. Gabriel Aubaret, having left to return to France just a few days before Captain Hood's arrival. Along with these officials, it is possible that Mrs. Anna Leonowens, the young English widow who was the governess of the royal children and confidential secretary to the king, was on the dock to get a look at this latest envoy from the United States. Her memoirs were later popularized by Margaret Landon under the title *Anna and the King of Siam*.[3]

Beside Captain Hood stood his young wife, Sarah, who had hoped to make this journey with her friend from Illinois, Mrs. Tucker. Unfortunately, for political reasons, Mr. Tucker had been unable to obtain the appointment as Captain Hood's marshal, and Sarah had to endure the long voyage in the presence of strangers. Just one month short of her 22nd birthday, she was a girl of the prairies and must have been apprehensive about this strange place to which her husband had brought her. The heat, the smells, and the throngs of Siamese would have assaulted her senses. Perhaps she smiled at the missionary wives in the hope of a kind glance and some civilized conversation.

As he stepped off the ship, Captain Hood was confident and had high expectations for a prosperous and successful tenure. He was an experienced merchant ship master, ship builder, land speculator, and politician. He had made and lost at least two fortunes and most recently had rebuilt his finances in the newly developing state of Illinois. This consular appointment was yet another step upwards in his career. Although he had never previously been to Asia, much less Siam, Captain Hood was acquainted with the ways of consuls from his many years of sailing between New England and the Caribbean islands, and he knew that the post could be lucrative. More than just a chance to make money, however, he saw the office as a prestigious appointment that would place him at the head of the American community in this distant and exotic land.

An examination of Hood's first dispatch from Bangkok tells much about his attitude. Although he headed it properly as being from the U.S. Consulate at Bangkok, in the body he referred to himself, incorrectly, as the United States consul for Siam, inferring that he saw himself as the United States diplomatic representative to the kingdom. In fact, U.S. consuls were always referred to by the city of their posting rather than the country in which they were stationed, and they were strictly forbidden from acting in any diplomatic capacity whatever without the explicit permission of the president.[4] Yet two days after his arrival, Hood presented himself as a United States diplomatic representative directly to the Siamese foreign minister, the phra khlang, who was a royal prince. The phra khlang granted him permission to act as consul, and he immediately agreed to seek an audience with First King Mongkut, to request his exequatur.[5] This was the formal document issued by the Siamese government officially recognizing his status as United States consul and giving him official permission to act as such.[6] This was the diplomatic equivalent of the U.S. consul at London requesting an audience with Queen Victoria. Both acts were in direct contradiction to the consular regulations, even if they were in accordance with local customs. This was Siam, however, a country where the king regularly met with ordinary foreigners, even as he distanced himself from his people.

Although the dispatch says that he arrived on September 12, the local English language newspaper, *The Recorder*, reported that Hood had actually disembarked in the city on Saturday, September 9.[7] He arranged temporary lodgings in the Presbyterian mission compound before presenting himself to the Siamese authorities on the following Monday. It was not until Wednesday, September 13, that he officially took up his duties and, with George W. Virgin, the vice-consul whom he was replacing, went through the property, books and records of the consulate.[8]

Virgin, an American merchant with many years of experience in Siam, had taken on the running of the consulate upon the abrupt departure of the previous appointee, Aaron J. Westervelt, two years before. Westervelt was the only previous non–Bangkok resident to hold the post. He had been driven to resign it by pressure from both factions in the American community, the merchants and the missionaries. Virgin had hoped to be confirmed in the office, a hope that Hood's arrival dashed.[9] Immediately, Hood grasped that something was wrong. The consulate was the back room of George Virgin's general store and rum shop. It had no proper furniture and the records and papers were stored in a haphazard and insecure fashion. From Virgin, Hood quickly discovered that the expense of running a proper consulate, one in keeping with the dignity of a great nation like the United States, was going to be far in excess of his salary and that, in spite of his warm welcome by the foreign minister, the United States was considered by the Siamese government to be a second-rate power behind France and Britain. This was due in part to the fact that during the Civil War, the United States had not been able to send any warships into these waters, while the French had deployed a squadron of them in support of their invasion of Cochin China, today's Vietnam, and the British maintained several in India, Burma, and Singapore.[10] He probably had some idea of this state of affairs before he left the United States, having had an opportunity to meet with Westervelt in New York City, but the Department of State undoubtedly had painted a rosier picture of the post. To see the situation for himself in his first week in the country must have been a shock. These observations were the facts that he promised to bring to the attention of the Department of State in his next communication.[11]

The dispatch was short and was written in haste in order to make sure that it could be taken to Singapore on the return trip of the steamer that had brought him. One of the drawbacks of a post like Bangkok was that it usually took five or six months for a round-trip exchange of dispatches with the Department of State in Washington, D.C. The telegraph would not reach Siam until several years after Hood's departure, so that, while he strove to keep the department informed of his actions and needs, any response was necessarily delayed to the point of uselessness. He was on his own.

When Captain Hood arrived, the independent Kingdom of Siam was ruled by Phra Bat Somdet Phra Poramenthramaha Mongkut Phra Chom Klao Chao Yu Hua, known in the West as King Mongkut, and later designated as Rama IV. Mongkut was an outward looking and progressive monarch who had opened the country to foreign trade and who wanted United States support to keep his country from being nibbled away by the British in Burma on the one hand and the French in Indochina on the other. Although the king was interested in expanding trade and diplomatic relationships with the United States, he had not been impressed with the former representatives of that country. Up to this time, the only real diplomatic contacts between Siam and the United States had been through special ministers, like Edmund Roberts, who visited to negotiate treaties and then departed.[12] The resident consuls, who lived in the capital, had no diplomatic powers and could only forward requests from the Siamese government to the Department of State for action. The first United States consul had been a Presbyterian missionary, Stephen Mattoon, who was viewed with suspicion by the devoutly Buddhist Siamese government. Mattoon was followed by a series of more or less disreputable American businessmen and traders, Chandler, Westervelt, and Virgin, who were more interested in making money than representing the United States.[13] Therefore, the king was only cautiously optimistic when Hood arrived as the first salaried United States consul, forbidden to trade and seemingly with no ulterior motives.

Over time, their relationship strengthened, with Hood providing information and advice to the palace and the Siamese government working to encourage American trade.

Who was this man, who traveled halfway around the world to an Asian backwater that he knew little about? He had started as the teenage captain of a tiny costal trading sloop and survived storms at sea and economic crises on land. By the time he reached Bangkok, he had developed into a shrewd businessman and politician, but the journey was long with many detours along the way. It was a life that could only have been lived in 19th century America, and it was lived by an American original, James Madison Hood.

2

Somerset, Massachusetts

The road to Southeast Asia started in southeastern Massachusetts. James Madison Hood was born in the town of Somerset, in Bristol County, on Saturday, January 14, 1815,[1] to a seafaring family. He was the tenth of twelve children of Capt. John Hood, a merchant master. His mother, Mary Ann Bowers, also came from a family of captains and ship-builders in that tightly knit community.[2]

The year 1815 marked the end of the War of 1812 between the United States and Great Britain. The Battle of New Orleans was fought just one week before James's birth. In June, the Battle of Waterloo, in Belgium, brought an end to the Napoleonic Wars. For Rhode Island and southeastern Massachusetts, the end of hostilities marked the beginning of a new era of prosperity based on the sea. Even before the war broke out, foreign trade had been suffering due to the Embargo Act of 1807 which forbade American ships to leave port. This was superseded by the Non-Intercourse Act of 1809 which forbade trade with England, France, and their colonies. During the war, the British Navy blockaded most major American ports, including Providence, Rhode Island, which effectively shut down almost all shipping from the Taunton River.[3] With the withdrawal of the British blockade, the New England states were able to resume trade with the southern states, the Caribbean, and the rest of the world. There was a demand for ships and the men who sailed them. John Hood was such a man, and he named his tenth child for President James Madison, who had successfully brought the war to an end.

The dutiable imports at the port of Bristol, Rhode Island, increased by a factor of eight from 1814 to 1815. Then, to promote domestic trade, President Monroe signed the Navigation Act of 1817. This act permanently closed the coastwise trade to foreign vessels by requiring that all

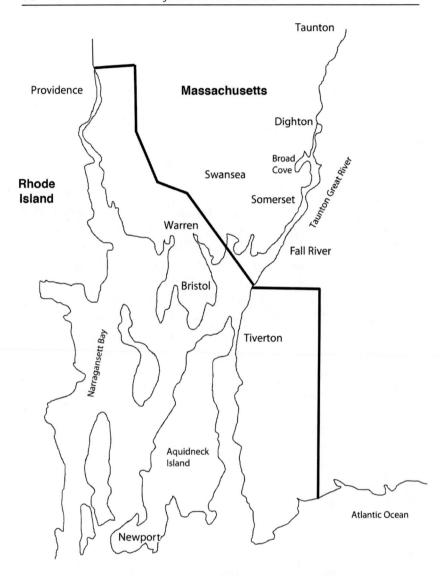

Southeastern Massachusetts and Rhode Island

cargo between American ports must be carried in ships entirely owned by American citizens or belonging to West Indian merchants. The duties on vessels licensed for coastwise trade were made eight times higher for foreign vessels than for American owned ones. This provided a huge boost for American shipping.[4]

Bristol County, which covers southeastern Massachusetts, looks southwards towards the Atlantic Ocean. Its principal rivers, the Taunton, Westport, and Acushnet, connected its towns to the coast more readily than its roads connected them to Boston. The county seat is Taunton, and the two principal cities are Fall River, which was a textile and iron manufacturing center, and New Bedford, a major whaling port. The county is bordered to the west by Rhode Island and shares a cultural heritage with that state. Both were settled by men and women who chafed at the heavy handed government of the Massachusetts Bay Colony and left to gain a measure of religious and personal freedom. Residents of Bristol County were more likely to travel to Providence than to Boston, and the boundary between the two states remained under dispute until well into the 19th century.

Somerset is situated across from the city of Fall River on the western bank of Taunton Great River where it empties into Mount Hope Bay. This bay, in turn, connects with Narragansett Bay in Rhode Island. The Taunton River is navigable to Somerset and a deep water channel swings close to shore along the town's waterfront. The area occupied by the town was originally known as the Shawmut Lands, and was purchased in 1677 by a group of thirty-three men from Plymouth led by Increase Robinson. Among the early settlers were the Eddy, Chase, and Slade families, which were still prominent during Captain Hood's lifetime. Somerset was originally a part of the town of Swansea, which was founded by Baptists from the town of Swansea in Wales who were seeking freedom to practice their religion. Somerset was set apart and received its own charter as a town in 1790.[5]

The origins of the Hood family of Somerset are obscure. They may be connected to the Hoods of Lynn, Massachusetts, through a Joseph Hood, who died in Newport, Rhode Island, in 1745. He was the son of Nathaniel Hood, who was the grandson of the original emigrant, John Hood, who came from Halstead, Essex, England, to Cambridge, Massachusetts, as early as 1638. Although the family genealogy asserts that Joseph had no issue, it does say that he was married and it is possible that he was the ancestor of the Somerset family as the records for this period are incomplete.[6] By 1790, there were also four Hood households in Taunton, headed by Joseph, Benjamin, Benjamin Landon, and Samuel, none of whom can be directly linked to the Somerset Hoods.[7]

The first known member of James Madison Hood's family was his grandfather, Noble Hood, who was born on August 16, 1748.[8] Noble was from Swansea, which at that time included the future town of Somerset. He served briefly as a private in Capt. Peleg Peck's company of the First Bristol Regiment of the Massachusetts Militia, commanded by Col. Thomas Carpenter III, during the American Revolution.[9] The British had occupied Newport, Rhode Island, and the rest of Aquidneck Island on December 7, 1776. While they remained there for approximately three years, Tiverton, which occupied the mainland across a narrow strait in the Sakonnet River from Newport, became a place of asylum for Americans fleeing from British occupation, and the town became a mustering point for Colonial forces who were assembling to drive the British off the island. Col. Carpenter distinguished himself for bravery in an attack on the British on August 29, 1778, which was part of an effort to coordinate American ground units with a French fleet to regain the island. Unfortunately, the French ran into a severe storm and had to divert to Boston, causing the failure of the campaign. The British occupation of Newport, combined with the presence of the British 20-gun frigate, HMS *Rose*, under Captain James Wallace, effectively blockaded both Providence and the towns along the Taunton river, closing off almost all trade for three years. The British finally withdrew in October 1779 after destroying their fortifications around Newport and the Beavertail Lighthouse on Conanicut Island south of Jamestown, Rhode Island.

On July 25, 1780, a report was received in Newport that the British commander-in-chief, Sir Henry Clinton, who was in New York City, was planning an attack on Rhode Island with 10,000 men. Clinton actually loaded 6,000 British troops onto transports at Throgs Neck in the Bronx but changed his mind when he realized that Washington was threatening Kingsbridge from the Hudson Highlands and disembarked the men at Whitestone, on Long Island, on July 31. In the interim, the Americans in Rhode Island scrambled to strengthen their defenses and activated two regiments of militia from Rhode Island and one from Massachusetts. On August 4, the company in which Noble was enrolled was called up to respond to the alarm and marched to Tiverton, Rhode Island, which is just south of Fall River. The men were assembled from several Swansea companies and placed under Captain Peck when the other militia officers refused to serve. When the news that General Clinton had called off the attack was confirmed, the men were sent home after serving only 6 days.[10]

Noble was a merchant and ship owner. In the winter of 1772, when he was only 24 years old, he brought the sloop *Industry*, of which he was the mate, back to Newport from North Carolina after its master, Nathan Simmons, was washed overboard in a gale.[11] From that time on he sailed as a captain. Noble married Hannah Perry and they had five children: Lydia, John, William, Martha, and Noble Jr. John Hood, the father of James, was born in the midst of the American Revolution on March 23, 1775.[12] His brother, Noble Hood, Jr., married Sarah Booshee on August 9, 1804, in Swansea.[13] The large Hood family lived, at various times, on both sides of the Rhode Island–Massachusetts border. In 1810 and 1820, Noble Jr. was living in Warren, Rhode Island. In 1810 William was living in Somerset, Massachusetts, and by 1820 he had been joined by his brother John and his nephew, John Jr.[14] Noble Sr. died before 1818, Hannah Perry after that date.[15]

John Hood was a man of some prominence in Somerset. During the War of 1812, he was appointed captain of the fourteen man militia company drafted from the town in 1814 to serve for 25 days at the barracks at Fairhaven.[16] When the federal tax collector came to town on January 13, 1816, John Hood's house was the location for paying the taxes. These were the Direct Tax of the United States, which was based on the value of the taxpayer's real estate and a separate duty imposed on household furniture and "gold and silver watches."[17]

Fifteen years later, the Somerset tax list of 1833 gives the assessments levied on all the adult male taxpayers. John Hood paid $5.27 in taxes on his real estate and an additional $1.55 on his personal property. Also listed as separate taxpayers are James' older brothers, George B. Hood and John Hood, Jr. The tax rate was $12 per thousand, so John Hood, Sr.'s, real estate was valued at $439. John's brother, William P. Hood, Sr., was one of the selectmen signing the tax list.[18]

Somerset was primarily an agricultural town, but it supported several industries, including shipbuilding and its associated crafts, and pottery making in the aptly named Pottersville. Many of the towns along the Taunton River had small industrial establishments that were dependent on ships to bring them raw materials and to carry their products to far-flung markets. Prominent among these industries were iron making and textiles in Fall River and silver and copper working in Taunton. These industries grew rapidly as trade developed. This provided opportunities for the master mariners of Somerset and the other towns along the Taunton River.

The Hoods were members of the Baptist Church. James' aunt, Sarah Booshee Hood, was baptized into the 1st Baptist Church of Warren, Rhode Island, in 1810, and her husband, Noble Hood, Jr., was baptized ten years later, on April 13, 1820, but was excluded from that church after only one year for unknown reasons.[19]

James went to sea at an early age. In those days, it was common for boys as young as 8 or 9 to sign on as crew members and we know that, later, James took his own son to Cuba at the tender age of 2. His father and uncles, including Noble Jr., were in the coastal trade, sailing from New England to the southern states and the West Indies. They had a strong connection to Matanzas, Cuba, a major port for the sugar growing region on the north shore of that island, about 50 miles east of Havana. James' uncle, Noble Hood, Jr., was trading between Cuba and Bristol, Rhode Island, in 1823,[20] and later died in Matanzas in May 1827.[21] Cuba had become a significant market for American traders even before the Revolution when it became an alternative to the British and French West Indies, which were closed to American ships. In the 1770s, Robert Morris, the American financier, obtained licenses from the Spanish to trade with Cuba, which needed to import food, and others followed his lead in opening up the island.[22]

Matanzas was well known for its molasses, which, when brought back to New England, was fermented and distilled into rum. With good winds, it was only a five-day sail from there to Narragansett Bay. Sailing with them during the warmer months, James probably attended school only in the winter when the Taunton Great River was frozen, supplementing his studies by reading from the Bible and the sailing instructions, and doing sums on bills of lading while at sea.

An incident involving James' uncle, Noble Hood, Jr., illustrates the commercial risks involved in these trading voyages. Noble had entered into joint ownership of the sloop *Lydia* with Joseph Alger and James and Daniel Salisbury of Warren, Rhode Island, to trade to the Carolinas. In October 1809, while the *Lydia* was in Edenton, North Carolina, waiting for a cargo, Daniel Salisbury secretly took $600 from the ship's funds and told the others that he was going to Plymouth, North Carolina, to see if there was any freight to be found there. Instead, he disappeared with the money and headed for Charleston, South Carolina. The other owners took out the following advertisement in the Edenton, North Carolina, *Gazette*:

STOP A VILLAIN!!

—$25 REWARD will be given to any person or persons within the United States that will apprehend and convey to Warren (R. Island) a certain DANIEL SALISBURY, Master and part owner of the Sloop Lydia of Warren, who left this place on the 13th instant, taking with him upwards of $600 in gold and silver, belonging to the subscribers. We are informed, that after he arrived at Plymouth, he made no application for a freight, but took himself off from thence, it is supposed, for Washington, as he was seen on the road in company with a blacksmith, 20 miles from Plymouth.—The said SALISBURY is about five feet eight or nine inches high, tolerably well set, stoops in his shoulders very much, red face, drinks pretty freely at times, has a scar on one of his cheeks, occasioned by a wound from a splinter, and is about 30 years of age.

It is supposed he will make for Charleston, (S.C.). Masters of vessels and others, would do an act of justice to their country, by refusing him a conveyance from one port to another, as he may, by that means, be brought to justice. The said SALISBURY is indebted to us more than his part of the Sloop amounts to.

> JOHN ALGER,
> JAMES SALISBURY,
> NOBLE HOOD, Part Owners

Edenton, Oct. 19, 1809 [23]

The resolution of this case remains a mystery.

This incident points out that in the early 19th century, trade was carried out in cash and a captain had to carry large sums aboard his ship. Partners, even when family, could prove unreliable, and law enforcement was practically non-existent, so that the aggrieved needed to take matters into their own hands to apprehend the offender.

Yet another risk was pirates, especially in the Caribbean and along the coasts of Cuba and Jamaica. As late as 1824, a Capt. Daniel Hood from Portland, Maine, sailing the brig *Castor*, was captured by pirates within sight of the dock at Matanzas and robbed. The *Boston Commercial Gazette* published the following letter from Capt. Hood to the owner of the *Castor*:

> When within four miles of the shipping, I was boarded by seven men in an open boat, and armed with swords, pistols, carabines, muskets and knives, who took my vessel from me and stood out of the Bay. They run down the coast about twenty miles, anchored my vessel, furled my sails, and commenced beating me and my men, and plundering us and the vessel. For the most part of the time they kept me below; calling me on deck at short intervals, beating me with their cutlasses and threatening

my life until I was as black as I could be, and my mate and men more or less so. They made me put into my boats and load them with such part of my cargo as they wanted, viz: Butter, Lard, Fish, Soap, Herring, Provisions, Stores, Cabin furniture, studding sails, spare rigging, tools, my new top-sail, and every article of our clothing except what we stood in. They took me about ten in the morning and kept till about eleven at night. They then cut my cable and ordered me to go, retaining my boats. The next morning I fell in with the brig Friendship, Capt. Hopkins, from Boston; being armed he took me under protection, and saw me safe to Havana. I dare not attempt to go to Matanzas having every reason to suspect there was no man of war there. I thought it best for the preservation of our lives and the vessel and cargo, to go to Havana, where I arrived on the 2d July. Last evening (5th) we had accounts from Matanzas of two brigs, one ship, and one schooner, being taken by the Pirates. The brig John, Capt. Norris, from Portland, was one — they let him go in. I was on the coast of Cuba nine days, becalmed, and during that time did not see one of our cruisers; nor is there one about Matanzas or Havana.[24]

Capt. Daniel Hood was from Maine, and was not related to the Somerset Hoods. He was usually engaged in the lumber trade and may have been carrying logs as a cargo, since the pirates only took the most portable goods on board and were probably incapable of unloading large items from the ship. His letter indicates that as the master of the vessel, he had the right to refuse to sail to the port in his orders if he felt that it was unsafe and to try to sell the cargo in a different port to the owner's advantage.[25]

This was the world that James Madison Hood grew up in, a world of entrepreneurs who looked out for themselves and their extended families and who built fortunes on their shrewd trades and a willingness to take risks.

3

Captain

By the time he was 16, in 1831, James was experienced enough take over his father's sloop, the *Rose Bud*, and assume the title of captain, a title he would proudly use for the rest of his life.[1] In the United States in the 1830s the only license a captain needed was the confidence of the owner, but gaining that trust took a lot more than passing some examination. The owner was entrusting the master of his ship with a considerable part of his fortune as well as the lives of the crew, which often included relatives. Capt. John Hood had carefully observed his son's performance as a mate and overseen his education in the business of a merchant trader before making this important promotion.

There is an account of a similar career path in the autobiography of Capt. Charles Ranlett, who was a contemporary of Captain James Hood, having been born in Maine in 1816.[2] Ranlett was not from a seafaring family and did not go to sea until he was 13, when he signed on as the sole crew member of a little 10-ton fishing schooner, the *Jane*. Over the next six years, he worked his way up in larger and larger ships and became a mate in 1836 at the age of 19. Two years later, when he was only 21, he was named master of the 150-ton, 84-foot-long topmast schooner *Waldoboro*. This was due in part to a friend who bought a one-eighth share of the vessel, and partly to his own purchase of another eighth.

The East Coast trade was constantly changing. It was dominated by New England ships sailed by New England masters but was centered on the port of New York. New York was the hub of commerce, capital, and maritime insurance. There, a captain could assemble a cargo of produce, livestock, or manufactured goods. He could also get intelligence about markets in the southern cities and the Caribbean. This was critical to his success. If a ship called at a port and there were no buyers for its cargo, it was a loss of both time and money, but prior to the widespread diffusion of the telegraph, the only way to find out where there was demand and where cargos could be found was by talking to those who had been there or reading newspapers that had been carried to New York on other ships. Thus, on September 11, 1832 the *Rhode Island American*, a Providence newspaper, reprinted the following note from the Norfolk, Virginia, *Beacon*;

> Scarcity of Salt.—We learn today from Capt. Hood of the brig Roveno, arrived this day from Rum Key, that there was no salt at that place, nor at Exuma or Crooked Island. At Turk's Island there was some, but at a high price.[3]

This Captain Hood may have been James or his father, John. The islands mentioned are in the Bahamas and the Turks and Caicos Islands.

There had always been a market for hats, shoes, and other manufactured goods from New England. This expanded when textile mills were established throughout the region during the first half of the 19th century. A major shift in trade occurred after the opening of the Erie Canal in 1825. Midwestern grain and flour, which had previously been shipped via New Orleans, now began to flow eastward and down the Hudson to New York City.[4] These products, along with lumber, lime, livestock, salt beef, dried fish, hardware, and cloth from the New England textile factories, including those in Fall River, were shipped to the southern ports of Wilmington, North Carolina; Charleston, South Carolina; and Savannah, Georgia. A typical cargo from 1841 might include calico cloth, bread, potatoes, and cheese.[5] In the southern states, the cargos were traded for rice, tobacco, and other local products which were carried to the Caribbean islands where sugar, molasses, oranges, tobacco, and salt were bought for the return voyage.

Another important trading partner for ships from the Fall River Customs District, which included Somerset, was Pictou, Nova Scotia. Quite a number of ships were involved in carrying coal from the Nova Scotia mines, much of which was purchased by the Fall River Iron Company. On the return trip, they brought food, cloth, and machinery to the mines.[6]

Somerset was well situated to participate in this trade. Located on the Taunton River just upstream and across the river from the city of

Fall River, it offered a sheltered, deep water anchorage, and was the head of navigation for large ships. The channel varies from 20 to 36 feet in depth along the shore of Somerset.[7] The town also had good connections to the interior, especially after 1836 when the Taunton Branch Railroad connected that city to the Boston and Providence Railroad in Mansfield, Massachusetts.[8] Shallow draft ships from Somerset could easily reach Taunton by sailing up the river. In 1834, the designated port of entry for the local customs district, where all ships had to call before proceeding to their destination port, had been moved from Dighton to the city of Fall River, which, being just across the Taunton River, was more convenient for ships headed for Somerset.[9] By water, it was just a quick sail down the Taunton River, around Hog Island, and up Narragansett Bay to Providence. New York City could be reached through the relatively sheltered waters of Long Island Sound. Schooners regularly made the round trip from Fall River to New York and back in three days.

There is an interesting record of one of these trading voyages assembled from the shipping news in various newspapers. On January 23, 1826, Capt. John Hood, James' father, brought the newly built brig *Ajax* from Somerset to Providence, Rhode Island.[10] The 126-ton *Ajax* had been built in Somerset in 1825. On February 7, the Providence newspapers carried an advertisement seeking freight for the *Ajax*.[11] On February 24, a month after he had arrived, Capt. Hood sailed from Providence, for Norfolk, City Point and Richmond, Virginia. On the way he spoke the brig *Rachel Ann* on March 6 and said he was headed for the James River, but instead of stopping at Norfolk, he arrived at Wilmington, North Carolina, on March 9. From there, he took the *Ajax* to New York, then back south, this time arriving at Norfolk on May 7. After that it was another round trip between Norfolk and New York in June and July, followed by a trip to Charleston, South Carolina, arriving on September 13.[12] This nine month voyage typified the life of a coastal trader, a series of relatively short hauls with long periods in port to waiting for the next cargo to be completed.

The captain of a trading vessel not only sailed the ship but was also responsible for selling its cargo at a good price and finding another cargo for the return trip. This was a heavy financial responsibility, but one that James embraced. In the 1830s, to keep his business active in winter when Taunton Great River was frozen over, Captain Hood opened a store at Wilmington, North Carolina, near the establishment of his cousin from

Somerset, George A. Marble.[13] He continued to do business in Wilmington through the 1840s, dealing with important merchants such as Aaron Lazarus, who owned a large brick mansion at 314 Grace St. there.[14]

The world of captains, ship owners, and merchants was a tightly connected one. In his dealings as a merchant master, Captain Hood built up a network of contacts that would serve him well in the future. He worked with and competed against many of the same firms for which he would later build ships and interact with as a politician and consul.

About this time, Captain Hood added real estate to his business interests. He began to buy and sell land in and around Somerset. In August 1836 he traveled to Albany, New York, where he bought two parcels of land comprising ten vacant building lots in Somerset from Oliver and Anne Eliz Kane of New York City. He paid $300 for them. The lots had been the property of John James Clark of Providence, Rhode Island, before his death. Captain Hood then returned home and resold the land to his father on September 8 for the same amount he had paid for it.[15]

Slowly, Hood's role shifted from master to merchant. He managed to remain solvent during the early part of the Panic of 1837. This started on May 10 when the New York City banks stopped payment in gold and silver following a series of business failures throughout the country. This resulted in a severe, immediate credit crunch followed by a depression that lasted for 5 years and caused many merchants to fail. The Panic had its roots during the presidency of Andrew Jackson, when an economic expansion, fueled by easy credit from banks, which issued paper money without backing it with sufficient bullion reserves, led to inflation. Sales of public lands had gone from about $1.5 million in 1829 to almost $25 million in 1836, a sixteen-fold increase. Then, towards the end of his second term in the summer of 1836, Jackson issued the Specie Circular which declared that purchases of federal land could be made only with specie, that is, gold or silver coin. It was a time of speculation in western lands, when people were borrowing paper money from the banks to purchase large tracts to hold until prices rose and they could sell at a profit. The Specie Circular pricked the bubble and led to a devaluation of the banks' paper currency. By the time the effects of the circular became apparent, Jackson was out of office and Martin Van Buren had become president. Van Buren refused to let the government intervene in the economy and let the circular stand. This led to runs on banks as people tried to redeem their paper money for specie. In response, the New York banks halted payments in specie and effectively shut down credit throughout the country. Four out of ten banks in the country went out of business, and within two months the losses from bank failures in New York alone approached 100 million dollars.[16]

Bucking the trend, on June 23, 1837, one month after the start of the panic, Captain Hood's brother, Capt. George B. Hood, took out a license at the customs house in Fall River, Massachusetts, for the 33-ton sloop *Independence* to engage in the coastal trade. Somerset was a part of the Fall River–Dighton customs district. Under federal law, all American ships engaged in the coasting trade, that is, trade within the United States, had to post a bond and be issued a license by their local customs district in order to be entitled to the rights of being considered an American ship. If the ship was greater than 20 tons, it also had to be enrolled by the customs district. The bonds ranged from $100 to $1,000 depending on the size of the ship. Ships engaged in foreign trade were registered rather than licensed.[17]

For some reason, possibly an inability to raise funds to buy a cargo, George Hood was unable to take the sloop to sea and on June 30, the license was transferred to Captain James M. Hood and Capt. Joseph Simmons, II, who was also from Somerset. The *Independence* had been built in Somerset in 1834. Simmons was listed as the master and Hood as the merchant. The license was for one year and was surrendered at Fall River on July 5, 1838, and not renewed.[18] This indicates that Captain Hood had access to capital to purchase a cargo and knew of customers with money to buy it. James E. Bradbury, relates a story that later during the Panic, when others were retrenching, Captain Hood loaded a ship with lumber in Wilmington and set out for the Caribbean, taking a risk that apparently paid off.[19]

Business must have continued to go well, for on June 15, 1839, James married Anna Maria Moison, daughter of the late Capt. William Moison, in Newport, Rhode Island.[20] He was 24 years old and she was only 16. On her mother, Elizabeth Standish's side, Anna was a lineal descendant of Myles Standish, who sailed with the Pilgrims on the *Mayflower* and served as the commander of the Plymouth militia.[21] William and Elizabeth had been married on April 28, 1816, in Dighton.[22] He was from Duxbury and she was from Wellington, both in Massachusetts.

Anna's brother, William Henry Moison, eventually moved to Somerset as well, where he died in 1845, leaving all of his estate to his wife, Caroline Bowers, the daughter of Philip Bowers, a relative of Captain Hood's mother.[23]

Anna's father, Capt. William Moison, had a moment of fame in 1826 when, six months before his death, as the master of the ship *Isaac Hicks,* he rescued Capt. Reid and the officers and crew of the British brig *Skipsey.*

> On the night of the 20th April the ship Isaac Hicks, Captain Moison, of New York, in lat. 47, long. 20W fell in with the above vessel in a sinking condition, took off the crew and brought them to New York. On the passage, the crew of the Skipsey was called on to assist in working the vessel that had taken them off the wreck, which order three of them refused to comply with, and one being very insolent, Captain Moison ordered corporal punishment to be inflicted on him. On the arrival of the Isaac Hicks in this port, the man who had received the punishment, prosecuted Captain William Moison in the Marine Court, and recovered 50 dols., 43 dols. expenses. It is not a part of the plan of our paper to impugn the Tribunals of this country; we therefore make no comment on the verdict of the Court alluded to, but content ourselves with giving the following letter from H.M. consul to Captain Moison. We are happy to say that the part taken by Mr. Buchanan on this occasion, has drawn forth the most unqualified approbation of the whole community.
>
> BRITISH CONSULATE, New York, 5th June, 1826
>
> Sir,— I regret you should have met so ungrateful a return for your successful and humane efforts, in saving the lives of the master and crew of the British brig Skipsey. Your generous conduct, in not requiring remuneration for the support you afforded the crew so long on board your ship, as also the terms in which Captain Reid spoke to me of your uniform sympathy and kindness, demand from me this public expression of my thanks.
>
> The fine and costs to which you have been subjected, by the ungrateful and scandalous conduct of one of the crew, whose life you saved, I feel it my duty to discharge, assuring you of the just feeling of respect your conduct calls forth.
>
> I remain, sir, your obedient servant,
> James Buchanan. [24]

James and Anna's only child, a son, James Madison, Jr., was born on October 7, 1841. At first, the Hoods lived in Newport and Providence.[25]

However, things did not always go well for Captain Hood. On February 5, 1842, he filed for bankruptcy in the Rhode Island Federal District

Court, listing debts of $14,819.76 and assets consisting only of $400 in sundry debts due him in Wilmington, North Carolina, his personal furniture, and a bed and bedding. He listed his residence as Providence. The list of creditors is interesting in that it shows the extent of Hood's business dealings. He had debts in Boston; New York City; Providence; Wilmington, North Carolina; and Havana, Cuba. His creditors included Aaron Lazarus, one of the most prominent merchants in Wilmington; Seth Padelford, a grocer who would later become governor of Rhode Island; seven merchants and a sail maker in New York City; Francisco D. Gyre & Co. in Havana; and his brother, George B. Hood.[26]

Samuel Peckham, who was appointed as the assignee to receive Hood's assets, exempted the bed and bedding and stated that with regard to the debts due in Wilmington, "whether good & collectible to that amount the assignee cannot state." The bankruptcy was granted on March 1, 1842, and the case closed and the debts discharged on July 5, only four months later.

The almost $15,000 in debts listed in the bankruptcy filing represents about $7 million in today's money and indicates the scope of Captain Hood's business enterprises. It is difficult to understand how someone with that large a business could have essentially no assets, and one can only conclude that either Hood had engaged in a series of exceptionally bad deals or that assets were being concealed. In light of the fact that the creditors were spread from Boston to Cuba, and that only one month elapsed between the filing and the granting of the bankruptcy, and only 4 more until the case was closed, it is not surprising that the claims were not disputed. This again points out the difficulties of commercial law in a time with limited communications and when many assets consisted of cash with no paper records. The bankruptcy was only the first of several questionable financial dealings that would come to mark turning points in the life of James Madison Hood.

On March 15, 1843, soon after the bankruptcy was granted, Captain Hood and his wife signed an agreement with Henry Cranston, the trustee of a sum of $709.14, the income from which Anna had inherited from her mother, Elizabeth Moison.[27] Because the money was held in trust for her, Hood's creditors had been unable to touch it. Cranston agreed to let them use the money to buy land in Somerset, rather than to keep it in the bank stock in which it was invested. This land was a lot on the Taunton River which was used as a fishing camp, and, on January 11,

1844, Hood petitioned the state legislature, through Representative Chaloner of Fall River, for the restoration of fishing privileges on the Taunton River.[28] After Captain Hood's death in 1871, this land became the object of a suit by Anna to recover what she considered to be her dower.[29] It was soon after this transaction took place that the Hoods moved back to Somerset.[30]

In the fall of the same year, Captain Hood set out on a voyage to Cuba, taking his wife and two-year-old son along. This was not unusual for a young, recently married merchant master. As master and part owner of the ship, he was able to provide as comfortable accommodations as possible on what was probably a vessel crowded with cargo. Unfortunately, this trip did not turn out well. Tragically, their son, James Madison, Jr., died in Havana, Cuba, on January 26, 1844, most likely of a tropical fever.[31] The loss of his son had a profound effect on Captain Hood, as evidenced by the fact that he erected memorial stones to James Jr. on the sites of both his own grave in Sycamore, Illinois, and the family cemetery of his first wife, Anna, in Dighton, Massachusetts.

Memorial Stone of James Hood, Jr., the son of Captain Hood, who died in Cuba. It is located in the Center Street cemetery, Dighton, Massachusetts. Photograph by G. Kingston.

Soon after the loss of his son, Captain Hood began to think about leaving the sea for a new career on land. For start-up capital, in July 1845, he persuaded his father to deed to him and his wife, Anna, a parcel of land on the Taunton River in Somerset that would later form part of the shipyard he established. John Hood gave them the land "in consideration of the love, good will & natural affection I bear towards [them]."[32] However, James was not ready to hang up his sea boots just yet.

In 1846, the Mexican War broke out. The independent Republic of Texas, which had seceded from Mexico in 1836, accepted annexation by the United States as the 28th state on July 4, 1845. There had never been an agreement on Texas' western border. The United States government insisted that it was the Rio Grande, but Mexico maintained that it was the Nueces River, farther east. President James Polk sent troops under General Zachary Taylor to Texas at the end of July 1845, and Taylor set up his camp on St. Joseph's Island on the seaward side of Aransas Bay, just east of the Nueces River, where he spent the winter.[33]

On March 8, 1846, General Taylor moved his forces into the disputed territory between the two rivers to pressure Mexico into negotiating the sale of California and New Mexico to the United States. He set up his base at Point Isabel, across the Brazos Santiago Pass from South Padre Island. It was just north of the Rio Grande and separated from that river by an extensive marsh. The base was connected to the mainland by a narrow peninsula, making it easily defensible, and could communicate with the sea through the pass at the south end of South Padre Island. Unfortunately, the bar across the pass was only 8½ feet deep and the bay inside was even shallower, which meant that the navy ships and heavier transports had to anchor outside and row reinforcements and supplies almost 4 miles to reach the base.

When his troops were assembled, Taylor marched them inland. Mexico responded by sending its own troops across the Rio Grande. Hostilities started on April 25, when a strong Mexican force attacked a small American patrol in the disputed territory. On May 7, a Mexican force under General Mariano Arista attacked Fort Texas, one of Taylor's outposts near present-day Brownsville, with around 6,000 men. Taylor heard the artillery fire at his base at Point Isabel, and hurried to relieve the fort with 2,300 men. The battle of Palo Alto, fought the next day, May 8, was a decisive American victory, largely due to the superior American artillery.[34]

The Mexican War was the first one in which the U.S. Army invaded an enemy's territory by sea. Both for its initial move across the Rio Grande from Texas and for its later attack on Monterey, the army required the use of a large number of oceangoing vessels to transport troops, munitions and supplies. Quartermaster General Thomas S. Jesup reported that the lack of suitable harbors in Texas necessitated "the debarkation of troops and heavy stores by the slow and precarious process of lightering, during what is, in the Gulf of Mexico, the dreaded hurricane season.... For the risks incident to the navigation of such a coast, for such purposes, and at such a season, the department had no alternative, but to submit to the exaction of indemnifying rates of compensation by the heavy transports chartered for the dangerous service."[35] In other words, ship owners were asking and getting exorbitant rates for their charters because they had to anchor close to shore while unloading to lighters or barges and would be unable to get away quickly if a hurricane or other storm struck.

Captain Hood decided to get a piece of the action. He was captain of the brig *Virginia*, which he co-owned with his friend, Daniel Brayton Eddy. The *Virginia* was a 13-year-old, 84-foot-long, 158-ton two-masted vessel, registered in Somerset but originally built in Warwick County,

Daniel Brayton Eddy House, a typical sea captain's house in Somerset, Massachusetts. Captain Eddy was a friend and business partner of Captain Hood. Photograph by G. Kingston.

Virginia, out of live oak and white oak with iron knees. By the standards of the day, she was a fairly old vessel but well suited for the coastal trade, capable of carrying 1800 barrels or 240 gross tons of cargo.[36] On May 5, he chartered the *Virginia* to Lieutenant J.L. Donaldson, of the Quartermaster Corps, "to transport from Pensacola harbor to Point Isabel, Texas, two companies of the 1st regiment of artillery, numbering (officers and men) about 100 (more or less) with their baggage, [for] the sum of $900, demurrage $50 per day."[37]

A Florida newspaper, *The Pensacola Democrat,* reported that on May 5, 1846, six days before the actual declaration of war by Congress,

> Maj. W.H. Chase arrived in this city from New Orleans, with orders for the forces stationed here under command of Col. Crane, to embark forthwith for the Rio Grande. The brig *Virginia*, Capt. Hood, was chartered for the transportation of the troops at 2 o'clock p.m., and at 4 o'clock had on board ballast, provisions and men, with the steamer *Gen. Taylor* alongside, ready to tow her to sea.[38]

The *Virginia* actually departed the following morning, May 6. On this first trip, Captain Hood carried 94 men accompanied by Captains Webster and Taylor, Lieutenants Donaldson and Bowen, a surgeon, Dr. Moore, and Lieutenant Hood, the regimental adjutant, to Brazos Santiago, where General Zachary Taylor had his camp.[39] These troops were meant to reinforce General Taylor's army, but they did not arrive in time to participate in the battle of Palo Alto, which was fought while the *Virginia* was still at sea.

Captain Hood returned to New Orleans on June 1 in ballast, having taken 10 days to sail from Brazos Santiago.[40] He did not immediately recharter the *Virginia* and apparently went back to his normal trading activities.

By July 10, Hood was in back Boston, advertising that the *Virginia* was available for sale, freight, or charter, with Nathaniel Winsor, Jr., a well-known Boston shipping broker, as his agent. The advertisements continued until September 18, and along with numerous other similar advertisements for other ships, indicates a glut of available bottoms during the summer of 1846.[41] Captain Hood may have terminated his charter to avoid being in the Gulf of Mexico during the yellow fever season, which ran from April to October, or it may have been terminated by the government since General Taylor's slow advance through northeastern Mexico could be supplied with fewer ships. Throughout the summer of

1846 and into the early months of 1847, there was little naval activity in the Gulf of Mexico.[42]

While waiting for something to turn up, Captain Hood visited Somerset and on August 7 he purchased a lot of about 12 acres on the highway there from the estate of his brother-in-law, Wheaton Luther, for $350, a sum which probably came from his profits on the *Virginia* lease.[43] Conveniently, the executor of Wheaton's estate was James' brother George B. Hood. In October, he renewed the license of the *Virginia* for the coastal trade in Fall River,[44] then sailed to Providence, Rhode Island, arriving on November 1.[45]

At the start of 1847, Captain Hood was back in New Orleans and on January 13, Major Thomas B. Eastland of the Quartermaster Corps again leased the *Virginia* for government use in support of the landing of the American forces under General Winfield Scott at Vera Cruz, Mexico. The terms of the lease were $1500 for the first month, $1300 for the second month, and $1000 for the third and each succeeding month.[46] Three thousand eight hundred dollars for a 3-month-lease with no cargo risk was a lot of money in those times.

On January 15, two days after Hood had renewed the lease, General Winfield Scott, who had taken over as the field commander, ordered all of his transports to rendezvous at Isla Lobos, a sheltered anchorage south of Tampico, Mexico, about halfway between Brazos Santiago and Veracruz. The choice of anchorage was important, because in the winter this section of the gulf was subject to dangerous storms known as northers and the transports were at risk from them. There was some confusion about the orders, with some transports sailing via Brazos as intended, while others went via Tampico or directly to Isla Lobos.[47]

During these operations, on February 11, the *Virginia* was hit by a norther with gale force winds and foundered off the Mexican coast. The crew took to the boats and all reached shore except George B. Luther, Captain Hood's nephew, the son of his sister Mary and her husband, Wheaton Luther, who drowned in the surf.[48] Hood claimed that he used his Yankee trader skills to convince the Mexicans that he and his men were English, rather than American, and to get the Mexicans to provide transportation for them back to New Orleans.[49] More likely, they were rescued by an American ship and taken back on an empty transport. While Captain Hood was making his way home, his mother, Mary Hood, died on March 30 in Somerset at the age of 70.

It took until late February 1847, for all of the transports to arrive at the rendezvous, but finally, on March 2, the flotilla sailed for Anton Lizardo, another sheltered anchorage just south of Veracruz, without the *Virginia*.

The ships arrived at Anton Lizardo on March 5 and the landings began on March 9. This was the first amphibious landing by American troops on foreign soil, and was carried out over Collado Beach just south of Veracruz using flat bottomed surf boats. The siege of the city began the next day, March 10, 1847. The landing of supplies and reinforcements was interrupted by a series of northers on March 12–17, March 21 and March 24–25. The last of these was the most destructive with 23 transport vessels being driven aground. In spite of the supply problems, the siege progressed rapidly, and Veracruz surrendered on March 27.[50]

With Veracruz secured as a base, General Scott moved his army inland, capturing Puebla without a fight on May 1 and moving against Mexico City on August 7. The campaign culminated in the battle of Chapultepec on September 13, which resulted in capture of the Mexican capital. After that, the war wound down, and ended with the treaty of Guadalupe-Hidalgo, which was signed on February 2, 1848.[51] Among the many results of this treaty was the cession of California to the United States, an action that opened the West Coast to American trade and that, combined with the discovery of gold at Sutter's Mill less than a week before the treaty was signed, would help set the stage for Captain Hood's next career move as a builder of clipper ships.

4

Shipbuilder, Somerset, Massachusetts

In 1848, the year after his shipwreck, Captain James M. Hood "swallowed the anchor" and came ashore for good. Instead of sailing ships, he decided to build them and he established a shipyard in his home town of Somerset, Massachusetts, just as the boom in clipper ship building was getting underway. He took in his brother and neighbor, George B. Hood, and associate Joseph Marble, both of whom were also ship captains and merchant ship owners, as partners. For his confidential secretary and business manager, Captain Hood hired his nephew, William Perry Hood, the son of his brother David B. Hood.[1] William Perry was only 23 years old at the time but was already an experienced fire, marine, and life insurance salesman. Thus the family firm of James M. Hood & Co. was founded, the first of many business ventures that these three men would collaborate on.

In the 19th century, it was not unusual for a captain to go into the shipbuilding business. In those days of wooden ships, a captain had to know everything about how his vessel was put together. Often, it was necessary for a captain to oversee repairs in a strange port or even on the high seas, using little more than hand tools and the available timber. Thus, of necessity, a captain acquired many of the skills of a shipwright. Moreover, as an experienced master, Captain Hood had seen firsthand how different hulls and different rigs behaved in all weather and sea conditions, from a dead calm to a hurricane. He had developed strong ideas about how a ship should be designed and built to maximize its profitability and was now in a position to put those ideas into action.

Somerset already had a long history of shipbuilding. In 1695,

34

Jonathan Bowers, an ancestor of James Hood's mother, established the first commercial shipyard there at the end of Main Street. Four years later, Thomas Coram, who had been invited to come from England specifically to build ships, established another shipyard upriver in the town of Dighton. Other yards in Somerset were later run by Samuel Lee, Jared Chace, and Edward Slade. Many of these early shipyards built only a few vessels and some built them only for the family of the owner. Around 1825, the Davis & Simmons shipyard was started at the location where Captain Hood later built his. More shipyards existed in Dighton, the next town upriver from Somerset.[2]

The most famous vessels built by Captain Hood were specialized ships called clippers. Unlike normal merchant ships, which had bluff bows, flat sterns, and wide beams to maximize their cargo capacity, clippers were designed with sharp angles at both bow and stern and narrower beams. The clippers were the wind-powered answer to steamships, greatly exceeding the speed and range of the early steamers, which needed expensive fuel and frequent stops to replenish fuel supplies. The clippers sacrificed cargo space for speed, and were less stable than more conventional ships, requiring more skilled handling. Their higher speeds, however, more than made up for their disadvantages when carrying passengers or perishable cargos. They were called the greyhounds of the sea, and, at first, commanded premium prices for their builders. The lengths of their passages between New York and China, California, Europe and Australia were widely reported and followed with the avid attention usually reserved for sporting events. A record voyage meant bragging rights for the builder, captain and owner. More speed also meant lower operating costs and higher freight rates and fares.[3]

The first generally acknowledged extreme clipper ship, as distinguished from the earlier Baltimore clippers, was the *Rainbow*, which was built by Smith and Dimon in New York City, based on a design by John Willis Griffiths. She was built for the firm of Howland and Aspinwall and launched in January 1845.[4] That same year the treaty ports in China, which had been conceded to the European powers after the Opium War, were opened to the United States.[5] The *Rainbow* headed to China. On her maiden voyage there under Capt. John Land, she set records for both round trip time (7 months 13 days) and the run from China to New York (105 days), going around Cape Horn both ways.[6]

Following that initial run, other yards began to build clippers as well. These first clippers made great profits by hauling valuable cargoes and more and more builders began to turn out ever faster ships.

John Hood, James' father, had given James and Anna about a third of an acre of land on the Taunton River in 1845,[7] and in May 1847, James had purchased an additional 12 acres of land in Somerset from the estate of Wheaton Luther.[8] This land, where the Davis & Simmons shipyard had operated in the early part of the century, sloped gently down to the Taunton River from Main Street between School and Cherry streets, where the deep water channel of the Taunton River swings close to the bank. While the depth of the river along most of the shore is only about three feet, here it drops rapidly to between 19 and 29 feet, making it easy to launch large ships. Appropriately, there is a municipal boat ramp on the site today.

While the shipyard was being established, Hood's path may have crossed that of Abraham Lincoln for the first time. In September 1848,

Hood Shipyard site, showing the slope to the river where the ship building ways were located at Main and School Streets, Somerset, Massachusetts. Today this is a municipal boat launch site. Photograph by G. Kingston.

Lincoln, who was at the time a freshman congressman from Illinois and a member of the national Whig Central Committee, agreed to come to Massachusetts to campaign for Zachary Taylor's presidential bid after Congress adjourned. Taylor had been nominated at the Whig national convention in Philadelphia, but because he was a slave owner from Louisiana, many of the Northern, anti-slavery Whigs broke away and nominated their own, Free Soil presidential candidate, the ex-president Martin Van Buren. Van Buren's third party bid threatened to divide the Whig vote and give the election to the Democratic candidate, Lewis Cass, a senator from Michigan. Massachusetts was a critical state for Taylor, because it was a heavily Whig state, but many of its Whigs were leaning towards the Free Soilers and he needed to bring them back in order to win the election in November. Lincoln traveled from Washington, D.C., to Worcester by train and arrived September 12, the day before the Whig state convention opened. He was unknown in the city and was not originally scheduled to speak. Alexander Bullock, the local Whig committee chairman, had called for a public pre-convention rally at the Worcester City Hall and invited some of the prominent state politicians present to speak, but as evening approached, none of them had accepted his invitation. Lincoln was largely unknown in New England, but when Bullock heard that the Illinois congressman was in town, he tracked him down and, in desperation, asked him to address the rally.[9]

At 7 in the evening, Lincoln was introduced as a proponent of free soil and he said nothing to dispel that label. He spoke for more than two hours, portraying Taylor as being the only Whig candidate who could carry both the North and the South, and, although a slave owner and a Southerner, a man of genuine Whig principles. He also spoke against Van Buren, cautioning that a vote for him was a vote for Cass. As was his habit, Lincoln studded his speech with anecdotes and jokes, a style that he had developed in Illinois, but that was new and interesting in Massachusetts where politicians tended towards more formality.

Hood was a Whig and may have been at the convention, but no list of attendees has survived. As evidenced by the government shipbuilding contracts he would get in the next few years, he was already politically connected, if not actively participating in politics yet. If he was not there, he may still have heard Lincoln speak at Taunton, which was only a few miles north of Somerset, on September 21. Lincoln had been invited to Taunton by Samuel L. Crocker, the president of the local

Taylor club, because the Free Soil Party was gathering strength in Bristol County, and Crocker knew that he had a tough campaign for Taylor ahead of him. Lincoln actually gave two speeches in Taunton that day, one in the afternoon at Mechanics Hall and another in the evening at Union Hall. Taunton was his next to last stop before he left the state and returned home. Although it is unlikely that Captain Hood actually met Lincoln at any of these events, which were attended by hundreds, if he did hear Lincoln speak, his exposure to the future president would have stood him in good stead when he moved to Illinois and entered politics in that state ten years later.

Lincoln was not the only politician stumping Massachusetts for Taylor that fall, but he did contribute in a small way to Taylor's victory in the state and the nation in the presidential election in November 1848. Although he never spoke publicly in Massachusetts again, the state made a deep impression on Lincoln and years later, when he had achieved the presidency himself, he remembered Samuel Crocker and others he had met there when they visited him in the White House.

The James M. Hood & Company shipyard laid down the keel of its first vessel, the schooner *Empire State*, in 1848. It was launched on Saturday afternoon, May 20, and was commanded by Capt. Salinas Marble.[10] The launch occurred just in time for the shipping boom caused by the California gold rush. This had been sparked by the discovery of gold at Sutter's Mill in January 1848, and for the next two years every available ship was pressed into service to take miners and supplies to the new United States territory of California, either via a land traverse at Panama or around Cape Horn. The *Springfield Republican* reported:

> A citizen of New York, with cash to the amount of $10,000, was smitten with California fever, bought one of the brigs sold at auction by the Government, at the close of the Mexican War, for $3,500, freighted it with wines and liquors, despatched his cargo for San Francisco, and took the Isthmus route himself, with the remainder of the money in his pocket, amounting to $500. On his arrival, he disposed of his cargo at a profit of 300 or 400 percent. He then sent his brig two trips to Oregon, for lumber, and then sold her for $45,000. He then gathered up his profits, and turned them into gold dust, and a few days ago returned in the *Crescent City* and deposited at the Philadelphia Mint, for coinage, $150,000 worth of dust. The truth of this narrative may be relied on.
>
> Rush for California. — The rush at Howland and Aspinwall's, New York, on Wednesday, for tickets for passage in the two new steamers, to

be started from Panama for San Francisco, was perfectly overwhelming. The applicants for tickets began to assemble as early as 4 o'clock in the morning, and before the doors were opened, hundreds had collected. The pressure was so great that the balustrade and windows were broken. — Five hundred tickets were run off for the two December steamers, as rapidly as the money could be counted, and the crowd calling loudly for more, 100 tickets were sold for the January steamer. The prices were $300 for a cabin passage and $150 for steerage.[11]

In the summer of 1849, the Hood shipyard also launched three other vessels, the brig *Somerset* and the ships *Milford* and *Fountain*. All told, in five years the yard launched at least 29 vessels including several important clippers, lightships and packets.[12]

The shipyard centered around the ways where the ships were built. The ways were massive blocks of wood lined up perpendicular to the shoreline on a natural slope. The keel, which was the backbone of the vessel, was laid down and assembled on these blocks as the first step in the actual construction. In addition to the ways, the yard included an

Hood Shipyard Steam House, School Street, Somerset, Massachusetts. Photograph by G. Kingston.

office, rope-walk, mould loft, steam house, and other specialized build-ings. The only one remaining today is the stone steam house which was used to steam the hull planking so that it could be bent to shape.[13]

The construction of a vessel began with the crafting of a scale model of the hull. Because a vessel is symmetrical about its longitudinal center line, only one-half of the hull was modeled and this was mounted on a flat board. When the builder and the client were satisfied with the shape of the hull, its lines were carefully measured and drawn on the floor of the mould loft at full scale in chalk. From these lines, moulds or patterns of the shapes of the timbers that were needed were constructed out of light wood. These moulds were then used to cut the timbers to tolerances of ⅛ inch. After the timbers were cut, they were joined together to make the frames. Structural timbers were crafted from naturally curved tree trunks, but less critical pieces were shaped in the steam house. The keel was laid down on the ways, the stem and stern posts were attached to it, and as each frame was completed, it was attached to the keel and the adjacent frames. When all the frames were in place, the hull was planked on the outside, ceiled, that is, covered on the inside, and caulked. The hull could then either be completed with decks while it was still on the ways, or it could be launched into the river and completed while afloat. The final assembly and rigging could be done in the original yard or at another one nearby. When the hull was complete, it was usually fitted out with masts and rigging while afloat, but some ships were launched fully rigged and ready to go to sea.[14]

Much of the material for shipbuilding was available locally. South-eastern Massachusetts had abundant pine and oak forests, although some of the larger timbers had to be brought from Maine, Delaware Bay, or the Carolinas on the same type of coastal trading ships that Captain Hood had sailed. He probably already knew many of his suppliers from his trading days. The keel and frames were crafted from oak, the inner lining of the hull, called the ceiling, was often made of Georgia pine, and the decking, masts and spars were pine. In building the clippers, small amounts of exotic woods such as mahogany, teak, and rosewood were used for railings and cabin fittings. These were imported from the Caribbean and South America.[15] The metal sheathing for the hull was manufactured just up the river in Taunton by Samuel L. Crocker, the local politician who had invited Lincoln to speak there. It was an alloy of copper and zinc known as Munz metal after its inventor, George

Munz, or simply called yellow metal. Crocker, who already produced copper at his Taunton Copper Manufacturing Company, had learned about this new invention on a trip to England in 1848. Crocker brought William H. Munz, the son of the inventor, back with him and made him the superintendent in the plant that he established.[16] Iron bolts and fittings were manufactured in Somerset, Fall River and Taunton, and rope was made locally as well.[17]

The major expenses for the shipbuilder were for the raw timbers and iron work and for the wages of the shipwrights. A skilled worker earned a little more than a dollar a day for ten hours of hard work. Each worker had to provide his own tools, and each specialty had its own unique ones. There were numerous specialists employed in building a ship. In addition to those doing the heavy labor of moving the timbers, there were the moulders who laid out the lines of the ship and transferred them to the light wooden moulds that served as patterns for shaping the timbers, and carpenters, who shaped and cut the timbers. There were also plankers, caulkers, finish carpenters, carvers, fasteners, painters, and others. All were under the direction of Captain James Hood, who was listed as their master carpenter, by virtue of his being the head of the shipyard.

It cost about $25 a register ton to build a fore-and-aft rigged ship, and a little more to build a square rigged one, due to its more complicated rigging.[18] That translated into a cost of $18,750 for a 700-ton, 3-masted schooner. This was a substantial investment. In most cases, ships were built on contract for shipping firms, which provided the capital or secured the loans needed to fund the construction. Captain Hood had gotten to know these companies during his days sailing the East Coast and the West Indies. Many of them were based in New York City but owned by native New Englanders. As the yard thrived, Captain Hood became a regular on the steam packets that plied between Fall River and Manhattan.

After that first successful summer of 1849, disaster struck. In the early hours of Wednesday, October 17, a fire of suspicious origin broke out in a ship being built for Howes, Godfrey & Co. in the yard. Fire in a shipyard was a great threat. The yard would normally be packed with dry timber and flammables such as tar, pitch and paint. In addition, the ground would be covered with wood chips from shaping the timbers. The *Taunton Whig* reported in an extra edition:

Great Fire at Somerset.— A fire was discovered this (Wednesday) morning about 1 o'clock, on board of the fine new ship now in process of
building, in the ship yard at Somerset landing, of Messrs. James M.
Hood & Co., which in a short time was totally destroyed, together with
a large quantity of ship timber and other materials, such as copper,
spikes &c. Loss amounting in all to between $30,000 and $40,000; partially insured in New York. The fire communicated to two stores and
sheds belonging to George B. Hood, which with contents, tools for ship
building, &c. were destroyed. Loss about $2,000; insured at the People's
Mutual Insurance Office, Taunton for $1,500. The dwelling house of
Baylies Davis, including part of their furniture — loss $1,000 — insured at
the Bristol County for $750. Next the dwelling house belonging to
Martha and Ann Chace and occupied by three families, was destroyed —
a portion of the furniture saved. Loss $2,000 — no insurance. The new
dwelling house of Jos. Simmons was next destroyed — it was occupied by
one family — furniture partially saved. Loss about $1,000 — insured for
$600, at the Bristol County office. Total loss nearly $50,000, besides
throwing a number of hands out of employment for the season. There
were no engines in this village, and the fire made such headway before it
was discovered, that all efforts to arrest its progress were fruitless. This is
a heavy loss for Somerset.[19]

The careful reporting of the losses, the insured amounts, and the
names of the insurance companies was done for more than idle curiosity.
In the mid-nineteenth century, insurance companies tended to be undercapitalized and heavy losses, like the $1,500 for People's Mutual and the
$1,350 for Bristol County, could endanger their financial stability. Their
members and stockholders wanted to know the amounts involved.

Adding to Captain Hood's troubles, the shipyard's insurance claim
was disputed. The Manhattan Insurance Company, which had issued a
policy covering the ship that was being built, insisted that although the
burnt frames were intended to be part of the ship, because they were not
yet attached to it, they were not covered. Hood filed suit in Superior
Court in New York City and won, but the insurance company appealed.
The case dragged on and eventually reached the Court of Appeals in
New York, which, six years later, ruled against Hood.[20] It is probable
that James Hood's nephew and secretary, William Perry Hood, played a
part in this dispute, because of his prior experience in the insurance
industry. Fortunately, the lumber and building materials in the shipyard
were insured separately, but only partially, by the New York Fire and
Marine Insurance Co.

In spite of the losses, Hood rebuilt and continued to turn out ships. The early part of 1850 was spent in rebuilding the yard and only three ships were launched that year. These were the 500-ton clipper *Rosario,* the 227-ton bark *Fanny Major,* and the 1039-ton packet *William Nelson.* Every ship is the creation of its builder, and once launched its career is a reflection on him. Its travels extend his name and reputation. Therefore, in discussing the ships built by Captain Hood, it is useful to give their history, where known.

The *Rosario* was a clipper built bark, that is, a ship with three masts, the fore and main being square rigged while the mizzen was rigged fore and aft. She was 136 feet long, 26 feet, 9 inches wide and 15 feet, 6 inches deep. She was built for the firm of Loring Brothers of Malaga, Spain, who were merchants and famous for their Malaga wines and raisins. The *Rosario* was launched on March 27 and initially commanded by Capt. Caleb Sprague, trading to Cuba.[21] Capt. Sprague was born in Barnstable, Massachusetts, and commanded several important clipper ships. He was intended to be the first commander of the *Raven* as well, but he was unable to get home in time and the command went to another master. The *Rosario* was named for the mother of the owners of Loring Brothers, Maria del Rosario Oyarzabal.[22]

The *Fanny Major* was named after the wife of her captain and part owner, Hugo R. Major of New York City. She was 105 feet 9 inches long with a breadth of 27 feet and a depth of 9 feet. She had one deck and three masts, but did not have a figurehead. In 1859, she was trading to Vancouver in the Pacific Northwest, bringing supplies to the growing settlements on Puget Sound and returning with timber. By then, she was under the command of a Capt. Woodley.[23]

The *William Nelson* was a large packet ship built for Capt. Charles Cheever of New York. Capt. Cheever owned ⅛ of the vessel, while Captain Hood owned the other ⅞, which he sold to the firm of Eagle & Hazard of New York while the ship was still being built. Her keel was laid on April 3, 1850, and she was 173 feet 11 inches long, 36 feet wide, and 18 feet deep. She had two decks, three masts, and a figurehead, though its design is not recorded.[24]

The *William Nelson* spent 15 years shuttling between North America and Europe, but it met a tragic end. On June 26, 1865, this ship caught fire while sailing from Flushing in the Netherlands to New York, full of German emigrants. When some of the passengers became sick, the captain, Levi Smith, decided to fumigate the ship by using hot irons to make tar smolder below decks, a common, but dangerous, procedure in those days. One of the tar buckets caught fire and boiled over, igniting the ship. According to the captain's statement:

> I was in command of the ship *William Nelson* ... with a crew of 30 men. I left Flessingen on the 4th [June] with six hundred tons of merchandise and four hundred and fifty emigrant passengers, for New York. On Saturday, June 26, at 12:30, lat. 41 21, long. 50 22 ... I was informed that the ship was set on fire while fumigating, and the flames spread so rapidly that I had only time to order the four boats to be lowered, which were immediately filled by those nearest, and finding all efforts useless I soon followed. The scene on board was horrible in the extreme. This morning, at 4 o'clock the ship had entirely disappeared. I stood out for the northwest, the other three boats keeping company as long as they could.[25]

Forty-five of the passengers and crew were rescued from the boats by the French mail packet *Lafayette*, commanded by Capt. A. Bocandi, and the Russian ship *Il Mari*, Capt. Adolph Niska, and taken by the *Lafayette* to Le Havre, France. Another forty passengers in the fourth boat were picked up by the steamer *Meteor* and carried to St. John's, Newfoundland. More than 400 lives were lost. A number of survivors alleged that the captain and crew were the first to abandon ship, but apparently Captain Smith was never prosecuted for the incident.

In addition to building ships, Captain Hood continued to invest in ships that were actively trading. In 1850, he acquired a part interest in the 60-ton schooner *Horatio Ames* and the 142-ton brig *Oregon*, of which John C. Berry was the master.[26] It was quite common for ships to have two or more owners, with their interest divided up into often unequal shares, as in Captain Hood's ⅞ ownership of the *William Nelson* during construction.

Captain Hood continued to build clippers with launches of the *Rip Van Winkle*, the *Raven*, the *Greenfield*, and the *Governor Morton* in 1851; the bark *Pathfinder* and the ship *Archer* in 1852; and the *Mischief* and the *Skylark* in 1853.[27]

The *Archer* went into service on the China run and experienced several accidents over the course of her career. In 1865, she grounded while under the guidance of a local pilot in the Min River and went into drydock in Foo Chow (Fuzhou, Fujian), China for repair. While there, the photograph reproduced in this book was taken by Herreshoff. It

Clipper ship *Archer*, built by Captain Hood, in dry dock in Foo Chow (Fuzhou, Fujian), China, 1865 after grounding in the Min River. Note the hollow bow. © Mystic Seaport, Photography Collection, #1984.141.2.

shows the lines of her hull as well as her standing rigging.[28] The contemporary marine artist Christopher Blossom has painted a seascape of the *Archer* entering San Francisco Bay, based on this photo.[29] She is one of the few Hood ships of which a photograph survives. In 1880, she foundered at sea on a voyage from New York to Le Havre but Capt. Harris and his crew were rescued by the steamer *Naworth Castle*.[30]

The *Mischief* was said to have had the sharpest ends of any clipper ever built.[31] She was built for W.H. Merrill and Capt. Martin Townsend of New York City, and Capt. Townsend was her master. She was 548 tons, 145 feet long, 29 feet wide and 16 feet, 6 inches deep. She was launched on March 26, 1853, and became part of Ogden & Hayne's Celestial Line of San Francisco and China packets. In late May, she sailed from New York Harbor on her maiden voyage to San Francisco, with Capt. Townsend hoping to make the voyage in 90 days or less. Unfortunately, she was damaged in a storm off Cape Horn and had to put into Valparaiso, Chile, for repairs. On September 25, she put to sea again in company with another Hood-built ship, the *Pathfinder*. She finally reached San Francisco on November 9, 172 days out of New York, with 133 of those sailing days.[32]

The *Mischief* remained in the San Francisco trade only until 1853, when she was sold for $22,000 and entered the China trade between New York and Foo Chow. In 1855 she was again sold, this time to Meyer & Stucken in Bremen, Germany, then sold again to the firm of Rossing and Mummy, also in Bremen, where she was renamed the *Felix* and sailed between the Baltic and North America. In 1862 she was again sold, this time to the Danish firm of A.N. Hansen in Copenhagen. For the next 18 years she sailed the North Sea until she was wrecked on the coast of Denmark with the loss of all hands on November 19, 1880.[33]

One of the pieces of the clipper ship mystique was the way they were named. For centuries, merchant ships had customarily been named rather prosaically for owners or their relatives, cities and states, as the *Jane B. Crocker* or the *Virginia*. But starting with the first generally accepted clipper, the *Rainbow*, these vessels were given romantic names that suggested speed or adventure. Thus some of the most famous ships were given names such as *Sea Witch, Typhoon,* and *Pathfinder*. These names were selected by the owners, who hoped that they would help with marketing the vessels to shippers and passengers.

The *Greenfield* was built for Capt. Tolmon Wakeman of Southport, Connecticut. She was 562 tons, 134 feet, 6 inches long, 30 feet, 4 inches wide, and 15 feet two inches deep. She had three masts, two decks, and a billethead, which was a spiral shaped decoration on the top of the stem.[34] In 1855, she loaded the first consignment of wheat ever exported from California, consisting of 4,752 bags.[35]

The *Governor Morton* was more prosaically named for Marcus Morton, a Whig who served as governor of Massachusetts for four months in 1825, and again for full one-year terms in 1839 and 1841. The ship was the largest ever built in the Hood shipyard at 1429 tons. It was 196 feet, 6 inches long, 39 feet wide, and 19 feet, 10 inches deep. It had one deck and three masts with a round, clipper stern. The ex-governor, who was from Taunton, owned a $\frac{1}{16}$ share in the vessel and Captain Hood owned a $\frac{19}{80}$ share. In all, the ship had 8 separate owners when it was first registered.[36] During its career, the *Governor Morton* made many voyages around Cape Horn to San Francisco for Coleman's California Line. Capt. John A. Burgess, of Somerset, was her master between 1851 and 1855, and Capt. Horton sailed her after 1861. The ship burned in 1877.[37]

The *Pathfinder* was built for William Merritt and Benjamin Trask of New York City, but Captain Hood retained a ⅔ ownership share and was listed as its first master. It was only 373 tons but very sharp, being 126 feet long but only 28 feet wide and 11 feet deep. It had one deck, three masts, and a billethead. She took her name from a book and character in James Fenimore Cooper's *Leatherstocking Tales* series. The name lives on today in a class of scout ships in the United States Navy.

The *Skylark* was an extreme clipper of 1209 tons. She had the reputation of being a fast sailing ship and made at least two passages from New York to San Francisco in 116 days, sailing for the Sutton & Co. Dispatch Line. In 1860 Capt. Bursley became her master. She was sold to a German company in 1866.[38]

In the design of his clipper ships, Hood collaborated with the marine architects John Willis Griffiths and Stephen Dickinson. Griffiths was the author of two books, *The Ship-Builders Manual* and *A Treatise on Marine and Naval Architecture,* which became the standard works on the subject during the mid-19th century.[39]

Many of Hood's ships were custom-built for various New York shipping companies. For example, the *Raven* was built for the firm of Crocker & Sturgis of Boston and later owned by the firm of Crocker and Warren of New York. Eventually, Crocker and Warren, which was engaged in the East India trade, owned at least three of the Hood clippers, *Raven, Archer,* and *Skylark.* Although the firm was based in New York, it was a partnership between Ebenezer Crocker, a native of Barnstable, and George Warren, a native of Plymouth, and had strong ties to the trade of southeastern Massachusetts.[40]

The *Rip Van Winkle,* named for Washington Irving's character, was launched on March 18, 1851, and went into service on the run from Europe to Australia. [41] The following is an advertisement for a sailing from Liverpool to Port Philip, Australia, in 1852 that captures the spirit of clipper ship travel.

> AUSTRALIA.— Emigration from Liverpool.—
> For PORT PHILIP direct, to sail positively the 20th of July, the clipper United States frigate-built ship RIP VAN WINKLE, A.F. house Dock. This new, powerful, and fast-sailing ship has cabins unequalled

for extent and splendour; her second cabins are unsurpassed for space
and comfortable accommodation, and her third cabins are arranged with
the utmost regard to the convenience of passengers. She will be fitted up
and provisioned with every attention to secure the comfort of passengers
on the voyage, under the inspection of Her Majesty's Emigration Agents,
and will carry an experienced surgeon. Cabins all enclosed. Captain
Smith has had many years' successful experience in the passenger trade.
The Rip Van Winkle has been built in the most elegant and substantial
manner, with all modern improvements, and with special regard to speed
in sailing, being intended for the regular New York packet service, from
which she is temporarily withdrawn for this voyage only. Apply to James
M'Henry, 5 Temple-place, Liverpool; or to Campbell and Rudd, bro-
kers, 2, King-street, Liverpool. This ship will carry Phillips' Patent Fire
Annihilator. [42]

The Phillips' Patent Fire Annihilator was an early carbon-dioxide
fire extinguisher which produced the gas by a chemical reaction. It performed well in most tests carried out by the inventor and his agents but
proved unreliable in practice.[43]

On this voyage, the *Rip Van Winkle* arrived at Melbourne on
November 11, 1852, after an eastward passage around the Cape of Good
Hope of only 101 days from Liverpool with 46 passengers in the cabin
and 256 in the steerage. Such a rapid passage was essential if large numbers of people were to be transported long distances with a minimum of
sickness.

The Melbourne *Argus* reported:

> The *Rip Van Winkle* is an American ship, chartered by Liverpool mer-
> chants, and a superior class of ship, both as regards her model, accom-
> modations and fittings, the latter being very superior. She entered the
> harbour with the American ensign flying from the peak, having fired a
> royal salute when about three miles below Williamstown. Little or no
> sickness has occurred on the passage — only two infants having died. She
> has upwards of three hundred passengers on board, and a small cargo, all
> for Melbourne.[44]

The most famous ship that Captain Hood built was the *Raven*. She
was considered to be an extreme clipper, meaning that she had very sharp
ends and sacrificed tonnage for speed. A small ship by comparison to
other clippers of the period, the *Raven* displaced only 711$\frac{32}{95}$ tons. She
was 151 feet long and only 33 feet wide with a depth of 13 feet. She had
two decks, three masts and a figurehead depicting a raven's head.[45]

In the summer of 1851 a race around Cape Horn developed between the *Typhoon*, the *Raven*, and the *Sea Witch*. The *Typhoon* was a large, extreme clipper ship of 1611 tons, more than twice as large as the *Raven*. She was designed by Samuel Harte Pook and was built by the yard of Ferdinand and Pettigrew in Portsmouth, New Hampshire, for the California and China trade. The *Sea Witch* was a very famous clipper of 908 tons, designed by John W. Griffiths, who also designed ships for Captain Hood. She was built by the firm of Howland and Aspinwall, which would later build the Panama Railroad to link packet routes between New York and San Francisco. The city of Aspinwall, now Colon, in Panama was named for one of the principals in this firm, William H. Aspinwall.

The *Raven* sailed from Boston on August 5 under the command of Captain William H. Henry, several days after the other two ships. The *Sea Witch* led the way south in the Atlantic to the equator, but the *Raven* caught up with her off Cape Horn, at the bottom of South America, with the *Typhoon* less than a day behind them. On the run back to the equator in the Pacific, the *Sea Witch* flew on ahead, crossing the line with a two-day lead over the *Raven*, and a four-day lead over the *Typhoon*. Then the winds changed and the *Typhoon's* size gave her the advantage. She flew on past the *Raven* and pulled ahead of the *Sea Witch*. The *Typhoon* arrived in San Francisco first, entering the harbor on November 18, followed by the *Raven* on November 19 and the *Sea Witch* on November 20, but because the *Raven* had sailed after the others, she emerged as the winner with a passage of 106 days from Boston Light.[46]

In 1863, the *Raven* put in to Rio de Janeiro, leaking badly and was condemned. However, she was repaired and in 1864 was sold to a Brazilian owner and renamed *Bessie*. The last known reference to her was in 1875 when she was registered under the name *Mondego* under a Portuguese owner.[47]

In July 1851, Hood began to speculate in real estate in a big way. He bought several lots of land, comprising more than 58 acres, in the nearby town of Norton for $2,488 from a consortium led by Leavitt Jackson of Brunswick, Maine, and including investors from Missouri, Massachusetts, Virginia, Ohio, and Illinois. This land was part of the Mine Farm which had been subdivided and was being sold off.[48] Since Hood had no other interests in Norton, this can be seen as a straightforward investment, probably of excess profits from his shipyard.

Eighteen fifty-three proved to be the top of the clipper ship bubble.

Almost 120 new fast ships were built that year, and the competition
meant that they were having trouble finding cargos. In 1854, the rate of
building slowed dramatically. But Captain Hood had seen this coming,
and in 1852 he had begun building revenue cutters for the U.S. Rev-
enue-Marine and lightships for the U.S. Lighthouse Board. Given the
state of political patronage in the 1850s, the granting of these contracts
indicates that Captain Hood had developed some powerful connections.
He resided in the 10th Massachusetts Congressional District and was
represented during these years by Joseph Grinnell of New Bedford and
Zeno Scudder of Barnstable, both of whom were Whigs like Captain
Hood. By 1853 he had established a second shipyard in Bristol, Rhode
Island, to help fulfill these government contracts.[49]

The revenue cutters were small, fast topsail schooners which were
charged with enforcing the laws regarding import duties. They acted
against smugglers and pirates in a continual game of cat and mouse. It
was not unusual for a shipyard to build both revenue cutters and smugglers' schooners side by side. The Hood-built cutters were named for
members of President Franklin Pierce's administration. The *James C.
Campbell* was named for the postmaster general, the *Robert McClelland*
for the secretary of the interior, the *J.C. Dobbin* for the secretary of the
navy, the *Caleb Cushing* for the attorney general, the *Jefferson Davis* for
the secretary of war who later became president of the Confederate States,
and the *William A. Marcy* for the secretary of state. These vessels were
significantly larger than the revenue cutters built in the same year by
Page and Allen. They were also quite different from the Joe Lane class
of cutters, being about 10 feet shorter on deck and 2 feet deeper in the
hold. They were rigged as topsail schooners and armed with a single 30
or 32 pounder rifle, supplemented in some cases with a 12 pounder.[50]

The first American lightship was deployed in 1820 in Chesapeake
Bay, and by the 1850s a number of them were in service. They were
anchored on dangerous reefs, shoals and sandbars where lighthouses
could not be built and were named for the place where they were sta-
tioned and given the designation LV followed by a number or a letter.
LV stood for light vessel. The Hood-built lightships included the LV-3,
Shovelful Shoal, named for the sandbar at the south end of Monomoy
Island off the south coast of Cape Cod; the LV-13, *Succonnessett Shoal*,
which served as a reference mark for vessels using the north channel of
Nantucket Sound; the LV-16, *Sandy Hook*, which marked the Ambrose

LV-3, Shovelful Shoal lightship, built by Captain Hood in 1852, 140 tons, contract price $12,000. Courtesy U.S. Coast Guard Historian's Office.

3ᵈ Dut. Phty. from 6 Dec. 1894 to 1 Dec. 1908 Sandy Hook Lt. V
Nº 16.

Channel into New York Bay; and, LV-E, *Rattlesnake*, which marked the entrance to Charleston, South Carolina. The LV-7, *Minot's Ledge*, was named for a rocky obstruction that is part of the dangerous Cohasset Rocks, about a mile offshore from the town of Scituate on the south shore of Massachusetts Bay. She was stationed on the ledge from 1854 to 1860, when a granite lighthouse was built there, and then repositioned in Vineyard Sound, between Martha's Vineyard and Cape Cod. A contract for a sixth lightship, the *Rough and Ready*, was cancelled for "failure to construct on time." The contract prices of these lightships ranged from $12,000 for the *Succonnessett Shoal* to $28,084 for the *Sandy Hook*. These prices were between 3 and 5 times as much as for a standard fore-and-aft rigged ship of the same size. The lightships carried one or two lanterns, each of which consisted of eight oil lamps, mounted on their masts. They also carried a large bell and horn, both of which were hand operated, for use in fog.[51]

The government contracts did not always go smoothly, however. There were disputes over the quality of Hood's materials and workmanship, and over the cost of the ships. In the spring of 1854, Hood had Capt. Ezekiel Jones of the U.S. Revenue Service arrested and held in Taunton on a charge of threatening to shoot him.[52] The *Milwaukee Sentinel* offered the following commentary:

> New Method of Enforcing Government Contracts — Capt. Ezekiel Jones — who by his name should be a Welshman, and therefore congenitally peppery — was ordered by Justice Ondronaux of Taunton, on Saturday, for threating to blow out the brains of James M. Hood, of Somerset, to pay the costs of prosecution, and to give bonds not to blow out any body's brains except his own during the next year. It appeared that Capt. Jones is a government superintendent, and that Capt. Hood is a contractor for five light boats. Light as these were, Capt. Jones felt that his responsibility was heavy, and that Capt. Hood was making too light of his contract as well as too much money out of it. Thus thwarted as to the thwarts and sternly repulsed in respect of the sterns, Capt. Jones took the novel method of bringing Capt. Hood up to the mark by making a mark of him. Although this might be pleasing to the secretary of the Treasury, who has just been all the way to Kentucky to help save his

Opposite — top: LV-13 *Succonnessett Shoal,* built by Captain Hood in 1854, 155 tons, contract price $12,000. *Bottom*: LV-16 *Sandy Hook,* built by Captain Hood in 1854, 250 tons, contract price $28,084. Photographs courtesy U.S. Coast Guard Historian's Office.

friend Ward from the scaffold, it was displeasing to the soul of the Taunton Justice, and Jones was at once made bonded goods of, as we have stated. Probably Capt. Ezekiel Jones thought that desperate diseases required desperate remedies. Perhaps he had seen the light-boat designed for Nantucket Shoals,— a craftily constructed craft, in every way fitted to go to pieces with commendable rapidity upon the very first blast of Boras, and capable of the highest degree of safety only upon being taken five thousand miles above the level of the sea. We should have been sorry to have had the brains of the builder of that boat blown out after the Jonesean method, but if, before its non-construction, that contractor had died an easy but certain death, it would have been several thousand dollars in the pocket of the venerable Samuel, and no loss at all to the maritime age in which we live.[53]

The lightship referred to in this article was LV-11, which was built in Baltimore, Maryland, by Tardy & Auld in 1853 and had not yet taken up its station when the article was written. It was, in fact, blown ashore at Montauk Point on Long Island after its moorings broke in February 1855, but in spite of the editor's allegation, there is no record that the grounding was due to faulty workmanship.[54] The secretary of the treasury he mentions was Thomas Corwin, but what the incident involving Ward was is unknown.

In addition to his shipbuilding activities, Captain Hood also had ownership interests in active merchant ships, including the brig *Oregon*, the schooner *Horatio Ames,* the schooner *Lady Adams* and the bark *Flight,* which was one of the last ships built in his yard. In 1855 he sold his ⅜₆ share of the *Lady Adams* to Joseph Marble for $280.[55]

The success of the shipyard spurred further industrial investment. In April 1853, the Somerset Iron Works was incorporated with James M. Hood as a director and president. Other directors included his brother George B. Hood, his cousin Joseph Marble, Edward Slade, Moses Buffington, David P. Davis, and the son of his neighbor, John Q. Pierce, who contributed land on the river next to the shipyard for the works. The start-up capital was $35,000. The works were nearly completed by November and included a wharf on the Taunton River and an 80 horsepower steam engine.[56] The company initially operated as an anchor forge and a brass foundry, providing some of the ironwork and fittings used in the shipyard.

Soon afterwards, James also established the Boston Stove Foundry on the other side of the shipyard. This company produced cast iron stoves for heating, ranges for cooking, iron sinks, chimney flues, pots, kettles, and a wide variety of other iron castings. The firm had a start-up capital of $25,000. Once again, his brothers and cousins were the principle investors and directors. Captain Hood's nephew William Perry Hood, the business manager of the shipyard, was also the managing director of the stove foundry.[57] Neither of these enterprises proved to be as profitable as the shipyard, but they limped along for several years before being taken over by others.

The *Fall River Monitor* commented on the increase in business in Somerset in 1853 as follows:

> During the present year many buildings have been erected, but the demand is greater than the supply. Arrangements are in progress for the erection of a large number of dwellings the coming year for the wants of the augmenting population.
>
> From the business now transacted, and the prospective arrangements of the future, we are led to assume, that Somerset is destined to become a place of importance, and eventually one of the most thriving towns in Bristol County. For the impulse given to enterprise, the community are indebted largely to Capt. James M. Hood, the enterprising ship builder.[58]

In spite of this rosy view, Captain Hood's enterprises ran into financial difficulties in 1854. The Somerset Iron Works was sold at auction on September 20,[59] and the next day, the Hoods' shipyard came to a sudden and dramatic end. On the night of Thursday, September 21, 1854, a fire started in the cabin of the large ship *Somerset*, of about 2,000 tons, that was being constructed on Hood's own account. It flared up quickly and spread to the buildings in the yard as well as to Captain Hood's home, which was also destroyed. By this time, Somerset had acquired a small fire engine, but it was unable to suppress the flames. Eventually the fire was seen from Fall River and the *Mazeppa* fire engine, named for a legendary Cossack hetman, was ferried over from there to help. It contributed to saving a large quantity of timber. It was estimated that the ship itself contained about one and a half million board feet of well-seasoned wood, which, assembled into the open work structure of a ship, burned fiercely. The light of the fire could be seen from as far away as New Bedford and Watch Hill, Rhode Island. Luckily, only one person died, Caleb Evans, an 83-year-old man who was asleep in one of the yard buildings at the time. The bark *Escort*, which was being constructed nearby in the yard, was saved by covering it with wet blankets. The fire put some 100 men out of work as well as burning up the chests and tools of the shipwrights. The total loss was estimated at $100,000, although the ship, the shipyard, and Hood's house were all insured, with the policies spread over some seven different insurance companies.[60]

Based on the rapid spread of the initial fire throughout the ship, arson was immediately suspected. A Mr. Brady happened to be passing by and noticed someone running from the ship soon after the fire started. Conveniently, Captain Hood was absent at the time, having left for New York that evening on the Fall River steamboat, but Brady thought that the person he saw leaving the ship was the general manager of the yard, Captain Hood's nephew, William Perry Hood. William was duly arrested on suspicion of setting the fire.[61]

The accusation of William Hood raises many questions about why the head clerk of the shipyard might have been led to burn one of his own ships. One possibility is that the company was under financial duress. It had invested heavily in new buildings and raw materials in 1853 in anticipation of continued strong demand for clipper ships, and the general fall off in orders which affected the entire industry in 1854, combined with the investments they had made in the iron and stove works, may have put the Hoods in a cash crunch. Perhaps they hoped that an insurance settlement would help them clear their debts. If this was the case, then the fact that the fire got out of control and destroyed the entire yard was an unexpected outcome.

On the other hand, there was widespread speculation that the fire had been set by a rival shipyard owner, or by a disgruntled worker who had also sabotaged several of the lightships by drilling holes in their bottoms. For those who held this opinion, the accusation against William Hood was an attempt to divert attention from the real perpetrators. A poem was even written and published in the *Taunton Gazette* giving this version of the incident and its aftermath. It ran on for 23 stanzas and included the following verses:

> It was all supposed to be
> The work of an incendiary
> Who could possess so vile a heart
> As to destroy that splendid Bark?
>
> Confined within the prison walls
> Are two who've labored very hard

They vainly set their wits to work
For the ruin of the head clerk.

T'was by those envious-hearted men,
The innocent was thus condemned,
So very strange it all seemed
He being worthily esteemed.

Possessed of a most noble mind,
Nothing against him could they find,
Nor reason for suspicion see —
An thus they did pronounce him free.[62]

The *Escort* was finished quickly and launched in October, the last vessel to come out of Captain Hood's Somerset shipyard. This was small vessel of 474⁵⁹⁄₉₅ tons, 127 feet long with a width of 29 feet and a depth of 14 feet. It was built for Capt. Talman B. Wakeman of Southport, Connecticut, and had two decks, three masts and a billethead.

William Perry's trial for arson was held on Saturday, November 4. The defense alleged that Olmstead and Brady, the two witnesses who claimed to have seen him at the scene, were actually agents of the insurance companies which had insured the ship that burned, and that they were trying to "fasten the guilt upon the nephew, and then, by establishing a relationship between him and the uncle, escape the payment of the insurance."[63] Hood called a large number of witnesses in his defense and before a favorably inclined jury of friends and neighbors, he was acquitted.[64] On November 8, at a meeting held in Mechanics' Hall in Somerset, a group of citizens passed the following series of resolves congratulating William Perry on his honorable acquittal and asserting their opinion of his honesty and good character.

Resolved, That it is our duty to make some public demonstration of our regard for him.
Resolved, That we congratulate him upon his honorable acquittal, after an impartial investigation.
Resolved, That we tender him our sympathies; and that our confidence is unshaken in the integrity of his character, which remains, as it ever had been, unimpeachable.[65]

Five days later, on November 13, William's friends and supporters gave a public banquet in his honor at Babbitt's Hall, which over 100 people attended. Music was provided by the Somerset Brass Band. After the meal, everyone adjourned to Mechanics' Hall, where they danced until dawn.[66]

Having been acquitted, William Perry Hood promptly accused Brady and Olmstead of perjury for falsely naming him as the arsonist. Brady went to trial and was acquitted, on the grounds that he only testified that he thought the person leaving the ship looked like William Hood and not that he knew positively that it was him. The verdict was appealed and upheld by the Supreme Judicial Court of Massachusetts.[67]

In the end, it was never determined who did set fire to the ship that dark September night, but the consequences for Captain James Hood were severe.

As if the fire was not enough of a shock, in December, the New York Court of Appeals finally ruled against Captain Hood in his suit against the Manhattan Insurance Company for damages from the fire of 1849.[68] Then the U.S. Lighthouse Service withheld payment for two of the lightships Hood had built, claiming that they were not fit for use. Hood was obliged to spend about $8,000 to pull them out of the water to fix holes in their hulls. It was said that the ships had been sabotaged, but no charges were ever brought.

With all these reverses coming at the same time, the *Providence Post* reported on December 18 that both Captain Hood and his brother George B. Hood were unable to meet their financial obligations.[69] That report was denied by William Perry Hood and was retracted the next day,[70] but James was unable to resolve his affairs and on March 24, 1855, he was officially declared insolvent. Interestingly, the trustees appointed to take possession of Captain Hood's property for the purposes of liquidating it and paying off his creditors were David Anthony, president of the Fall River Bank, and Hood's own nephew and business manager, William Perry Hood, the very man accused of setting the fire.[71] The decree of insolvency under Massachusetts law was not a bankruptcy, and did not technically discharge Captain Hood's debts, but simply distributed his assets to his creditors, many of whom would attempt to collect the remainder due when he returned home from Siam.[72]

The claims against Captain Hood totaled $67,257.98 and give us a picture of the wide ranging contacts that he had established as a shipbuilder. They ranged from $4.00 owed to one Henry Pratt of Fall River, Massachusetts, up to a $5,229.32 debt to Benjamin J.H. Trask, Jr., a ship chandler on South Street in New York City. Among the creditors were Wilson L. Cannen of Leipsic, Delaware, who claimed that Captain Hood owed him $3,709 for ship timber; the Crocker Bros. Copper

Works in Taunton; Sillock Nichols, a maker of ships' blocks in New York; Stoddard & McLauchlin of Boston, ship carvers; and George W. Robinson & Co., locksmiths, also of Boston. Lumber dealers to whom Hood owed money included William B. Giles of Savannah, Georgia, for sawn pine boards, Campbell & Moody of New York, and Joseph H. Crane of Fall River. He had purchased spars from A. Denike & Co. of New York, paint from Henry Waldron of New York, pottery from the Somerset Pottery Works, tools from the Providence Tool Company, and various iron fittings from the Somerset Iron Works, the Somerset Foundry and Machine Co., and Edgar M. Brown of New York. His carriages and harness came from Sargent, Gunnison & Co. of Boston.

Among his family and friends, he owed money to his nephew Alfred H. Hood, who was living in San Francisco at the time. Alfred was the son of his brother David B. Hood.

In addition, Hood owed back taxes of $500 to Bristol County and $109.25 to the Town of Somerset, and he had an outstanding loan of $3,455.03 from the Marine Bank of New York. Finally, he owed almost $400 to his New York lawyers, the firm of Bovee and Bromley.[73]

All of these creditors were initially paid off at the rate of ten cents on the dollar, an amount that was increased to nineteen cents and eight mils ($0.198) in 1858.[74]

The trustees started selling off the lands owned by Captain Hood in August 1855. Over the next three years they engaged in ten separate land sales, the last one occurring in July 1858. Not surprisingly, the assets were selectively disposed of. For example, the land on which the shipyard stood was taken over by James' brother George B. Hood, who had managed to stay solvent, for a payment of $2,800, and some of the land was sold to the Mount Hope Iron Company in which the Hoods had interests. With this resolution of his debts, Captain Hood began to recover his fortunes and by October 1857 was buying land in Somerset back from his nephew William Perry.[75]

This second bankruptcy was a setback for James, but not a fatal one. The year before the fire, he had been elected to the Great and General Court of Massachusetts, as the state legislature is known. He was also looking west, planning for a move to Illinois. The first two chapters in his life, as ship captain and shipbuilder, were over, but there was much more to come.

Ships Built by the James M. Hood Shipyard, Somerset, Massachusetts.

Year	Name	Type	Size	Cost
1848	Empire State	Schooner		
1849	Somerset	Brig		
	Milford	Ship		
	Fountain	Ship		
1850	Rosario	Clipper Bark	528 tons	
	Fanny Major	Bark	227 tons	
	William Nelson	Ship	1039 tons	
1851	Raven	Clipper	711 tons	
	Greenfield	Clipper Bark	562 tons	
	Pathfinder	Clipper Bark	373 tons	
	Gov. Morton	Clipper	1429 tons	
1852	Archer	Clipper	1095 tons	
	Rip Van Winkle	Clipper	1095 tons	
	William Mason			
	Mary and Susan	Schooner		
	James C. Campbell	Revenue Cutter	174 tons	
	Robert McClelland	Revenue Cutter	174 tons	
	James C. Dobbin	Revenue Cutter	174 tons	
	Caleb Cushing	Revenue Cutter	153 tons	
	LV-3 Shovelful	Lightship	140 tons	$12,000
	Rough and Ready	Lightship		
	LV-E Rattlesnake	Lightship		
1853	Skylark	Clipper	1209 tons	
	Mischief	Clipper	561 tons	
1854	Escort	Bark	475 tons	
	Flight	Bark		
	Casanova	Bark		
	LV-7 Minot's Ledge	Lightship	142 tons	$18,304
	LV-13 Succonnessett Shoal	Lightship	155 tons	$12,000
	LV-16 Sandy Hook	Lightship	250 tons	$28,084

Ships built in the Hood shipyard in Bristol Rhode Island

1853	William A. Marcy	Revenue Cutter	179 tons	
	Jefferson Davis	Revenue Cutter	176 tons	

5

Whig Legislator

The 1850s were a time of political turmoil in the United States, and Massachusetts was no exception. The question of the expansion of slavery into the Midwest and the new territories recently won from Mexico excited national debate and threatened old party lines. The Democratic Party, in particular, was showing signs of stress as northern Democrats aligned themselves with the Free Soil Party while southern Democrats staunchly defended their intent to bring their peculiar institution to the new states.

As a successful businessman, Captain James Hood joined the conservative Whig Party. This was the party of wealth and industry, as well as the party of many of his immediate family. The Whig Party had been founded in the 1830s to oppose President Andrew Jackson's Democrats. The issue of the day was the economy, and specifically, whether or not the federal government should have a central bank. The Democrats believed that a central bank favored moneyed interests over farmers and small businessmen, and opposed the bank. Upon his election to the presidency in 1828, Jackson started a campaign to revoke the charter of the Second Bank of the United States. In response, the loose Anti-Jacksonian coalition came together to form the new party.

The First Bank of the United States had been established by Alexander Hamilton in 1791 under President George Washington. The Democratic Party opposed it throughout its life and defeated an attempt to extend its charter when it ran out in 1811, even though the bank was supported by the sitting president, James Madison. Four years later, in 1816, after experiencing severe inflation during the War of 1812, and with the government deeply in debt, Madison persuaded Congress to go back to a central bank by creating the Second Bank of the United States.

Jackson and his colleagues in the Democratic Party had always been opposed to the Bank of the United States, which they saw as a tool of the rich and an excessive concentration of power in the federal government. They preferred to place deposits of United States government funds in state banks, where they would be more available for loans to small businesses. Although the bank's 20-year charter ran until 1836, a bill to renew it was introduced in 1832 at the end of Jackson's first term. When this bill was defeated, Jackson began withdrawing funds from the bank and redistributing them to the state banks. Without the federal deposits, the Bank of the United States could not survive. In response, in early 1834, when James Hood was 18, Senators Henry Clay of Kentucky and Daniel Webster of Massachusetts, both of whom would become Whigs, called for petitions to Congress from anti–Jacksonians in all the states to restore the federal deposits to the Bank of the United States. This drive marked the birth of the Whig Party.[1]

The petition from Bristol County, Massachusetts, dated March 31, 1834, began by stating:

> That during the last summer the condition of our country was flourishing, and the facilities of credit equal to the necessities of business; but so much embarrassment is now experienced, that without relief much business must be suspended.

It then went on to list specific problems, including falling prices, a collapsing real estate market, and business failures, before fixing blame for the recession as follows:

> We do not undertake to point out the cause of these calamities; we know that they were nearly coeval with the removal of the revenue deposits from the Bank of the United States, and we would, therefore, suggest a restoration of the Deposits, and an extension of the charter of the Bank for two years, as a remedy which might be tried without injury to any of the national interests. If present relief was afforded, the future contingencies of business might be met by gradual preparation; and it is possible that some system, agreeable to all, may be devised hereafter, which will prevent the manifold evils of an irregular, unequal, and fluctuating currency.[2]

This petition was signed by more than 2,000 residents of Bristol County, including James Hood's father, John, and his older brothers John Jr., and George B. The petition did not sway Jackson and his supporters, and the charter of the Second Bank of the United States was allowed to expire in 1836. It received a new charter from the state of Pennsylvania and survived as an ordinary bank for five more years, before entering bankruptcy in 1841.[3]

By 1852, when Hood's shipyard was flourishing, the Whigs were the dominant party in Massachusetts, but a curious thing happened early in 1853. The Legislature had called for a constitutional convention in the state, which was to meet in May. It is likely that Hood was the Whig candidate from Somerset for convention delegate, and he would have had every expectation of getting elected. However, to the surprise of the Whigs, the Democrats and the Free Soil Party formed a coalition, and swept the election on March 7. On March 8, the day after the election, with 100 towns reporting, the count stood at 88 Whig delegates to 111 coalition delegates, giving the coalition a majority at the convention.[4] The small towns voted for the coalition and Boston was the only major city won by the Whigs. The race for delegate from Somerset was won by Daniel Wilbur, who ran as a Democrat. The Taunton *Daily Gazette* was jubilant at the Whig defeat.

> "Old Bristol" is the Banner County
> We publish, with no ordinary pleasure, the returns of delegates recently elected in Bristol County. "Total — 28 members; ALL *friends of the Convention*; No whigs — NO vacancies!" Is the message that Old Bristol sends greeting, with a solid phalanx of reformers to her sister counties in the Convention.[5]

The Constitutional Convention met in the chamber of the House of Representatives in Boston from May 4 to August 2, with 405 delegates.[6] In spite of speculation that the results of the convention had been decided by the coalition in advance, there was much spirited debate on the floor and not all of the anti–Whig measures passed. There was even serious consideration of women's suffrage, with Lucy Stone, a prominent proponent of women's rights, allowed to address the delegates.[7]

In the end, the convention produced a revised constitution plus seven separate amendments, all of which would need to be approved by the voters at the November elections. The amendments dealt with writs of *habeas corpus,* the role of the jury in criminal trials, claims against the commonwealth, imprisonment for debt, prohibiting state funding for religious schools, general incorporation, and the chartering of banks. The amendments were not controversial, but the rewritten constitution was. In particular, the constitution did not change the method of allocating representatives. This was done by towns, rather than by population, and it gave a disproportionate number of seats to the small towns in the western part of the state. The new constitution also truncated the terms of judges from life to 10 years for the Supreme Judicial Court and the Court of Common Pleas. Both changes were extremely unpopular. The representation issue was opposed in the cities, which had a larger number of voters. The judicial term limit issue was seen as politicizing the judiciary.[8,9]

In the backlash caused by the unpopularity of the proposed new constitution that the Democrats had produced, the Whigs came back to power in the fall elections of 1853. Captain Hood ran for the state representative's seat from Somerset and on Monday, November 14, he won, as a part of the Whig landslide. The Whigs achieved an overwhelming majority of 196 out of 308 representatives in the House and 30 out of 40 senators in the state Senate.[10] In the same election, the proposed new state constitution was defeated by about 5,000 votes, or about 4 percent.[11]

Eighteen fifty-four would be a pivotal year in American politics, seeing the split of the Democratic Party into regional factions and the effective death of the Whig Party, but these events were still just a cloud on the horizon when Captain Hood was sworn in and took his seat in the Great and General Court of the Commonwealth of Massachusetts on Wednesday, January 4, and became the Honorable Mr. Hood.[12] He was appointed to the joint standing committee on Mercantile Affairs and Insurance, an interesting assignment considering his history of problems with insurance companies. He also served on the joint special committee on establishing hours of labor and the joint special committee to ascertain when the standing committees would report.[13]

Although there was a rail connection between Boston and Somerset via the Boston and Providence Railroad and the Fall River branch, Captain Hood probably stayed in Boston during the week while the legislature was in session, returning home only on the weekends. Whether or not his wife, Anna, joined him there is unknown, but it is likely that she stayed in Somerset, where she was closer to her family. Such a separation could have introduced stresses into their relationship that would become manifest five years later in Illinois.

Governor Emory Washburn addressed a joint session of the House and Senate on January 12, 1854. His speech, which, in the official record, is nine pages long, deals exclusively with state issues. There is no mention of the brewing national debate over slavery. Instead, the governor reviewed the state of the commonwealth in glowing terms and offered little in the way of recommendations for new legislation, other than to urge the members to find a way to deal with the apportionment issue so as to provide for more equal representation across the state. He stated, "Coming, as I do, from the engrossing duties of a profession whose business is to interpret existing laws, rather than to devise new ones, I cannot be expected ... to offer many suggestions respecting the business of the session."[14]

In his first term, Hood kept a low profile. The *Boston Daily Atlas*, which reported extensively on each day's legislative session, did not report any speeches by him; however, he was not idle. One of his first actions was to introduce a bill to incorporate the Boston Stove Foundry Company at Somerset, the company which he had helped found the previous year and of which he was a director. It was to be capitalized for $25,000, or about $10 million in today's money.[15] He looked after his constituents, sponsoring a bill which authorized Israel Brayton to plant oysters in Taunton Great River at Somerset.[16] He also began to cultivate contacts among business interests in Boston, and on February 21, he introduced a bill to increase the capital stock of the East Boston Dry Dock Company.[17]

One of the longstanding issues for the Town of Somerset was the detour that townspeople had to make around a large inlet called Broad Cove on their way north to Dighton and the county seat at Taunton. Hood supported a bill transferring a small amount of land from Dighton to Somerset, which gave Somerset a bridgehead on the north shore of Broad Cove. He then introduced another bill to allow the Town of Somerset to build a bridge over the cove. Hood and others had petitioned for this bridge in 1853 before he got elected, but the last legislature had not acted on their petition, so he shepherded it through the legislature himself.[18] This bill may also have had the effect of increasing the value of his wife's land on the river near Broad Cove.[19] Hood was also occasionally noticed as reporting bills out from the Mercantile Affairs Committee.

The accounts of the legislative session reveal that it concerned itself with many minutiae. Since there was no general law regarding incorporation, the formation of almost every corporation required a separate act of the legislature. These acts specified the business that the corporation could engage in, the amount of capital they could raise, and often, how much time they had to raise that capital. If a corporation wanted to raise additional capital, it had to come back to the legislature for approval. A separate act was required for each city or town that wanted to form a fire department or a police court, as local courts were known, because these were relatively new institutions at the time. Many acts related to railroads, which were also new and constantly presenting unforeseen problems as they came into conflict with roads and landowners. Among these were a bill to protect landowners from encroachment by the railroads and a bill to resolve conflicts between railroads and street traffic.[20]

The *Boston Courier* ran the following profile of Captain Hood as one of a series it did on selected legislators. It is the earliest known character sketch of him, and is consistent with later descriptions.

> James M. Hood was born in that town [Somerset], January 14, 1815, and this is his first year of legislative life. He is an attentive member and a hard worker in committee. If as faithful an adherent of his Church doctrines as he is his Whig creed, there can be little doubt of his salvation. Like a true sailor, he hates sophistry; and he who would treat with him must come divested of sentimentality and cant. There are various anecdotes in circulation concerning him. One is that during the Fugitive Slave bill excitement of 1850, the local clergyman of Somerset was holding forth in the town-hall, in true Abolition style. When the reverend clergyman had got about half through his discourse, Mr. Hood rose and said: "Ladies and gentlemen, enough of this! Fellow-citizens, those of you that are of the opinion that our parson had better attend to his prayers and let politics alone, will say aye" — and the response was almost unanimous against the political parson. During the present session of the Legislature, he was appointed a member of the Committee to nominate Overseers of Harvard College. The chairman, who is a high-toned gentleman, suggested the names of many gentlemen whose abilities were undoubted, but they were mostly of one religious sect. Mr. Hood broke in upon the chairman with sailor-like frankness: "I don't like that deal! Our folks down my way don't believe in the infallibility of a Unitarian Board of Overseers. They'd like a man after their own heart." "Pray, Mr. Hood," said the chairman, in a tone of characteristic meekness, "may I ask to what denomination you belong?" "Yes, sir," said the other, "I am a Baptist — by God." But this is a rough view of Mr. Hood's character. He is really a kind-hearted man, and is the idol of his neighbors. By his own industry he has acquired a large fortune, and at his ship-building establishment in Somerset he gives employment and the highest wages to a

large number of men. His ships are among the most substantial afloat, and he has furnished many vessels for the United States government. Mr. Hood is a man after Julius Caesar's heart. Had the Roman warrior seen him when he cried out to Antony — "Let me have men about me that are fat: Sleek headed men, and such as sleep of nights!" — he would have embraced him, as one to be relied upon and trusted in the greatest emergency.[21]

One railroad question which was especially contentious was a proposal to lend state money to the Troy and Greenfield Railroad. This company, led by Fitchburg paper mill owner Alvah Crocker, wanted to construct a railroad tunnel through Hoosac Mountain, in the towns of Florida and North Adams in northwestern Massachusetts. This was supported by the towns across the northern part of the state, which would benefit from a rail link between Albany and Boston, but opposed by those along the route of the already existing Western Railroad through Worcester and Springfield. Work on the tunnel had started in 1851, but the estimated $2 million cost was beyond the ability of the company to raise in the private capital markets. In spite of determined opposition, the bill to grant the loan eventually passed.[22] Unfortunately, the loan was so loaded with restrictions and regulations, that the company was unable to live up to its part of the agreement. This was the start of decades of state interference with the construction of the tunnel. The first train would not pass through it for another twenty-one years, in 1875, when Hood was already dead. Yet the Hoosac Tunnel was considered an engineering marvel, and, with some modifications and widening, it is still in use today by Pan Am Railways, a division of Guildford Transportation Company, over a century and a half after it was begun.[23]

Captain Hood's most important piece of legislation was an act to regulate insurance companies. At the time, insurance companies were only lightly regulated. Many were small and undercapitalized, leaving them unable to cover major losses. As a result, firms seeking insurance limited their exposure to any one company by taking out policies with many different ones, including companies from out of state which were not subject to local laws. This complicated the settling of claims and the resolution of disputes.

Given his negative experiences with insurers, Hood crafted an extensive bill that contained 45 sections governing everything from the way insurance companies could be incorporated and the amount of capital they were required to have, to details of their business practices. For example, section 9 of the bill stated:

> Every person Acting for an Insurance Company incorporated in this Commonwealth, shall exhibit, in conspicuous letters, on the sign designating his place of business, the name of the State under whose authority the Company here present has been incorporated. And said Company and agent shall also have printed, in large type, the name of such State, upon all policies issued to citizens of this Commonwealth, on all cards, placards, and pamphlets, and in all advertisements published, issued or circulated in this State, relating to the business of such Company.[24]

It imposed strict reporting requirements on the companies, and generally attempted to make sure that their funds were safely invested and that they would be able to pay any claims against them. Penalties for violations of the act were severe, ranging from fines of $100 per day for late reporting to $1,000 or imprisonment for six months for false or fraudulent representations. The bill established a board of insurance commissioners consisting of the secretary, treasurer, and auditor of the commonwealth and empowered them to examine the statements and bonds of all insurance companies. To supplement his own experience, Hood probably relied on his nephew William Perry Hood for advice on how insurance companies operated. In addition to his work for the family companies, William was an insurance agent and so had knowledge of how the industry operated from the inside.

The bill was introduced on April 21, 1854, only 8 days before the end of the session and extensively debated and amended. It passed both houses of the legislature as part of a last minute rush of legislation and was signed into law by Governor Washburn. Because of this success and his contributions throughout the session, the Whig leadership recognized Captain Hood's abilities and after the session was over, appointed him as one of the twenty-eight members of the State Central Committee of the Whig Party.[25] This was a powerful position which gave him a voice in the selection of candidates and the formulation of Whig policies and platforms.

Local issues were not the only things that occupied the Massachusetts Great and General Court in 1854. The question of the extension of slavery into newly organized territories and states was a contentious one that year. The Missouri Compromise of 1820, passed at the time when the Louisiana Purchase was the westernmost territory of the United States, had prohibited slavery in any new territories or states north of 36° 30' north latitude with the exception of Missouri. When the organization of the Nebraska Territory was taken up by the U.S. Congress in 1853, the southern states tried to repeal this prohibition. It was agreed that the Nebraska Territory would be reorganized into the two new territories of Kansas and Nebraska which could then begin the process of becoming states. The problem was that if they were both admitted as free states, as required by the Missouri Compromise, the slave states would have their power in the U.S. Senate reduced. The southern legislators therefore proposed that slavery should be allowed in Kansas, even though it was north of the Compromise Line. No resolution of the issues was immediately possible, so Congress tabled the measure before it adjourned that summer.

When Congress re-convened in Washington in December 1853, the bill was immediately reintroduced. To avoid declaring the status of Kansas directly, Senator Stephen Douglas of Illinois introduced the controversial principle of popular sovereignty into the bill. This stated that the residents of a territory had the right to decide for themselves whether to allow slavery or not when they adopted their new state constitution. Douglas did this to gain support from the South, effectively revoking the Missouri Compromise and opening up the new territories in the West, which had been acquired in the Mexican War, to slavery. The popular sovereignty clause of the act led to the invasion of Kansas by armed gangs from Missouri in an attempt to force a pro-slavery state constitution, even before the act was passed. The resulting conflict was known as Bleeding Kansas.[26]

This caused a fierce outcry from the northern states. In early February 1854, the Massachusetts legislature began debating a resolve opposing the Kansas-Nebraska Act and directing its delegation in Washington to vote against it. On February 16, in the midst of the debate on this resolve, the Free Soil Party held a convention at Faneuil Hall in Boston. Attendees came from as far away as New Hampshire. For several hours in the late afternoon and evening the hundreds of attendees heard speech after speech denouncing the "Nebraska bill" while shouting down anyone who favored it. This convention adopted some of the strongest anti–Kansas-Nebraska bill resolutions yet, with clear abolitionist language. The following two are good examples of the tone adopted:

> Resolved, that it would be wicked and impious for Congress, in legislating for any territory, to say to its inhabitants "here ye may kill, here ye

may steal" — so it is wicked and impious to say, "here ye may possess your neighbor, his wife and his children, and make them your cattle."

Resolved, that if this conspiracy against liberty in America shall be consummated, if force is to be the only standard of justice and honor with the South, it cannot complain if the fire thus kindled at the North, consuming all Compromises which have given shelter to slavery, shall spread into a conflagration which will not be checked until it has swept away slavery itself.[27]

Similar meetings were held in Dedham and Fall River. Two days later, on February 18, the legislature passed the resolve. Governor Washburn approved it the next day.

Then, on March 30, 1854, the Whig Party held a legislative convention in the statehouse to elect its central committee for the following year and at that convention, passed the following resolution:

Resolved, That the bill now pending in Congress, known as the Nebraska bill, and involving the repeal of the Missouri Compromise, is a measure iniquitous in its character, so hostile to every principle of justice, and involves so gross a violation of public honor, that we are only surprised that an honest man, either North or South, can be found to sustain it.[28]

In spite of this opposition, which was echoed in all of the northern states, the Kansas-Nebraska Act finally passed the U.S. Congress on May 30.

Then, on June 2, anger over slavery issues in Massachusetts was further stoked by the case of Anthony Burns. Burns was a man who escaped from slavery in Richmond, Virginia, in 1853 and managed to reach Boston by ship. He got a job, but was arrested on May 24, while walking in the street. President Franklin Pierce chose this case to show that he was enforcing the Fugitive Slave Act, which had been passed in 1850, and ordered Burns' prosecution. A riotous mob of Bostonians tried to free Burns from the courthouse and in the melee, a U.S. marshal was fatally stabbed. In spite of the protests, Burns was tried by Edward G. Loring, the federal commissioner of the U.S. Circuit Court in Boston. Although Burns was defended by the prominent attorney and author Richard Henry Dana, the commissioner ruled against him, inciting further massive demonstrations in the city. Federal troops had to be called out to control the crowds so that Burns could be escorted to the ship that was to take him back to the South.[29]

Almost immediately upon the passage of the Kansas-Nebraska Act, impromptu conventions were called in several northern states to craft a unified response. In Massachusetts, some Whigs wanted to call a convention right away, in part so as to hold onto their leadership position in the anti-slavery movement and to prevent the Know-Nothing Party from preempting them on the issue. In mid–June, a general meeting of all citizens was called in the town hall at Concord "for the purpose of expressing their opinions in relation to the passage of the Nebraska bill, and to take such action thereon as the present exigency might seem to demand." A committee, which included the transcendental poet and abolitionist Ralph Waldo Emerson, was appointed to draft resolutions and the meeting was adjourned until Friday, June 23. When it reconvened, the meeting adopted the following resolutions, which provide a concise summary of the general opinion in New England.

Resolved, That the citizens of Concord, whose fathers were among the first to resist the tyranny of 1775, will not be the last to resist that of 1854.

Resolved, That the passage of the Nebraska and Kansas bill by the present Congress, is an unprovoked and wanton outrage upon the principles and feelings of the freemen of the North and West, and destroys all confidence in the integrity, good faith and honor of the National Government.

Resolved, That the Compromise of 1820 was in the nature of a compact between the slaveholding and non-slaveholding States, and in as much as that compact has been repudiated by one party, the other party is thereby absolved from all the obligations supposed to be imposed by it.

Resolved, That the free States are at full liberty to resist the admission of any slave State into the Union hereafter, and that it is their solemn duty so to do.

Therefore, resolved, That the whole system of compromise measures has received a fatal stab in the house of its friends, and that the fugitive slave law of 1850 was a part of that system, and cannot stand without its support.

Therefore, resolved, That the fugitive slave law of 1850 must be repealed. And whereas there are unmistakable indications of a settled purpose on the part of the administration and many of those who represent the slave States, to extend the area of slavery by conquest or annexation; And whereas we believe a large majority of the people of this State are decidedly opposed to any further encroachments of the slave power:

Therefore, resolved, That we believe it to be a duty immediately to take such steps as will unite the people of this Commonwealth for the recovery of the ground already lost to freedom, and to prevent the further aggressions of slavery.

Resolved, That a committee of six be chosen, whose duty it shall be to correspond with eminent individuals in various parts of the State, and to invite them to meet at an early day in Boston, for the purpose of making arrangements for a meeting of delegates from every town in the Commonwealth, to decide what measures shall be adopted to avert the alarming inroads of the slave power.[30]

The Whig Central State Committee, of which Captain Hood was a member, recognized that this kind of popular protest threatened its leadership position on the anti-slavery question, but, unlike the Maine Whigs who convened in Portland on June 29, it was not prepared to immediately call a convention to address the issue. Instead, the committee decided to compromise by moving their annual convention from September to August 16, which would give them a month to see how popular opinion was trending, but still appear to be proactive. In the address to the Whig Party announcing their decision, published in the Boston *Daily Atlas* on June 26, just prior to the Maine convention, and other papers throughout the state on the following days, the committee stated:

We have not been unmindful of the intense degree of sensibility which has pervaded the entire body of our party throughout the Northern and Western States consequent upon the late unprecedented action of the National Legislature, nor of the anxious forebodings which this action has excited in the bosoms of the upright and patriotic throughout the whole Union. We have been deeply solicitous that no lukewarmness should be manifested in relation to events so grievous to every patriotic spirit, and have desired in some fitting manner to respond to the universal sentiment of indignation which these events have aroused, both among our immediate constituents and our fellow Whigs in other States, equally interested with us in the honor and welfare of our common country. We have therefore anxiously considered whether any measure should be proposed to the friends of freedom and of the honor and integrity of the free States, in view of the present unexampled emergency.

The propriety of calling a Grand Mass Convention of the people of Massachusetts, or of calling a convention of delegates authorized to speak the sentiments of every town and city of this ancient Commonwealth in anticipation of the regular annual Convention, have both been suggested and considered by the Committee. Had such suggestions been presented at any other season than so shortly before the time for holding the State Convention, and had we felt that any doubt could exist as to the true sentiments and attitude of the Whig Party of Massachusetts; or indeed, of the great body of her citizens upon the subject which now so agitates the public mind, we might have deemed it incumbent upon us to issue an immediate call for such a Convention; but we believe that no such doubts can anywhere exist, and that the sentiments which have been so nobly and fearlessly proclaimed on a recent occasion on the floor of Congress, by the entire Massachusetts delegation, and which have been echoed from every Whig press throughout the State, find a deep response in the heart of every member of the Whig party and in the hearts of the great mass of the people of whatever name; and we are therefore led to the conclusion that such a demonstration may be safely deferred till the time when it has been usual to consider great questions, both of the State and National policy, at our hands. In view, however of the magnitude and importance of the question to be considered, and of a general desire for an early expression, we have decided to anticipate by a month the usual time for holding the State Convention, and to hold it this year early in August, instead of September. The inconvenience of assembling so large a body of men twice, with so brief an interval, will readily be perceived, and we have no fears the stern, inborn constitutional repugnance of the Whig party of Massachusetts, alike to human slavery and to corrupt and perfidious breaches of solemn compacts, will be lessened by delay.

The usual notice of the time and place for holding this Convention will be given, and it is superfluous for us to express the hope and belief that the importance of the occasion will bring together our wisest, purest and bravest men, who shall resolve upon and initiate such action as their duty to themselves and their country imperiously demands.

We cannot allow this occasion to pass without congratulating the Whigs of Massachusetts upon the proudly eminent position their party now occupies with the eyes of all men turned towards them, as at this momentous crisis the vanguard of the great army of constitutional liberty. But two short years since the whole country, wearied by the prolonged conflict between the free and slave States, acquiesced at last in the measures called the Compromise of 1850, as a compact for the final cessation of slavery agitation. The Whigs of Massachusetts, with great reluctance and many misgivings it is true, yet in sincere good faith, determined that they would not be the first to open afresh that exciting question. And well have they kept their pledge. Yet scarcely a year has passed of the Administration called into power, because it was supposed to have 'set its face as flint' against a renewal of the sectional conflict, when in the very face of the solemn pledges of the South, of the Democratic party and of its chosen President, a majority of Congress, without solicitation from any quarter, to the utter amazement of the whole country wantonly and ruthlessly tear down the mighty barrier erected by a past generation of patriots against the extension of slavery. Upon the recklessness, the perfidy, and the infamy of this deed, it is needless to enlarge, because upon these characteristics of the act there is no difference of opinion among the Whigs of Massachusetts or of any of the free States. And if there be one among us, who does not regard himself and his party as absolutely released from every contract, compromise or understanding, moral or conventional, expressed or implied on the subject of slavery, the plain and direct provisions of the constitution always excepted, we can only say that his name has been unspoken in our ears.

Of course, it cannot be supposed that under such an outrage as the repeal of the Missouri Compromise to say nothing of the other enormities, the rumors of which have floated to us on every breeze, the free States will lie down in meek submission. Even now, from the lips of every freeman, comes the demand for the instant restoration of that great bulwark of freedom. And it will be among the great matters for consideration of the next Convention, it is already the subject of earnest inquiry among individuals, whether we can now satisfy ourselves with the simple restoration of that which has been torn down, or whether we ought not to resolve upon some further action having for its object not merely the recovery of the ground lost for a time to freedom, but the erection of impregnable barriers against the extension of slavery and against the unceasing assaults of the slave power.

With no responsibility for the renewal of the agitation of slavery, and with the lesson so lately taught us that no compact is sacred to the South, the moment they have nothing to gain by it, we have only now to seek what measures are best adapted "to promote the general welfare and to secure the blessings of liberty to ourselves and posterity," and to this end to invoke the aid of every member of the Whig party and the co-operation of all who sincerely desire to check the encroachments of slavery and to secure the triumph of free principles throughout our vast territories.[31]

This document was signed by the entire State Central Committee of the Whig Party, including Captain Hood.

The Maine convention passed 13 separate resolutions against the Kansas-Nebraska Act and the Fugitive Slave Act. These resolutions set a pattern that would be followed by the Massachusetts Whig convention in August, with some of them being copied verbatim.[32]

The Free Soil Party held a preliminary convention in Worcester on July 20 to attempt to forge a coalition between themselves, the Know-Nothings, and anti-slavery Whigs and Democrats. Almost 2,000 men attended, but not as formally elected delegates. They heard an afternoon of speeches and voted in favor of a number of anti-slavery resolutions, but did not succeed in establishing a permanent organization or party. They agreed to hold another, more formal convention in September.[33]

The Whig state convention was held in the Music Hall in Boston on August 16, 1854. Each town was allowed five delegates for each member of the state House of Representatives to which it was entitled. Hood was a member of the Whig State Committee and a state representative, and he attended as one of five delegates from Somerset. The railroads allowed the delegates to travel to and from the convention at half the usual fare. The organizers claimed that there were exactly 1,776 delegates, an auspicious number matching the year that the Declaration of Independence was signed, but, in fact, only 929 men voted in the balloting for governor.[34]

The convention was dominated by the question of slavery and the passage of the Kansas-Nebraska Act two and a half months earlier. For five hours, from 11 in the morning to 1:30 in the afternoon and again from 3 to 5:30 in the evening, the delegates listened to speaker after speaker denounce the "Nebraska Fraud" and the spinelessness of the Democratic Party. No other issues were discussed. While the delegates listened, a committee met in a smoke filled back room to finalize a set of 14 pre-drafted resolutions. Of these, 11 were in opposition to the Kansas-Nebraska Act and the Fugitive Slave Law, including the following:

> Resolved, that the repeated and long continued aggressions of the advocates of slavery extension, have awakened the people of Massachusetts, and of the Free States, to the fact, that their end and aim is political supremacy; that by this last crowning act, the repeal of the Missouri compromise, effected through Southern faithlessness and Northern treachery, stimulated by the corrupt use of excessive influence, the naked question of liberty or slavery as the controlling influence of the government, is presented to the people; and for ourselves we declare our readiness to meet that issue, and our determination at all times and under all circumstances, so to exercise our constitutional rights as to "secure the blessings of liberty to ourselves and our posterity."[35]

In addition, there was a resolution of Whig solidarity, a resolution to support the adoption of the state constitutional amendments passed in the last session of the legislature, and a denunciation of the Democratic Party and President Franklin Pierce. In the end, the delegates adopted all of the resolutions unanimously. They also nominated Emory Washburn and William Plunkett for another 2-year term as governor and lieutenant governor.

Not every newspaper in Massachusetts agreed with the Whig opposition to the Kansas-Nebraska Act. The Democratic *Pittsfield Sun* reported that:

> The Resolutions adopted by the Convention were such as might be expected from Massachusetts whigs, who have passed more anti-patriotic, absurd and ridiculous resolutions than the whigs of all other States of the Union.
>
> The Hon. Josiah Quincy,— a Hartford Convention federalist, who has always adhered to his *political platform*— was one of the speakers. Nothing could be more appropriate than the appearance of this gentleman at the Convention. It shows conclusively that the Federalism of 1812–14 and the Whiggery of 1854 are alike, and that the lapse of forty years have changed them only in name.[36]

After the convention, Captain Hood headed back to Somerset to prepare for his next campaign.

6

Know-Nothing

The Whig Party seemed to be strong, but cracks were beginning to appear in the organization because, for many, it did not go far enough. Disenchanted Whigs who wanted to push for no extension of slavery at all had broken away and formed the Free Soil Party. Another threat to the Whigs was the American Party, better known as the Know-Nothings. It had abolitionist leanings, supported temperance, and opposed immigration, a policy known as nativism. In 1854, the Know-Nothings were preparing a surprise for the establishment by establishing a grass-roots base through local lodges, called Twigs. In the spring, they won the municipal elections in Boston, Roxbury, Cambridge, and Salem and established Twigs in most of the towns in the state.[1] The Know-Nothing movement was surprisingly short lived. In Greenfield, Massachusetts, the local Twig was organized in August 1854 as a weak coalition of Whigs and Free Soilers, but after the elections it split into two factions and quickly fell apart.[2] However, the party survived long enough to help change the political landscape in Massachusetts in 1855.

In close-knit Somerset, Captain Hood was well aware of the movement. Unlike Abraham Lincoln, who refused to compromise his principles in return for Know-Nothing support and declined an invitation to join the party,[3] Captain Hood bowed to political expediency and joined the local Twig.[4] This was more of a pragmatic political move than an ideological shift on his part. He gave no indications that he had been converted to nativism and was clearly not a supporter of the temperance movement. He retained his Whig affiliation and position on the state committee, but he realized that in the fall elections the Know-Nothings would be a force to be reckoned with.

The Free-Soil coalition of dissident Whigs, Democrats, and Free

Soilers held their formal nominating convention on September 7, 1855, in Worcester. Their intent was to form a new party, to be called the Republicans, which would be staunchly anti-slavery and prohibitionist. The *Massachusetts Spy* noted,

> A large number of the delegates appointed to the Convention, are men who last year belonged to the old parties, and we have no doubt that many of those to be appointed will be of that class. Such men are doubly welcome, because they place themselves where their action will tell for the principles they love, and not be so controlled by pro-slavery leaders, as to aid the cause of oppression and wrong.[5]

This convention was smaller by half than the Whig convention, with only 480 voting delegates. Charles Sumner, the strongly anti-slavery U.S. senator from Massachusetts, gave a stirring speech to open the proceedings. The convention was a partial success and adopted strong anti-slavery resolutions, including the following:

> Resolved, That the Republican Party is pre-eminently the party of the Union and the Constitution; of law and order, and may justly claim to be the true National and Democratic party, because it is opposed in its principles, sentiments, and aims to sectionalism, secession, and disunion; is equally desirous of the welfare of every part of the country, and disregarding the aristocratic, hereditary distinctions of birth and color, maintains the right of all men to freedom and equality before the law.
>
> Resolved, That the Republicans of Massachusetts in cooperation with the friends of freedom in other States, are pledged to make the question of freedom paramount to all other political questions, and to labor for the accomplishment of the following purposes:
>
> To bring the administration of the General Government back to the national principle of liberty;
>
> To repeal the fugitive slave law;
>
> To restore the prohibition of slavery in Kansas and Nebraska;
>
> To prohibit slavery in all the Territories;
>
> To resist the acquisition of Cuba or any other territory unless slavery therein shall be prohibited;
>
> To refuse admission into the Union of any more slave states;
>
> To abolish slavery in the District of Columbia;
>
> To protect the Constitutional rights of citizens going to other States and to sustain all other constitutional measures of opposition to slavery.[6]

The delegates nominated Henry Wilson, of Boston, for governor and Increase Sumner, of Great Barrington, for lieutenant governor. Henry Wilson was a former member of the state legislature and a newspaperman who owned and edited the *Boston Republican* from 1848 to 1851. He would go on to become a Republican United States senator from Massachusetts and vice-president under Ulysses S. Grant.[7] However, the Republican Party thus formed did not gain the needed momentum, in part because many Whigs were not yet ready to abandon their party. A viable Republican Party did not come together in Massachusetts for several years.[8] Given his later membership in the Republican Party in Illinois, it is possible that Captain Hood attended the convention as either a delegate or a spectator, but his name is not mentioned in any of the published accounts of the convention and he ran as a Whig-Know-Nothing in the November elections.

The Massachusetts Know-Nothings held their convention on October 18, 1855, and nominated Henry J. Gardner for governor. He was a dry goods merchant and member of the Boston Common Council, as the city's ruling body was known, but a relative unknown in statewide politics. Simon Brown was nominated for lieutenant governor.[9]

The great fire that destroyed Captain Hood's shipyard occurred not long after the Republican convention, but this did not prevent him from running for a second term in the legislature. This time Hood ran as a Whig–Know-Nothing candidate and on election day, November 14, he again won.[10] His victory was part of a Know-Nothing landslide which saw Henry Gardner and Simon Brown win the executive offices by a majority in a field of 4 major parties. Not widely known at the time was the fact that that Henry Wilson, the Republican candidate, had thrown his support to Gardner in return for Gardner's promise to get him elected to the U.S. Senate seat that was being contested in 1855. At that time, senators were elected by the legislature, and with a Know-Nothing majority, Gardner could deliver on his promise.[11] When this deal was revealed, there was a loud outcry from the Whig press denouncing it, but Wilson went to the Senate anyway, with Hood casting his vote with the other Know-Nothing representatives in Wilson's favor.[12]

The 1855 legislative session opened in the Statehouse on Wednesday, January 3.[13] At eleven in the morning, the House of Representatives was called to order by its oldest member, Mr. Allen Presbrey of Taunton, as was traditional. The *Barre Patriot* reported that he said, "It may be easy to get a ship under way and put to sea, but not so easy to control the length or circumstances of the voyage."[14] He then called on the members who were in favor of a short and productive session to say aye, and received unanimous agreement.

Most of the representatives were new to the legislature.[15] As one of
the few returning members, Captain Hood took a leadership role from
the start, getting himself appointed to the ceremonial committee that
went to the secretary of the commonwealth to inform him that the House
had been called to order. When the credentials of the members had been
collected and it was established that a quorum was present, the governor
was informed and, with his council, came into the House and adminis-
tered the oaths of office. The House then proceeded to elect Mr. D.C.
Eddy of Lowell as its speaker and to elect its other officers. They
adjourned at two thirty and assembled under the statehouse dome with
the Senate, governor and council. From there, they walked in procession
to Old South Church, preceded by the sheriff of Suffolk County and
accompanied by a company of cadets. At the church, they listened to the
annual election sermon, which was preached by the congregational minister, the Reverend Dr. Lothrop, who took as his text the 15th verse of
the 11th chapter of Revelations, "The kingdoms of this world are become
the kingdoms of our Lord and of his Christ." In the sermon he urged
the legislators to avoid partisanship and to strive for good government.[16]

The next few days were spent on organizational and procedural
matters. On the following Tuesday, January 9, Governor Gardner
addressed the Great and General Court. The printed transcript of the
governor's speech runs to 24 pages. Unlike Governor Washburn's speech
in 1854, which focused on state issues, more than half of Gardner's address
was devoted to an anti-immigration rant, in which he pointed out the
evils of foreign influences on the nation and called for severe restrictions
on naturalization, voting, and office holding for the non-native born. At
the beginning of his address, after a few preliminaries, and in spite of
the ongoing anti-slavery debate, he stated:

> The most prominent subject before our State and Nation at the present
> moment, and that which most naturally commends itself today, and in
> this place, to our attention, concerns our foreign population;—the duties
> of republicanism towards them, its dangers from them.[17]

If this sounds like Arizona in 2012, it is important to remember
that in 1855 there were no controls on foreign immigration, and so all
immigrants were legal and naturalization was a simpler process than it
is today. A large percentage of new immigrants were impoverished Irish
fleeing from the effects of the famine of the 1840s. As with immigrants

today, they were seen as a threat to jobs and wages for native workers, as well as being culturally distinct.

The governor particularly singled out the Catholic Church as a threat and proposed legislation against the establishment of parochial schools. The only other issues that he addressed briefly in his speech were the sectional issues dividing the country, especially the Kansas-Nebraska Act and the Fugitive Slave Act; the state budget, which was in poor shape; and a populist proposal to end incarceration for debtors unless they were fraudulent.

The governor noted, "The financial condition of the Commonwealth is not a flattering one." He urged the legislators:

> Introduce into every branch of expenditure rigorous and minute economy; remembering, however, that parsimony is not true economy in fostering the noble and Christian, charitable and humane institutions of Massachusetts ... there is one item especially that can be, should be, and the people expect will be diminished, and that is the expense of the Legislature. Whatever additional cause of grateful regard the session of 1855 may bring to our constituents, let it have the special merit of being a working and a short one.
>
> A large and increasing annual expenditure of money is made to various Commissions created by the Legislature. In many cases, the duties performed are not commensurate to the price charged. It is hoped no commission will be created that is not indispensable, and perhaps the Legislature can safely terminate some now in existence. I earnestly recommend that in all cases hereafter, where, commissions are created, and the amount of labor can be approximately estimated, the Legislature will [set] the specific sum that shall be paid each Commissioner. The system of per diem pay should be avoided.[18]

In spite of the emphasis in the governor's speech on limiting foreign influences, the legislature, recognizing that the new immigrants were also voters, did not carry out his agenda. Only two acts were passed in this session that dealt with the issue. These were an act to ban Massachusetts courts from issuing naturalization papers, leaving that to the federal courts, and a constitutional amendment to ban the expenditure of public funds on sectarian, that is, Catholic, schools.[19] Captain Hood did not take an active part in the passage of either of these measures.

In the 1855 legislative session, in spite of his financial difficulties, Hood assumed more of a leadership role. As mentioned above, he was one of the few representatives in the session who had served before, and he managed to get himself appointed to the chair of the Mercantile Affairs and Insurance Committee.[20] The committee had a dual role. It considered bills sent to it and either took no action, or reported them back to the House for a vote. It also considered orders adopted by the House and either originated legislation in response to them, or reported that the order was inexpedient, meaning that they recommended no action. In his capacity as chair, Captain Hood reported out a number of bills that had been prepared by the committee over the course of the session.

In reaction to the extensive regulation of insurance companies adopted by the legislature on Hood's instigation in 1854, the question of insurance company regulation was raised again on January 26 by Mr. William Kimball of Salem, who proposed an order to have the Committee on Mercantile Affairs and Insurance

> consider the expediency of reporting a bill declaring that the provisions of sec. 31, chap. 453, of the acts of 1854, entitled "an act concerning Insurance Companies" enacting that no foreign insurance company, by their agent in the Commonwealth, shall insure property in the Commonwealth, or contract for insurance with any residents in the Commonwealth, unless the capital stock of the company amounts to $100,000, all of which amount shall have been paid in and invested, exclusive of stockholder's obligations of any description, and the debts of the Company, not unless the company is restricted by its charter or otherwise, from incurring any greater hazard in one risk than one-tenth of its capital, do not apply to foreign mutual insurance companies.[21]

Kimball's connection with the insurance industry is unknown, but it is likely that he had the backing of one or more out of state, that is, foreign, insurance companies who wanted these restrictions lifted. Some of the members objected that the proposed order was incomprehensible and it was at rejected on those grounds, but Dr. Stone, of Boston, moved for reconsideration. His motion was taken up the next day and the order was adopted. Kimball then also proposed that the insurance regulation act passed in the previous session be amended to make it consistent with the other laws of the commonwealth, which was a backhanded way of calling for a full review of the act with the intent to gut it.[22]

A month later, on February 20, instead of proposing to reduce the regulations, the bill that Captain Hood reported from his committee tightened the existing regulations by establishing a permanent enforcement mechanism. The committee noted that the value of the property insured in the state was close to $400 million and that the amount of the premiums paid on this insurance was almost $8 million, divided among 124 insurance companies in the state and more than 40 outside of it. Given the size of the industry, it was necessary to institute greater oversight in order to prevent fraud and to look out for the interests of the policyholders.[23]

The act set up a board of three insurance commissioners, each to be paid $5 a day plus $1 per mile of official travel, in direct opposition to Governor Gardner's admonition to avoid per diem pay for commissioners. They were charged to visit every insurance company in the state once every two years and conduct a detailed audit to determine if the companies could meet their obligations to their policyholders. They were also required to do this for any new insurance company within one year of its establishment, and at any time when petitioned by 5 or more members or creditors of any insurance company. The penalty for failing to cooperate with the commissioners was a steep $1,000 per incident. If the commissioners found a company to be insolvent, they were authorized to obtain an injunction from the Supreme Judicial Court restraining the company from further conducting business and, after a hearing by the court, shut the company down and put it into receivership.[24]

Hood managed to get this legislation through the House with no significant debate. The bill was ordered to be printed with one amendment on March 6 and passed on March 12. It was signed by Governor Gardener on March 31 as Chapter 124 of the Acts of 1855. The principles embodied in this bill still underlie Chapter 175 of the Massachusetts General Laws today.

These tough new regulations went against the Know-Nothing policy of small government and minimal regulation of business, but that did not matter to Captain Hood. Mr. David Wilmot, who had the opportunity to interview Hood reported:

> In the case of the Insurance Commission, James M. Hood, chair of the Committee on Mercantile Affairs, pointed to the deficient "security offered by the policies of a number of different [insurance] companies" in the state. The industry's rampant speculation threatened consumers. For legal precedent, Hood invoked the state's banking commission, which was "universally regarded as successful" and necessary. To Hood and his colleagues, it was "obvious" that "without any supervision of State authority," the public's confidence in the insurance industry and the safety of policy holders would be jeopardized.[25]

Hood, who had been personally affected by the inability or unwillingness of insurance companies to pay claims, was in favor of additional regulation when it benefited him.

On February 14, the House took up the first of the constitutional amendments that had been passed in the previous session, an amendment to allow election by plurality. This measure made the candidate with the most votes the winner of an election, even if he did not get a majority. This was a significant issue for local elections where several candidates might be running for a single office and it might take two or more elections for one of them to gain a majority. The amendment passed by a two-thirds majority with Captain Hood voting for it. In subsequent votes over the rest of the session, Captain Hood supported all of the amendments that had been proposed, most of which concerned making elections for various state offices direct rather than through the legislature. The most controversial of the amendments was the third, which proposed substituting a district system based on population for allocating representatives to the statehouse for the current system of allocating them by town. Hood voted for this, but it lost by a vote of 142 to 192.[26]

Captain Hood was not above a bit of political maneuvering. The Commissioners of Alien Paupers were members of a board that was charged with dealing with insolvent aliens in the state. Many of these were Irish, and a good proportion of them were considered insane by the standards of the day. The commissioners were authorized to pay for their deportation back to the country they had come from. When the annual report of the commission was presented to the House to be read and printed on the 22nd of February, the *Daily Atlas* reported, "Mr. Hood, in the most innocent manner possible, and without any instructions of course, moved that it be referred to a special committee with instructions to print those portions of the report as it may deem expedient." A debate ensued and it turned out that the report included an inflammatory note from one of the commissioners, Peleg W. Chandler, who was also a member of the Executive Council. He pointed out that, under state law, any justice of the peace could order the deportation, at state expense, of any alien who was a ward of the state or otherwise could be considered a pauper. However, the law was being ignored and alien paupers were being deported without the required orders. But Chandler went further and questioned the arbitrariness of the deportation process, especially the deportation of the insane. He wrote:

It is said that these people *consented* to go. *The consent of lunatics!* when it is one of the wisest and most humane maxims of the law that a lunatic can not give consent to anything.

But Chandler went further, and compared the law allowing the deportation of paupers without trial or consent to the Fugitive Slave Law, which allowed the removal of blacks to the South without trial. He finished by writing:

> And while we have the present law on our statue books, and especially when our public officers do not even resort to it, but on their own motion exercise the powers therein granted to Justices of the Peace, we cannot well declaim against the act of Congress for the extradition of fugitive slaves, upon the order, not of any Justice of the Peace, but of officers specially appointed by the Courts of the United States as Commissioners.
>
> A black man is no better, and is entitled to no more security as to personal rights, in the opinion of the undersigned, than a white man, although the former may be a fugitive slave, and the latter a pauper and an Irishman. [27]

It appears that this note made the leadership of the House, which was, at least theoretically, opposed to all aliens, uncomfortable and they got Hood to try to bury it. The ploy did not work, and the full report was printed. On March 8, the House appointed a special committee to consider new legislation with regard to foreign paupers; however, no new laws were passed.

Although Captain Hood concerned himself mostly with commercial issues, the passage of the Kansas-Nebraska Act in the previous year and the victory of the anti-slavery Whig-Know-Nothing coalition meant that slavery was an important agenda item in 1855 and he was drawn into the debate. He voted with the majority to pass an act to make it more difficult to arrest and reclaim fugitive slaves in Massachusetts. Chapter 489 of the Acts of 1855 enabled any justice of any court in the commonwealth, or any justice of the peace in the absence of a judge, to issue a writ of *habeas corpus* for any person arrested or restrained as a fugitive slave. It also required a jury trial to determine if the claim that the person was actually a fugitive was true, with the burden of the proof being on the person asserting the claim. It established steep fines and imprisonment for anyone removing an alleged fugitive slave from the state without winning at trial and prohibited any person holding an office of "honor, trust or emolument" from the Commonwealth from assisting in the arrest or detention of fugitive slaves. It forbade the use of state and local facilities for detaining fugitive slaves. Finally, it required the governor to appoint commissioners in each county to act to protect any persons accused of being a fugitive slave at state expense.[28] The act was vetoed by the governor,[29] but the veto was overridden by both houses of the legislature with Captain Hood voting for the override.[30] The Legislature then passed a resolution declaring the Fugitive Slave Act unconstitutional and another resolution against the Kansas-Nebraska Act.[31]

Captain Hood, as the chair of the Mercantile Affairs Committee, became involved in a rather acrimonious issue with regard to the Boston Wharf Company, which was seeking legislative approval to extend its wharf in South Boston, near where the Boston World Trade Center is located today. This company, which was founded in the 1830s, was responsible for the development of the area on the south side of the Fort Point Channel and is still in existence. The bill was opposed by some who claimed that the extension would take from them title and rights to tidal flats that they currently enjoyed. The opponents first attempted to extend the authority of the Commissioners on the Back Bay, who controlled development in that area along the Charles River, to cover all of Boston Harbor and the South Boston Flats, but this move was defeated. From the reports of the debate, it appears that the opposition may have been an attempt prevent the development of South Boston in competition with the existing wharfs to the north.[32]

Hood fought for the Boston Wharf Company, and continually amended the bill to try to come up with something that could pass the House. On March 27, Mr. Bryant of Boston moved that the Committee on Public Lands "report a plan and form for all the riparian land owners on the northern shore of South Boston, that they may be entitled to extend their limits to the one hundred rods ... with power to send for persons and papers." This would have probably killed the bill, since there was not time enough left in the session for this to be done. The next day, Captain Hood moved for reconsideration and produced a new version of the bill that avoided specific bounds or measurements for the wharf extension, but merely stated that the company must conform to the legal front of their own flats and the true legal front was to be fixed by the Supreme Judicial Court.[33]

On April 20, Captain Hood addressed the House on the bill. He stated:

Mr. Speaker, I do believe that this bill will do more than justice to the petitioners [who opposed it]. It will injure the rights of no man. It will increase the commercial advantages of Boston. The flats proposed to be improved are useless now: nay, they are worse than useless — they are a nuisance. This bill will bring a portion of them into use.

It has been said, sir, that the man who makes two blades of grass grow in the place of one, is a public benefactor. Certainly, then, sir, the man or the company who changes a nuisance into a public convenience is entitled to our favor.[34]

The fact that Hood led the effort to get this bill through, even though neither the company, nor its project, was in his district, indicates that he probably had a financial interest in the outcome. He was not an officer of the company but he many have held some of its stock. The *Daily Atlas* reported:

Mr. Hood [stated that he] had carefully looked into the subject matter, and after spending two or three weeks in investigation, had come to the deliberate conclusion that it was a just bill, and would not injure the harbor of Boston, but would be a great benefit to South Boston; and if members of the House had not been deceived they would give it their hearty support, as he did. If the opponents of the first bill were not satisfied now, there was no such thing as satisfaction. There had been hundreds of bills passed, granting other parties the same rights as was proposed to give to the Boston Wharf Company. The Company claimed at their hands special considerations, and instead of giving them the chance to make a great speculation, they were simply giving them the chance to escape from a great public undertaking without loss.[35]

After several additional days of debate, the bill was passed into law on April 26, but the heated nature of the debate, when similar bills had sailed through the legislature without any, indicates that others had some financial interest in blocking it.[36]

Perhaps the most time consuming item taken up by the legislature in 1855 was the Maine Law, which would prohibit the sale of alcoholic beverages in the state. It was known as the Maine Law because it was based on legislation written by Neal Dow, the mayor of Portland, Maine, and first passed in the Maine legislature in 1846. The initial legislation was considered too weak, so in 1851, Dow engineered a new bill that strengthened prohibition with more stringent controls and more drastic punishments, including heavy fines and imprisonment for selling alcohol. This law marked the first successful move away from the early temperance movement's emphasis on moral persuasion towards state sponsored coercion.[37]

The temperance movement had a long history in Massachusetts. The first important organization formed to promote restraint in the consumption of ardent spirits was the Massachusetts Society for the Suppression of Intemperance, founded in Boston in 1813. While the society was ultimately unsuccessful, in part because it advocated for moderate alcohol consumption rather than total abstinence, it laid the groundwork for the temperance movement. The Massachusetts Society for the Suppression of Intemperance was followed by the American Society for the Promotion of Temperance, better known as the American Temperance Society, which was founded in 1826, also in Boston. Unlike the Massachusetts Society for the Suppression of Intemperance, which was organized by upper class social reformers, the American Temperance Society was closely linked to the evangelical Christian movement. The society urged total abstinence from distilled liquors, but not from fermented products such as wine, beer, and cider. It achieved great success through moral persuasion but failed to solve the problem of drunkenness in the lower classes. It was the failure of this movement that led to the campaign for state coercion in the form of rigorously enforced prohibition.[38]

In Massachusetts, this first took the form of the no-license movement. Sellers of alcohol were required to obtain a license from the county commissioners, who had total discretion over the issuance of the licenses. Starting in the 1840s, pro-temperance county commissioners were elected in most counties in the state. Once elected, they refused to issue or renew alcohol licenses, effectively shutting down the legal outlets for the product. In practice, this did little to limit the trade, because innkeepers and dram shop owners continued to operate without the licenses. In many cases, the local police refused to enforce the law, and even when formal complaints were lodged, convictions were hard to obtain.[39] This led the Massachusetts legislature to pass a strong prohibition law in 1852, modeled on the law passed in Maine the previous year. The Massachusetts law was soon declared unconstitutional because of its heavy handed search and seizure provisions, so the 1855 bill was the second attempt to institute prohibition. The Know-Nothing majority greatly increased the chances of success in that session.[40]

One of the basic beliefs of the Know-Nothing party was temperance, but this was not an issue that Captain Hood personally believed in. He came from a family and district where the shipping of rum and molasses was an important source of income. Moreover, it was well known that he had a taste for spirits himself, so he was probably involved in making sure that, even if passed, the law would never actually go into effect, because portions of it would be found to be unconstitutional. In its slow course through the legislature, this bill went through many days of debate, beginning on March 8, when the Committee on Commerce produced both a majority report in favor of it and a minority report opposed to it. In response, the House resolved itself into a Committee of the Whole to consider the bill. Numerous amendments were offered, most of which were rejected.

As an example of the debate, Mr. Monroe of Boston declared:

> It would not be denied that he was a temperance man. Three years ago he voted for the Maine law, but with some reluctance. He declared then that they could not enforce the law, unless they essentially modified it... Neither the present law, nor the one proposed could be enforced. Men could as easily stop the cataract of Niagara. He wanted the temperance men to do something for Boston, where there were now 1,500 tippling shops, and if they would give him a law such as he wanted he could shut up 1,400 of them, at short notice. He would have the license $1,000, and nothing less. The present bill might be tinkered with until doomsday, and then it would be a dead letter.[41]

The law, as eventually passed, included a comprehensive ban on the sale or public consumption of all alcoholic beverages. Exceptions were made for chemists, pharmacists, sacramental wine, and industrial use, but strict record keeping was required for those. One curious exception was that, to avoid violating the interstate commerce clause of the United States Constitution, foreign liquors could be sold, but only in their original containers or packaging and in the original size. This meant that if Kentucky bourbon was imported in 20 gallon barrels, it had to be sold the same way.[42] Although Hood did not take an active part in the debate, he did vote for the law in the end.[43] In spite of all the energy devoted to it, or perhaps because of the crafty amendments of its opponents, the law was eventually declared unconstitutional.[44]

Finally, at noon on May 21, 1855, the legislature adjourned for the last time and Hood headed home with his eyes fixed on a new opportunity.[45]

7

Somerset County, Illinois

During the summer of 1855, after the Massachusetts legislative session ended, Captain Hood and his wife, Anna, moved to the township of Loda, Illinois. This was not a sudden decision, made to escape the stigma of insolvency, but a long planned move to capitalize on the newly developing midwestern states.

Originally a part of the Northwest Territory, Illinois became the 21st state in 1818, fifteen years after the Louisiana Purchase had opened navigation on the Mississippi River to the United States and three years after Captain Hood's birth. At first, settlement in the state was heavily concentrated in the south, where the confluence of the Mississippi and Ohio rivers at Cairo provided connections to the north, south and east. Settlement then moved north, up the Illinois River, until the increasing population came into conflict with the native inhabitants. The Black Hawk War broke out in 1832 when Hood was just starting his career as a merchant ship master. A number of men who would go on to become prominent politicians, including the future presidents on opposite sides in the American Civil War, Abraham Lincoln and Jefferson Davis, acquired military credentials in this conflict.[1] That experience would later stand them in good stead with voters. The defeat of the Black Hawk confederacy at the battle of Bad Axe in August effectively ended Native American power in Illinois and opened the state up to development, but the lack of transportation infrastructure kept the northern and eastern portions of the state underdeveloped.[2]

The town that later would become the city of Chicago was not laid out until 1830. Although it did have a link with the east through the Great Lakes, the route was a long one, requiring ships to sail north in Lake Michigan to Sault St. Marie before turning south through Lakes

Huron and Erie to reach the Erie Canal at Buffalo. It was not until the arrival of the railroads, especially the Northern Indiana and Chicago Railroad in 1852, which provided a faster link to the east, that the city really came into its own.[3] By the time the Hoods moved to the state, they were able to travel by rail all the way from Taunton, Massachusetts, to Springfield, Illinois, via Boston, Albany, Buffalo, Toledo and Chicago. The fare from Taunton to Chicago was $22.00 in first class or $11.00 in emigrant class.[4]

Loda, where the Hoods settled, is located in the southwest corner of Iroquois County in east-central Illinois near the border with Indiana.

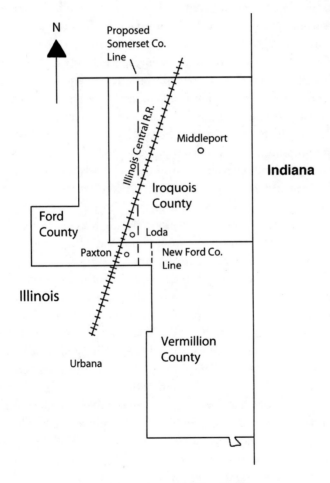

The Somerset County, Illinois Scheme

It is about halfway between the state capitals of Springfield and Indianapolis. Although the area's first settler, Alexander Henry, had arrived as early as 1843, the town did not begin to develop until the Illinois Central Railroad linked it to Chicago in 1854 and gave it an outlet for its agricultural products. When the railroad was being built, the town was laid out by the Associated Land Company, which was made up of men who had interests in the railroad. In 1855, when he moved there permanently, Captain Hood went as the leader of a group of men from southeastern Massachusetts which included his nephew Elisha S. Hood, the son of James' brother George, as well as Horace Barstow and Eldridge Harrington. They were recruited by Adam Smith, who had come to Loda in 1854 from Chicago when the Illinois Central Railroad started operations. Smith bought 16,000 acres of land around the site of the town from the railroad with no down payment, speculating that he could resell them at a good profit before payment was due. He also built a mill complex to process and store grain from the farms he expected to be established, a large house for himself, and a hotel to accommodate settlers until they could build their own houses.[5] In the early 1850s, prior to coming to Illinois, Smith had been in the shipping business in New York City and owned and chartered a number of vessels. He made a fortune shipping men and goods to California, but when that trade became less profitable, he turned his attention to the Midwest. It is likely that he became acquainted with Captain Hood during his days in the shipping business and that he had been corresponding with Hood about his plans for Loda even before he acquired the land.

When the Hoods arrived in that summer of 1855, they found that the town consisted of only three houses clustered around the Loda depot with its freight shed and railroad section maintenance buildings. Smith's house and mill were yet to be built. The town was surrounded by flat prairie grasslands as far as the eye could see. This landscape was as different from the rolling hills and broad seascapes of southeastern Massachusetts as could be. The only landmark was the straight line of the Illinois Central pointing north, one hundred miles to Chicago. Even in the summer, it must have looked bleak, especially to Anna. The scenery is much the same today, with fields of corn substituted for the grasslands and stretching to a horizon punctuated only by the grain silos that mark the location of the neighboring towns.

The origin of the name Loda is obscure, but the town had a curious distinction. In order to avoid confusion with the similarly named town of Lodi in Kane County, Illinois, Senator Stephen Douglas arranged for the post office to be named Oakalla, in honor of a woman who had nursed him through an illness. Thus Loda became one of the few towns to have a postal address with a different name from that of the town itself.[6]

In addition to serving as a market and social center for the farms, Loda quickly developed into a small manufacturing hub, beginning with Addison Goodell's lumber business and expanding throughout the late 1850s to include a brick and tile factory that utilized local clay deposits, a hemp rope factory that used locally grown fiber, and a large distillery to turn locally grown grain into whiskey, established by a British firm. The first religious congregation to be organized in the town was the Baptist Church in 1857. This was founded under the leadership of Adam Smith, and Captain Hood was a member of the congregation. A four room schoolhouse was erected in 1859 to replace the original one room log school.[7]

Initially, Captain Hood purchased a half-section farm of 320 acres from Smith. It was adjacent to the railroad and about half a mile south of the Loda depot in Section 32, Township 24 North, Range 10 East. Then, on January 4, 1856, he bought an additional 151 acres of land about four miles east of town from Parker Dresfer, a resident of Tippecanoe County, Indiana, for the sum of $600, or about $4.00 an acre. This land was in the northwest quarter of section 19 in Township 24 North, Range 14 West.[8] These curious designations had to do with the way the U.S. government surveyed the western lands. Base lines of latitude and longitude were chosen and the land divided into townships six miles on a side, that is, of thirty-six square miles. These were arranged into ranges, which ran north and south and were numbered by their position east or west of the base longitude. The townships were then numbered by their position north or south of the base latitude. The townships were further divided into numbered sections of one square mile. A quarter section had 160 acres and was the typical size of a family farm.

Captain Hood settled in and began calling himself a farmer, but he actually brought in the family of Amos Ford to work the land for him while he pursued his political and entrepreneurial goals. In June 1856, his nephew and business partner William P. Hood gave Captain Hood a power of attorney to act as William's agent in Illinois.[9] William was also speculating in land in that state and needed a local contact to transact deals, collect rents, and look after his interests.

As an ex–Whig and Know-Nothing, Captain Hood quickly became immersed in party politics, identifying himself as a Republican, and became involved with the movement to form an official Republican party in Illinois. This movement began with an informal convention of newspaper editors in Decatur on February 22, 1856. Although not a newspaper man, Abraham Lincoln attended and had a major influence on the anti-slavery platform they adopted. Out of this meeting came a call for a convention to be held in Bloomington, Illinois on May 29, 1856, to formally organize an Illinois Republican Party.[10] The recruiting of delegates and organization of the convention was orchestrated largely by Lincoln through his law partner, William Herndon. There is no record of the names of the delegates, but Hood likely attended the convention because he was already enmeshed in local issues. Although he may have heard Lincoln speak in Massachusetts in 1848, this was probably his first direct encounter with the Springfield lawyer who was up and coming in Republican politics. Lincoln declined to run for governor since he was already looking forward to the U.S. Senate race in 1858, so the convention nominated William H. Bissell, a former Democrat who opposed the Kansas-Nebraska Act.[11] Bissell had served with distinction as the colonel of the Second Illinois Volunteer Infantry in the Mexican War. While serving as a congressman from Illinois, he had been challenged to a duel by Jefferson Davis because of a speech he made denouncing the attitude of Southern members of Congress who claimed that the entire credit for winning the Mexican War was due to Southern troops. The duel did not take place due to the intervention of President Taylor.[12]

The campaign for governor went on throughout the summer and included a large rally at Middleport, now known as Watseka, which was the Iroquois County seat. The crowd was addressed by Owen Lovejoy, who was an abolitionist and a Republican candidate for Congress. He spoke for two hours. The *Middleport Press* reported:

> He moved the hearts of the great throng as we never saw them moved before, and the up-turned eyes oft filled with tears told in language stronger than mere utterance that humanity had its instinctive, spontaneous, irresistible sympathies for human woe and bondage in whatever of its Protean horrors it presents itself ... His apostrophe to the Constitution we expect never to hear surpassed in patriotic eloquence.[13]

Bissel went on to be elected governor and served until his death in 1860, and Lovejoy, who would later support Captain Hood's application for a consulship, was elected to Congress.

Although the area around Loda was first settled in 1844, it was not organized as a town when Hood and his companions arrived. That happened in 1856, and Captain Hood played an important role in organizing it. He was one of the leaders of a scheme to create a new county out of parts of Iroquois and the adjacent Vermillion County, with Loda to become the county seat. The new county was to be called Somerset after Captain Hood's hometown. One of the attractions of Loda was that it was a station on the Illinois Central Railroad that ran from Chicago to Cairo at the southern tip of the state where the Ohio River flows into the Mississippi. When the railroad started operations, Loda was the third stop south of Chicago. At that time, the population of Illinois was growing quickly and counties were being split into smaller and more manageable units as soon as their population was large enough. Iroquois County itself had been set off from Vermillion County in 1833, so the scheme was not unrealistic. As a landowner in Loda, Hood stood to see the value of his land rise significantly if the town became the seat of a new county. Because the courts were located in county seats, these towns tended to become business hubs. It is probable that this scheme was part of Smith's pitch for Hood to settle in Loda with his Massachusetts colony.

A meeting was held at the Loda hotel on December 20, 1856, at which Captain Hood and David Crandall, the publisher of *Garden City*, the Loda newspaper, presented a verbal report on the proposed boundaries of the new county. Hood, Crandall, R.D. Foster and I.O. Butler were appointed as a committee to write a petition to the legislature in favor of the proposal. Addison Goodell, who was the local banker, George Shafer and Moses Walker were appointed to circulate the petition and they gathered one hundred and fifty signatures from residents in southwest corner of Iroquois County and several hundred more from residents of Vermillion County. Hood and David Crandall were also appointed to take the petition to the Illinois legislature and lobby in its favor, but there was opposition to the scheme.

On December 23, another meeting was held in the town of Onarga to protest against the Loda scheme and to organize resistance to the project. A committee was appointed to draw up a formal remonstrance against having any portion of Iroquois County being taken to form a new one, and another committee of ten men was appointed to circulate that petition throughout the county. Both John Chamberlin, the first Iroquois county judge, and Franklin Blades joined the fight to keep the county from losing any area. Blades was one of the state representatives from Iroquois County, the editor of the *Iroquois Republican* newspaper, and a former judge who would go on to serve in the state Court of Appeals. There was an intense war of words between the two publishers, Blades and Crandall, in their newspapers. In addition, a group from Paxton, a town that was just over the county line in Vermillion County, was working to make Paxton the seat of the new county by excluding Loda. This group included Ransom R. Murdock, Leander Britt, and William H. Pells, who had originally met while living in Orleans County, New York. They came out to Illinois and, in 1855, bought up land around Paxton on the advice of Judge Chamberlin, who was also from Orleans County and who assured them that when a new county was formed, it would not include Loda. Although it was too close to Loda to qualify for a station on the Illinois Central under their normal standards, Murdock persuaded the railroad to construct a sidetrack for freight loading at Paxton by agreeing to build the depot himself. Murdock, Britt, and Pells encouraged their surveyor, James Mix, to assume leadership of the Vermillion County residents who remonstrated against the Somerset County bill.[14]

Although Hood succeeded in getting a bill introduced, in a caper typical of frontier politics, it was stolen from the hopper before it could come to the floor. Eventually it was found and passed, but after it was signed by the governor, it was discovered that the bill had been altered, and instead of calling for the transfer of six miles of the west side of Iroquois and a small portion of Vermillion to the new county, it called for 12 miles to be cut out of Iroquois and a six mile square to be contributed by Vermillion. This change proved to be fatal when the bill went to the residents of the two counties for a vote and it was soundly defeated. The author of the change in the bill was never discovered, but suspicion fell on Franklin Blades, the most experienced legislator on the opposition side.[15]

Having failed to get their new county through lobbying, Captain Hood, with Adam Smith's support, ran for the state legislature in the November election and won. At the start of the 1859 legislative session, on January 5, he presented a petition from Robert D. Foster and others to join the township of Loda to Vermillion County and the next day he introduced a bill to create the new county of Somerset from parts of Iroquois and Vermillion counties. On January 11, two petitions opposing the division of Iroquois County were presented to the legislature. One was signed by 260 residents headed by Henry Troup, a merchant from Middleport, the county seat of Iroquois County, now called Watseka. The other was from the Iroquois County Supervisors.

Judge Chamberlin, who had opposed the bill in the previous session, arranged to be in Springfield, supposedly on other business, when the bill was introduced. Although Chamberlin was no longer a member of the legislature, he was still a leader of the Democratic Party and had great political influence. The *Iroquois Republican* described the maneuvering around the bill as follows:

> Capt. Hood, your Representative, introduced a bill for the formation of the county of Somerset, out of the "arm" of Vermillion and the southwest corner of Iroquois. This bill he urged forward by all honorable and fair means, and he should have obtained its passage beyond a doubt had not trickery, "bargain and sale" and "party drill" been contrived against him. Opposed to him was Mr. Harmon of Vermillion, (and a majority of the Committee on Counties to help him) with his Summit County bill. It will be remembered that, before this election, he pledged himself to Mr. Mix and his Prospect City friends, to use all his power to prevent any portion of Iroquois county from being added to the Vermillion "strip," and he has fully kept his promise, with too little scrupulousness, I fear, as to the means he has employed to accomplish his end. The bills for the formation of Somerset and Summit, as a matter of course, were referred to the Committee on Counties. Mix and his tools contrived, by some means, to buy up all the Democrats on that committee, and, by promising the Republican member from Whiteside that the Democrats should support one of his local measures, they secured him too. The consequence was that the committee reported favorably upon Mr. Harmon's bill and unfavorably upon Capt. Hood's.
>
> The matter came up for final action in the House on Saturday. The discussion on it was very able, occupying most of the forenoon, but it was all of no use. It appeared that the Douglasites had endorsed Mr. Harmon's bill as a party measure, and were determined to "put it through" as such. Several of them made speeches in favor of it; and, on its final passage, every Democrat in the House but three voted for it, while nearly all the Republicans voted against it. Why the Douglas members should thus draw the party lines upon a local measure, confined to a Republican district is a question which I leave Mr. Harmon to settle with his constituents as best he can.[16]

The altered bill passed on February 17, 1859, and authorized the formation of a new county, to be called Ford, not Summit, the 102nd and last county to be formed in Illinois, with Paxton as its seat. It was named for the eighth governor of Illinois, Thomas Ford, who served from 1842 to 1846. The Paxton group had won, and the Loda boosters were defeated. As Murdock wrote, "Loda had lost and was sad. She was out generaled and her county seat boom was busted. Paxton had won the battle and was happy."[17]

In 2010, the City of Paxton had a population of almost 4,500 while the town of Loda had fewer than 400 residents.[18]

8

Lincoln, Douglas and Hood

Although Adam Smith and his other backers had persuaded Captain Hood to run for the legislature for the primary purpose of supporting the Somerset County scheme, his decision to do so put him into the midst of one of the most famous elections in Illinois history. At the county Republican convention on March 25, 1858, Hood was nominated for the Iroquois County seat in the 45th district, and in that solidly Republican district had high hopes of winning.[1]

When the Illinois Republican state convention met at Springfield on June 16, 1858, and nominated Abraham Lincoln for the U.S. Senate, Hood was in attendance as a Lincoln supporter. The nomination itself was unusual, because a party did not normally endorse a senatorial candidate before the election of the legislators who would select the winner, but the acclamation for Lincoln was so great that the convention ignored precedent and passed a resolution endorsing him. Hood was present that night when Lincoln gave the famous speech in which he declared "a house divided against itself cannot stand." The convention gave Hood an opportunity to meet the state political leaders and gain support for his own run.[2]

As provided by the U.S. Constitution at the time, senators were elected by the state legislatures, not by direct popular vote.[3] Therefore, Abraham Lincoln's campaign for the Senate actually consisted of working for the election of Republican legislators who would then vote for him. He spent the fall traveling around the state, speaking on his own and debating the incumbent Democratic candidate, Senator Stephen A. Douglas.

Douglas was a powerful politician. In 1858 he was finishing his second term as United States senator from Illinois. During those twelve years he had risen in the Senate leadership to become chair of the important Committee on Territories. In that capacity he had been responsible for the passage of the Kansas-Nebraska Act that had raised such an outcry in the North. In the Senate, he was opposed by the other senator from Illinois, Lyman Trumbull, who had been elected with Lincoln's support in 1856.[4] Trumbull was one of the few politicians who could successfully debate Douglas, and early in 1858 he had returned to Illinois where he somewhat reluctantly began to stump for Lincoln. Since it was widely believed that Lincoln and Trumbull were close, Douglas claimed that they had made a deal, and that Lincoln was going to rely on Trumbull to get him elected. It was to counteract this charge and to prove to the voters that he had what it took to be successful in the rough and tumble debates of the Senate that Lincoln challenged Douglas to debate the issues of the day in public.[5]

It was during these historic debates that Lincoln crystallized his anti-slavery and pro–Union positions. The reports of these debates were carried by newspapers around the nation and made Lincoln's name familiar in households on both sides of the issues. Captain Hood may have been among the 12,000 people who heard Lincoln debate Douglas at Charleston, Illinois, on September 18, as that town was only 70 miles from Loda and reachable by railroad. He also may have heard Lincoln's solo speech at Urbana, several days later, which was only 30 miles south of Loda on the Illinois Central.[6] As he plotted this campaign, Lincoln considered the 45th District to be safe, implying that Hood had the full support of the local Republican organization, and that that organization was strong. Because it was safe, Lincoln did not visit the 45th District during that historic campaign, but concentrated his efforts elsewhere.[7]

During the campaign, Captain Hood traveled the district, giving speeches at Martinsburgh on October 18, Chebanse on October 19, and Middleport on October 22.[8] In spite of Franklin Blades' opposition to the Somerset County scheme, Hood gained the endorsement of Blades' *Iroquois Republican*. He did run into a problem when a letter of his to the *Middleport Press* surfaced in which he stated, "I endorse S.A. Douglas' policy throughout." The *Garden State* defended him in the following paragraph:

Capt. Hood's Antecedents
  While Douglas was opposing the Lecompton bill "as the only course by which he could hope to carry Illinois" he was acting and voting with

Lovejoy, Giddings, Hale, Seward and the united Republican phalanx in Congress. The New York *Tribune* and the Albany *Journal* endorsed "Douglas policy throughout." So did Lyman Trumbull and many other sincere Republicans. Capt. Hood probably did the same thing; though the assertion in the *Press* that he did so will raise a doubt in the mind of every one who knows the villainous character of that sheet and its conductors. But where are Douglas, and Greeley, and Weed, and Trumbull, and Capt. Hood now? Douglas and his slavery extending schemes are hurrying to perdition together; while Greeley, Weed, Trumbull, Lincoln, and Hood are bashing his receding carcass with the liquid lava of eternal truth.[9]

The Lecompton bill mentioned in this article was the bill before Congress at that time that would have accepted the proposed pro-slavery constitution adopted by the legislature of the Kansas Territory meeting at Lecompton, Kansas, in 1857. This was the second proposed constitution for the territory, the first being a free-state constitution written by a separate convention in Topeka in 1855. When votes within the territory failed to establish the legitimacy of either document, due to boycotts, intimidation, and widespread fraud, the issue was thrown to the U.S. Congress. Eventually, another constitution, the anti-slavery Leavenworth Constitution, was adopted, but the debate in Congress split the Democratic Party, helping to lead to Lincoln's presidential win in 1860.[10]

Captain Hood's candidacy was even noted back in Massachusetts. The *Springfield Republican* reported,

> Capt. James M. Hood, formerly of Somerset, and a representative of that town in the legislatures of 1854 and 1855, is one of the republican candidates for representatives in the legislature of Illinois, from Iroquois county, his present place of residence. The captain is a capable legislator, a staunch republican, and a good fellow generally. We cordially wish him success.[11]

On election day, November 2, 1858, Captain Hood justified Lincoln's confidence by winning the Iroquois County seat in the 45th District with 319 votes. His Democratic Party opponent, a Mr. Paddock, polled only 4 votes. Hood was surely helped by the support of his followers from Massachusetts and his associate, Adam Smith. Statewide, all 75 of the representative seats were up for election, along with 12 of the 25 State Senate seats. Of these 86 contested seats, the Democrats won 46 and the Republicans won 41. When combined with the 8 Democrat and 5 Republican state senators who were in their mid-term and

not up for re-election, this gave the Democrats a majority in the combined houses of 54 to 46. This result occurred in spite of the fact that
the Republicans received a majority of the popular vote in elections for
both houses, 190,468 to 166,374 in the House and 53,784 to 44,750 in
the Senate. The discrepancy comes from the fact that in the 8 years since
the last federal census, the northern part of the state had seen a heavy
influx of Republican-leaning voters from the northeastern states, but the
apportionment of 1850 favored the more heavily Democratic counties in
the southern part.[12]

The 21st general assembly of the Illinois legislature convened on
January 3, 1859, but Hood did not arrive in Springfield and present his
credentials until January 4.[13] He was appointed to the Committee on
Counties and the Committee on Swamps and Overflowed Land.[14] The
appointment to the Committee on Counties was significant because the
creation of a new county was Hood's main legislative agenda item. The
fact that he got the appointment meant that he had the support of at
least a part of the House leadership. On the morning of January 5, Governor Bissell's address was read to the House of Representatives. He stated
that government of Illinois was financially sound and that he expected
that the state debt could be retired in six years, and further that "the
annual income from the Illinois Central Railroad and the Illinois and
Michigan canal will be sufficient to meet the expenses of the State government, independent of taxation."[15] He also spoke briefly against the
expansion of slavery under the Kansas-Nebraska Act. This drew a sharp
response from the editor of the *Chicago Times*, a Democratic newspaper.

> We cannot better begin than by saying that on this question Gov. Bissell
> has evidently been constrained to adopt the Abolition shibboleth, and
> denounce the Democratic party in general, and the Supreme Court in
> particular. He never did this, we have the charity to believe, of his own
> free judgment, but was beset and behounded by the Republican leaders
> in this State, until he felt obliged to interlope into his message a para-
> graph or two for their benefit... The Governor says that "it is important
> that we should not shrink from such a declaration of our opinions, as
> will effectually arrest further aggressions," &c... In the name of the peo-
> ple of Illinois — for in their name he assumes to speak — he asserts that,
> in view of the present condition of national politics, with reference to
> the institution of slavery, some new and bold stand ought to be taken by
> the Illinois legislature; but he neither intimates what position he individ-
> ually holds, nor indicates the position he would have the State occupy.[16]

At 2 o'clock in the afternoon, the House and Senate convened in joint session to elect the senator from Illinois. Stephen A. Douglas was nominated by Representative Barrett and Abraham Lincoln was nominated by Senator Judd. The joint session then voted along party lines to re-elect Stephen Douglas. Hood, with the Republican minority, voted for Abraham Lincoln, who lost by a vote of 54 to 46.[17] In spite of this loss, the campaign had made Abraham Lincoln a national figure and the leading candidate for the Republican nomination for president the following year. Lincoln, ever the careful politician, did not forget those who supported him in his losing bid for the Senate, and remembered Captain Hood when he petitioned for a federal job five years later.[18]

During the legislative session, Captain Hood kept the *Iroquois Republican* supplied with tidbits from the House. At one point he forwarded a report from the warden of the state penitentiary in the same mail as a reapportionment bill sponsored by the Democrats. The paper commented that,

> It would have been appropriate had these documents been bound in one volume, not that we wish to be understood in a disparaging sense, so far as the Warden's report is concerned, for it is really a sensible document. But, what we regret is that the Democratic — or rather Lecompton — Apportionment Bill should have been printed upon the same pages with the list of the convicts in the State Penitentiary, together with its author's name.[19]

One interesting act that came before Hood in that session was the granting of a charter of incorporation to the Chicago Board of Trade. The charter recognized the Board of Trade and gave it the power to set quality controls for the commodities its members traded in. The Board of Trade had been established in Chicago in 1848 by a group of 25 local businessmen as a marketplace for buying and selling futures contracts for commodities. It originally dealt only with grain, primarily wheat, corn, and oats, and by 1859 had grown large enough to need a more formal organization backed by a state charter. Today, the Board of Trade is a part of the Chicago Mercantile Exchange, the premier commodities market in the United States. It is one of the oldest futures markets currently operating in the world.[20]

Even after Hood's Somerset County bill had failed, Judge Chamberlain continued to harass him, and, towards the end of the session, Hood decided that he had had enough of Illinois-style politics. "Sidney," a correspondent from the legislature in Springfield, reported to the *Iroquois Republican* as follows:

> Judge Chamberlin has been here for sometime using his influence to prevent the sale of the eastern portion of the Peoria and Oquawka Railroad, in which I have no doubt he will succeed.
> "Douglas Monkey"—as you appropriately style him—has been here almost during the entire session, making himself exceedingly busy in all the rascally work the bogus Democracy have had in hand. He has, at the same time, used every means in his power to injure the reputation of your Representative, in which I am happy to say, he has most signally failed. No man on this floor is more generally respected than Capt. Hood.
> In conversation with the Captain today, I find that this one term has satisfied his ambition for legislative honors, and that he will freely make over to any one of his constituents all right, title or interest he may have in a future election—especially if there is any prospect that, as at this session, he will have to submit to the unjust, tyrannical and dictatorial rule of the Democratic majority.[21]

The legislative session ended on February 24, just two months after it started. Hood packed up his bags and returned to Loda. When he got there, a break occurred between him and his wife, Anna. Whether this was because she was tired of life on the prairie, or because she had learned of some infidelity of her husband's while he was away in Springfield, is not clear. Whatever the reason, on February 26, immediately after his return, Anna left him and started back to Massachusetts.[22]

The next two years were quiet ones in Captain Hood's life. There was no state legislative session in 1860. He did not run for re-election that year and seems to have retired from electoral politics, although he remained active in the Republican Party and maintained contact with prominent Illinois politicians.

In February 1860, he traveled back to Massachusetts and visited his wife where she was staying at his brother George's house in Somerset. He agreed to a separation, but did not obtain a divorce, and offered Anna a settlement of $3 a week as long as she remained single. Because the separation was voluntary, there was no division of property and no legal decision regarding the land in Somerset that had been purchased with Anna's trust fund. She accepted this agreement and at the end of March, Captain Hood returned to Illinois.[23]

In the summer of 1860, when the census was taken, Hood was still living on his farm in Loda, and claimed to have real estate worth $10,000 and a personal estate of $2,600. Also on the farm was the family of Amos Ford, who actually worked the land, two farm hands, and Mary Patton, a 24-year-old single mother, who was either Hood's housekeeper, or his mistress, or both.[24] This was a fairly substantial establishment at that time in the Prairie State, especially for a man who had been declared insolvent only five years earlier. It indicates that at least some of Hood's land speculation had worked out and that he had managed to retain some assets after the fire. He had also apparently remained aloof from politics, as he was not a delegate to the Republican state convention which nominated Abraham Lincoln for president, in May 1860.

It was at that convention that Judge Oglesby gave Lincoln the nickname "The Railsplitter" by having John Hanks parade through the hall with two chestnut fence rails from a batch of 3,000 that Hanks had split with Lincoln in 1830. This caused a sensation and contributed to the unanimous nomination of Lincoln for president.[25] As a Lincoln supporter, Captain Hood was probably present at the great rally held in Springfield in August when some 30,000 of Lincoln's followers marched past his house and later persuaded him to come to the fairgrounds where he gave a brief speech before escaping back home.[26]

Around this time, however, the fortunes of Loda began to wane as the east-west railroads that were being built to connect the north-south trunk lines bypassed the town. In 1857, the Peoria and Oquawka Railroad was completed from Logansport, Indiana, to Burlington, Iowa. It crossed the Illinois Central at Gilman, 20 miles north of Loda and started Middleport, today's Watseka, the county seat, on its rise to prominence. Trade began to decline, and Adam Smith sold his holdings, moving to Chicago where he settled for good, while continuing to speculate in land in Nebraska.[27]

In the spring of 1861, when the Civil War was breaking out, Captain Hood also left Loda and moved to Kane County, Illinois, northwest of Chicago. There, on May 22, 1861, he was granted a divorce from Anna and two days later, on May 24, married the 17-year-old Sarah Alexandra Botsford. The ceremony was performed by the Rev. I.S. Mahan, a Baptist minister.[28] At the time, Hood was 46. According to an affidavit of Anna Hood in a later proceeding, James Hood had been living with Sarah for almost a year before the marriage.[29] It is possible that Sarah was the reason that Hood had traveled to Somerset and made a financial settlement with Anna in 1860, as related above. The grounds for the divorce were abandonment, as a result of Anna's abrupt departure for Massachusetts in 1858. The court found that Anna had "means and property in her own private right sufficient for her support" and the divorce decree did not provide any financial settlement for her. Conveniently, the papers concerning the suit never reached Anna until after the divorce was final, even though Hood knew exactly where she was staying in Somerset.[30]

Sarah Botsford was born in Saugerties, New York, the daughter of Reuben Lay Botsford and Nellie Elizabeth Smith, and was brought out to Waukegan, Illinois, by her parents when she was eight years old.[31] They had met on one of Captain Hood's visits to Waukegan.[32]

One month after his marriage, Captain Hood would have first noticed the Great Comet of 1861. This bright comet appeared at the end of June, with its tail spanning half the night sky. From the dark prairie of Illinois, it was especially visible and, appearing so soon after the outbreak of the Civil War, was seen as a dire omen of death and destruction. The first Battle of Bull Run was fought in July, with the comet hanging over the battlefield at night.[33]

Too old for the draft, and probably out of shape, Hood settled with his new wife in Sycamore, the seat of DeKalb County, Illinois, where he sat out the war. His nephew Elisha S. Hood, who was still living in Loda, enlisted in Company C of the 10th Illinois Cavalry in September 1861 and served in Missouri and Arkansas over the next two years. He was discharged for disability at Rolla, Missouri, in March 1863.[34]

Sycamore was a booming town. The Sycamore and Cortland Railroad, completed in 1859, had connected it to the rapidly growing rail network in the Midwest, and there were many opportunities for an enterprising entrepreneur like Captain Hood. He became involved in a number of business and civic enterprises and was an active member of the local social scene. In the autumn of 1863, he purchased several lots just south of downtown Sycamore, intending to build a new house there in the spring of 1864.[35]

The local newspaper in Sycamore, *The True Republican*, described Hood as being "an ardent patriot, short, thick set, and a sporty dresser. He had, by reason of his genial qualities and generous nature, a host of friends, political and otherwise. The captain, however, had one failing. He occasionally mixed his patriotic spirit with another kind, that, at

times, seriously impeded his straight thinking and gentlemanly bearing."[36] This penchant for alcohol belies Hood's occasional flirtation with
the temperance movement for political purposes, and gives some insight
into his future initial good relations with the American merchant community in Bangkok, which was a hard drinking society.

9

Becoming a Consul

By the winter of 1863, Captain Hood was beginning to get restless. His fortunes seem to have reversed and, after 30 years as an entrepreneur, he decided to try to use his political connections to obtain a federal government job with a steady salary. In early January 1864, he persuaded John F. Farnsworth, Owen Lovejoy, Lyman Trumbull, Isaac Arnold, Jesse O. Norton and Elihu B. Washburne, six prominent Illinois Republican politicians, to sign the following letter to President Abraham Lincoln.

> Captain James M. Hood, of Illinois, having been a number of years connected with the shipping interest in the Eastern States as a ship-builder and also as master of a vessel, and having in that capacity visited many of the ports of Europe, and having also spent many years in travel upon the European continent, the undersigned members of Congress from Illinois respectfully represent to you our belief in his peculiar fitness for the position of consul, diplomatic attaché or commercial agent in some foreign country.
>
> Capt. Hood stands high in our State as a man of public spirit, respectability and social worth. His many and varied accomplishments are sustained by native good sense and he will do credit to your Department and the Government, in whatever position you may see proper to place him.
>
> Capt. Hood was a member of the Legislature in Massachusetts before coming to our State and was chosen to a seat in our own Legislature. In every position that he has filled, he has done his duty to himself and the public.
>
> We trust you will find some place where his practical talents may be made useful to the Government at this time.[1]

When the letter was written, Lovejoy, Washburne, Arnold, Norton and Farnsworth were all representing Illinois in Congress and were close associates of Lincoln. Washburne would later go on to become secretary of state and minister resident to France under President Ulysses S. Grant. Trumbull represented Illinois in the U.S. Senate, having originally been elected in 1855 when Lincoln threw his own supporters into Trumbull's camp.[2]

The letter was probably written by Hood himself, and it contains at least one inaccuracy. There is no evidence that Hood ever sailed to Europe, much less that he visited many of the major ports there. There was also insufficient unaccounted time during his seafaring career for him to have "spent many years in travel upon the European continent." In spite of this bit of padding in his resume, the strong endorsement of these members of Congress proves that he was known to them as a reliable man who would not do anything to make them regret their support for him.

Lincoln endorsed the request of these powerful politicians, as follows, and sent it to his secretary of state, William H. Seward.

> I personally have known Captain Hood since he went to Illinois and know that his position and standing there are such as above represented. I shall be really glad if a place, such as sought, can be found for him in the Department of State.[3]

The positions mentioned in Hood's recommendation were all concerned with American trade relations with foreign countries but differed substantially from each other. A consul was an official representative of the United States, recognized as such by the government of the country where he was stationed, and with certain rights guaranteed by treaty. The consul's chief duties were to encourage and expedite United States trade and commerce at his post and to provide aid and relief to American citizens, especially sailors. In some countries, particularly in Asia, where, by treaty, citizens of the United States had extraterritorial rights, the consul also had a judicial role, adjudicating disputes between American citizens, and between Americans and subjects of other countries. Some consuls were salaried and forbidden from running a business on the side, but others supported themselves by the fees they collected for their services and by private trading.

A commercial agent, although appointed by the U.S. government, was not officially recognized by the country in which he resided, had a much more limited role in supporting American commerce, and had no judicial authority. A diplomatic attaché served under a U.S. minister resident, as the chief U.S. diplomats were known, the title of ambassador not coming into use by the United States until 1893, and carried out duties similar to those of a consul. Of the three, the position of consul was the most independent and potentially the most lucrative one; however, a lot depended on the post to which the consul was assigned. The consul at a major port like Hamburg or London was in a much better position to make money than one at a minor port in South America or Asia.[4]

All such positions were filled by presidential appointment, with the advice and consent of the Senate. In the mid-nineteenth century, patronage was an accepted and important engine of government and politics. Civil service reforms would not go fully into effect for another twenty years. Lincoln filled thousands of positions from postmasters to cabinet secretaries based on recommendations from his political supporters in Congress and the states, even as most of his energy was directed towards the ongoing Civil War. The greater the position, the more political clout was needed to gain his support. In most cases, the Senate went along with the president's nominations, although all were reviewed by one committee or another and a few were rejected when the nominee proved to have an unsavory background. The process could move slowly, and Captain Hood probably did not expect an immediate appointment.

At the time, the Hoods were living in "a pretty cottage residence on the corner of Somonauk and High Streets"[5] in Sycamore, Illinois, which they were renting from Mrs. J.S. Waterman. Mr. James S. Waterman, her husband, was a wealthy dry goods merchant, real estate speculator, and banker with whom Captain Hood was associated in a number of business and civic enterprises. In April, a fire broke out in the house in the middle of the night. The Hoods were not present at the time. The local newspaper reported that the fire "was so far advanced at the time that help was obtained that little alarm was made and the building quietly burned down, not more than twenty people being present."[6] As in the case of the fires in Somerset, arson was suspected, and, again, no one was ever charged with the crime. The Hoods claimed to have lost about $1300 in furniture, clothing and silverware, which they had insured with the Hartford Insurance Company for $800. The building was valued at $700 and insured for $400. This was the third time that Captain Hood had been associated with a suspicious blaze from which he received an insurance settlement, and, combined with his request for a federal job, it adds weight to the conclusion that he was once again in financial difficulties.

Seward first recommended Hood for the post of consul at Payta (Paita), Peru, and Lincoln sent his nomination to the Senate on April 21.[7] Paita is a seaport on the northwest coast of Peru, over 600 miles north of the capital, Lima. Although today it is an important regional city and port, in 1864 it was a sleepy little town of about 2,500 people, exporting Peruvian agricultural products, including cacao, sugar, and orchilla weed.[8] The latter is a lichen which yields a purple dye and was much in demand in Europe.[9] Paita was also a trans-shipment point for whale oil. American and British whalers operating in the Pacific Ocean brought their oil there, where it was stored before being transferred to other ships for the voyage home. The whalers could also restock with provisions in the port and thus stay on the whaling grounds much longer.[10] The position of U.S. consul at Paita had a salary of $500 a year.[11] The Senate approved the nomination on May 18, but Hood quickly declined the appointment.[12] He was looking for something with a larger salary and in a less isolated location.

As the Civil War ground on through the bloody summer of 1864, with Ulysses S. Grant facing Robert E. Lee in Virginia and William Tecumseh Sherman taking Atlanta, Captain Hood's petition for a position did not progress, but he was not forgotten. At the beginning of the new year, Lincoln, on Seward's recommendation, sent Hood's nomination as U.S. consul at Bangkok to the Senate for confirmation. This position had been converted to a salaried status on July 1, 1864, and offered $2,000 per year,[13] a significant sum in 1865, equivalent to the salary of a major general. In spite of this, the post, which had been open for a year and a half, had been declined by three other candidates before it was offered to Hood.[14] This time, Hood accepted in his Dispatch No. 1 dated January 14. His dispatch states that he was born in Massachusetts, appointed in Illinois and had never resided in Siam.[15] At the same time he sent in his notarized oath and a bond to secure his financial responsibilities to the government, as required.

The next day, he wrote a letter to Congressman Farnsworth asking that Richard E. Tucker, who was a close friend and the owner of the Excelsior Hardware Store in Sycamore,[16] be appointed as marshal of the Consular Court at Bangkok. Although it was run by the consul, the court was a separate legal and financial entity from the consulate. The court provided a venue for settling disputes between American citizens, or between Americans and other, non–Siamese, foreign nationals. The marshal was the chief officer of the Consular Court, charged with maintaining its records and carrying out its functions under the direction of the consul. The marshal could also act as an administrative assistant to the consul when not engaged in court business. The post paid $1,000 a year, all of which went to the marshal because the expenses of the court were supposed to be covered by fees.[17]

Having Tucker as his marshal would have given Hood a strong ally inside the consulate. Hood also hoped that they could make the voyage to Siam together, so that Tucker's wife could be a companion for Sarah during the long trip. This request for the appointment of a friend or associate to a position on his staff was only the first of many that Hood would make over the course of his tenure as consul.

Captain Hood wrote:

> I ... am ready to leave for Siam in the first ship that sails. Now, my dear sir, I am about to inform you that we have a gentleman here who desires to accompany me as Marshal, and who has a charming wife, a dear friend of Mrs. Hood. They are anxious to go and we very much desire their company in this service — He is in every way qualified for the position of Marshal — His name is Richard E. Tucker & has lived here for the last twelve years — is an admirer of yours and a staunch supporter of the administration — He wrote to you today in regard to the matter — trusting that you will present his name to Mr. Seward for appointment and that his commission will follow in a short time — Hoping to hear from you soon and of your restoration to health–
>
> > I remain, yours truly,
> > J.M. Hood
> > P.S. Mrs. Hood desires to be remembered.[18]

Tucker's letter to Farnsworth followed.

> Enclosed I hand you a petition from some of the leading administration men of this place desiring you to use your influence to secure my appointment as Marshal of the United States Consular Court at Bangkok, Siam.
>
> I have been solicited to offer my name for the position by J.M. Hood, Esq. recently appointed to the consulship at that port. Having been acquainted with him since he first came to this place, and as my wife is an intimate friend of his, it would be very pleasant for the parties concerned if I would receive the appointment.
>
> Asking your pardon for intruding myself in this manner, yet trusting,

sir, that under all the circumstances you will use your influence in this matter in my behalf, and assuring you that I shall consider it a great favor which I shall not ever forget.

I am Sir, your Obdt Servant,
Richard E. Tucker.[19]

This was accompanied by a petition in his favor signed by twenty leading citizens of Sycamore, including Captain Hood and James Waterman. Congressman Farnsworth forwarded these to the Department of State with a positive recommendation, but Tucker did not get the appointment. Either Hood did not have the political clout needed to sway the patronage machine in the White House and the Department of State, or Tucker was not seen as a strong enough supporter of the administration to merit the job.

Now began a flurry of activity. In late January, Captain Hood received his credentials, along with the following letter from the Department of State.

Your official bond having been approved by the Treasury, herewith your letter of credence to the Siamese Government and your commission as the Consul at Bangkok, the receipt of which you will acknowledge.

You are instructed to proceed without unnecessary delay to your post of duty and report your arrival there to this Department.

A copy of the consular Regulations and several circulars of the Department have been transmitted to you and your careful attention is invited to [them].[20]

On February 2, Captain Hood wrote three dispatches to the Department of State, acknowledging the receipt of his passport and requesting one for his wife, Sarah, as well. He told the department that he was planning to take ship at Boston on February 15, less than two weeks later.[21]

Over the next few days, James and Sarah Hood traveled to Boston and by February 5 they were established at the Tremont House, a four-story, granite-faced, neoclassical building at the corner of Beacon and Tremont streets.[22] It was one of the finest hotels in Boston and is remembered as being the first hotel with indoor plumbing and running water in that city.[23] There he received a new passport that included both himself and Sarah, and was requested to return the solo passport previously issued. He was still planning on sailing on February 15, but for some reason, either because the ship was delayed or because he needed more time to prepare, that plan was soon abandoned.

Instead, the couple left Boston and traveled to Hood's hometown of Somerset, in southeastern Massachusetts, where they stayed from late February to late March.[24] Captain Hood had business affairs to arrange with his brother George and his nephew William before he left for the far side of the world. Whether he saw his ex-wife Anna, who was living in the city of Fall River, just across the Taunton River from Somerset, is not known.

By now, Hood had booked passage on the barquentine *Amaranth*, a ship registered in Bremen, Germany, which had been docked in New York since mid–January. As was typical in the days of sail, the departure date kept being pushed back as the ship loaded cargo and awaited favorable weather. Originally meant to sail on March 1, the estimated departure first moved to April 1, then was delayed for another week.[25]

Around March 21, Hood left Somerset and made a brief visit to the Department of State in Washington, D.C., where he received his instructions and arranged for the payment of his salary.[26] This was to be paid quarterly, but Hood was authorized to draw drafts for the money only after his accounts had been reviewed and approved by the fifth auditor at the Department of State. Since there were no Western banks in Siam, the drafts, which were essentially checks written against the United States Treasury, had to be sold to local merchants at a discount to their full value. The merchants would then cash them in Singapore or Hong Kong. The discount would be made up to Hood by the treasury, but only after receipts for it had also been submitted to Washington and approved. This arrangement was to cause Hood some consternation after he arrived in Bangkok and realized that it usually took six months for the accounts to reach Washington, be audited, and the authorization to come back to him, leaving him permanently half a year in arrears on his salary.

On this trip to Washington, Hood was accompanied by William T. Luther, a relative from Somerset then living in Rhode Island. Hood had recommended him for the post of marshal after Tucker, his first choice, had been denied the appointment. Luther carried a letter of recommendation from Frank Mauran, a prominent local politician in Providence, to Rhode Island congressman H.B. Anthony. Mauran wrote, "I have been personally acquainted with Mr. Luther since boyhood and for integrity, energy, & close attention to any pursuit in which he may be engaged recommend him as every way qualified for the position he seeks. Any thing you may do for him will be esteemed as a personal favor."[27]

Although Anthony endorsed the nomination, saying "his recommendation is entitled to the highest consideration,"[28] Luther did not obtain the appointment either.

Captain Hood's continued efforts to bring a close associate along as his marshal indicate that he knew something of the political situation in the American community in Bangkok and wanted a strong supporter to help overcome the resistance he expected to meet as an outsider. He must have known that he was only the second non–Bangkok resident to be appointed to the post, and the first person to have been appointed without having previously visited Siam. In the next few weeks, he would be in close proximity to two individuals who had extensive personal knowledge of the members of that community.

After his visit to Washington, the Hoods moved to New York City where they received their mail at the firm of Messrs. J.C. Jewett & Co. at 113 Pearl St.[29] This was a firm of ship owners and merchants which was the agent for the *Amaranth* and which also had a shipyard in Brooklyn. They were probably business associates of Hood's during his earlier years as a merchant ship master and shipbuilder. While there, Hood received a case containing a supply of stationary for the consulate, blank official consular forms, three flags, and ten copies of the *Diplomatic Correspondence of the United States for 1864*, which he was expected to distribute to the Siamese government and the other consulates in Bangkok.[30] The *Diplomatic Correspondence* was an annual publication prepared for the United States Congress and delivered with the president's State of the Union message. It contained copies of the most significant public diplomatic messages between the Department of State and foreign governments.[31]

While in New York, Captain Hood would have taken the opportunity to consult with Aaron J. Westervelt, who had been consul at Bangkok from 1862 to 1863. Westervelt was the son of Jacob Westervelt, a former mayor of New York who was also involved in ship and dock building. Jacob established a shipyard with William McKay at Lewis and Seventh streets near Corlear's Hook in New York City and constructed at least two clipper ships, the *Hornet* and the *N.B. Palmer*, both built in 1851.[32] With his sons, Aaron and Daniel, Jacob then built the 1100 ton clipper ship *Contest* in 1852, after ending his partnership with McKay, who should not be confused with the more famous Canadian clipper designer, Donald L. McKay, whose shipyard was in East Boston.[33] The following year, Aaron and Daniel took over the shipyard and built the 1680 ton clipper ship *Sweepstakes*.[34] In all, the Westervelts built some 181 ships. Because of these common business interests, Captain Hood was probably already acquainted with Westervelt.

Aaron Westervelt had acquired an unsavory reputation among the American community in Bangkok. Before his appointment as consul, he had spent several months there as a businessman, then returned to the United States for a few years. When he returned to Siam in his official capacity, he found that the missionaries disliked him for his reputedly dissolute ways, including the fact that, during his first residence in Bangkok, he had fathered a daughter with a Siamese mistress.[35] In addition, Dr. Bradley, a prominent medical missionary and newspaper publisher in Bangkok, accused him of attempting to seduce a Chinese girl who had been brought up by Baptist missionaries. On the other hand, the merchants resented him as an outsider who had once before tried to move into their territory. It appears that the two camps had combined against him and forced him out after only one year in office. On his departure in September 1863, Westervelt had appointed George W. Virgin, one of the merchants who opposed him, as the acting vice-consul, to carry out the functions of the consulate until a replacement could be appointed by the president. As acting vice-consul, Virgin could handle the paperwork and receive the fees paid to the consulate, but he did not have official status.[36]

For these reasons, Westervelt was in a good position to advise Hood on the political situation in Bangkok and on the more practical aspects of the consulate there. It would have been uncharacteristic for an experienced businessman like Hood not to seek out an interview with him.

Evidence discussed in chapter 11 suggests that William Burdon, a manufacturer of steam engines and related equipment in Brooklyn, sought out Captain Hood to solicit his aid in settling a lawsuit worth several thousand dollars that he had pending in Bangkok.[37] The news of Captain Hood's appointment as consul at Bangkok had been reported in the *New York Times* on January 7, 1865, and he was well known in the New York business community, so Burdon would have been aware of his presence in the city.[38] Burdon's factory at 102 Front Street in Brooklyn was almost directly across the East River from where Hood was staying in lower Manhattan. The lawsuit involved the failure of John Chandler, an American merchant in Bangkok, to pay for certain goods that Burdon

Leather trunk belonging to Captain Hood, made by the Richard McKensie Saddlery and Coach Harness Company of Philadelphia and New York, now in the Somerset Historical Society's James E. Bradbury Museum in Somerset, Massachusetts. Photograph by G. Kingston.

had shipped to him in Siam. The suit had been pending for several years, with the previous consul, George Virgin, refusing to act on it. Hood's actions in regard to this suit would come to have an important influence on his tenure as consul.[39]

Finally, on April 8, 1865, the day before Lee surrendered to Grant at Appomattox Court House in Virginia, the *Amaranth* sailed from New York under the command of Capt. Heidorn, with James and Sarah Hood on board.[40] It remained in the lower bay for a few days, waiting for a fair wind, and it was there that Hood learned of the assassination of President Lincoln, which had occurred on April 14. The assassination did not affect his appointment directly, but it presented certain difficulties for him. Hood did not know the new president, Andrew Johnson, who was from Tennessee, nor did he know if William Seward would continue in office as secretary of state in the new administration. He did know that news of the event would precede him to Bangkok, traveling by fast packet across the Atlantic to London and from there by telegraph to India and on through Singapore to Siam by sea, but he did not know what effect the news would have on relations between the United States and Siam.[41] With a long sea voyage ahead of him and little opportunity for gathering news along the way, all he could do was to wait and see what developed.

Taking a leaf from Captain Hood's own book, his ex-wife, Anna, waited for him to leave the country and then filed for divorce in Massachusetts, on the grounds that his Illinois divorce had been fraudulent, and that he was therefore in an adulterous relationship with Sarah. She did this to try to regain the property Captain Hood had purchased with her dowry many years before. Unlike Anna, who was not represented when the Illinois divorce was issued, Captain Hood had family and friends in Somerset who hired a good lawyer to defend him. In October, soon after Hood's arrival in Bangkok, the court would rule that the divorce that he had obtained in Illinois was valid, as he was a resident of that state at the time, and a Massachusetts court had no standing to challenge the facts presented to a court of another state. Therefore, Anna's suit was dismissed and she was unable to obtain a financial settlement.[42]

The *Amaranth* took the most direct passage, sailing south in the Atlantic and around the Cape of Good Hope at the tip of Africa, before setting out across the Indian Ocean towards the Sunda Strait and Singapore.[43] Although there is no written record of the passage, given Captain Hood's sense of the dignity of his new position and his reputation for living well, he would have booked a comfortable cabin for the voyage.

At Singapore, the Hoods disembarked and settled in to wait for the next visit of the Siamese steamer *Chao Phraya*, which sailed regularly between Singapore and Bangkok, while the *Amaranth* continued to Hong Kong. At the time, few ships went directly from the United States or Europe to Bangkok, as the trip up the Gulf of Siam was a long detour and, in spite of the commercial treaty between the two countries, there was little trade. There is no record of the Hoods' stay in Singapore, but they probably enjoyed the hospitality of the United States consul, Isaac Stone. Stone had been born in New York and, like Captain Hood, had moved to the Midwest, in his case, Wisconsin. He would eventually settle in Northampton, Massachusetts.[44] Based on the comings and goings of the *Chao Phraya*, as reported in the *Bangkok Recorder*, the Hoods' stay was probably less than two weeks. This was in sharp contrast to the experience of Dr. Dan Beach Bradley who had come out 30 years earlier, when he had to wait six months for a ship from Singapore to Bangkok.[45]

Finally, on Friday, September 8, the spire of Wat Phra-Cha-Dei appeared on the northern horizon and the steamer dropped anchor about 3 miles from the mouth of the Chao Phraya River, also known as the Meinam or Mother of Waters. Under Siamese law, the captain was required to send a boat to the Customs House at Paknam (modern Samut Prakan) where the ship's papers were checked and another boat sent upriver to the palace of the phra khlang, who acted as the foreign minister. It was the phra khlang who granted permission in the king's name for the ship to proceed up the river to Bangkok itself. While waiting for a reply, any guns or gunpowder had to be removed from the ship and taken into custody by the customs officials. This procedure took the better part of a day, so that the ship did not enter the river until the next morning, Saturday, September 9, 1865.[46]

Because the water over the bar across the mouth of the river was quite shallow, the ship had to wait for the morning high tide before steaming over it. It was twenty-five twisting miles from the mouth of the river to the city, with the river becoming steadily narrower and more congested every mile along the way. Soon, the banks of the river became lined with densely packed houseboats, which formed a floating city. At last, the ship reached its berth in the heart of Bangkok.

Amidst the bustle of mooring, Captain Hood was probably received by agents of the government and by the man he was replacing, Acting Vice-Consul George W. Virgin.

Captain Hood's hometown newspaper, the *Sycamore True Republican*, reprinted the following from the *Siam Times* of September 13.

> James M. Hood, Esq., U.S. consul, with Mrs. Hood, arrived in the steamer Chao Phraya on Saturday last. The customary calls on the Siamese officials and the consuls of the treaty powers were made on Monday, and he assumed the duties of his position on Wednesday the 13th inst. Mr. Hood has received a most cordial welcome from all sources, and especially from the American citizens.[47]

Captain Hood's term as U.S. consul at Bangkok had begun.

10

Bangkok Beginnings

Of course, not everyone was excited about the arrival of the new United States consul. On September 9, Dr. Dan Beach Bradley, an American medical missionary and newspaper publisher, made no mention of Captain Hood's arrival in his diary. Instead he wrote:

> The Chow Phraya arrived and bring a European mail with news from the U.S. down to the 8 or 10th of July. Political affairs seem to be moving on in our beloved country pretty well. Negro suffrage is now the stirring topic of all the papers and well it may for it is one of vital importance scarcely less than the one of Emancipation before President Lincoln sent forth the Emancipation edict. I hope and pray that President Johnson will be specially guided by Divine Providence as his illustrious predecessor was in his great work. Without the privileges of the ballot box the blacks cannot be accounted as citizens and if not citizens then they are aliens.[1]

This lack of enthusiasm did not deter Captain Hood. Two days after his arrival, on Monday, September 11, accompanied by George Virgin, the acting vice-consul, he called at the palace of the phra khlang, where he presented his credentials. The phra khlang was the minister of the South. Although King Mongkut had taken direct charge of foreign affairs, the phra khlang still carried out the duties of a foreign minister and was also in charge of the treasury.[2] After examining Captain Hood's commission and letter of credence, the phra khlang granted Hood the right to act as United States consul, but did not give him an exequatur, the document that would formally recognized him as such. The phra khlang suggested that the new consul present his request for an exequatur directly to the first king, Mongkut, and, when Hood agreed, the phra khlang offered to make the necessary arrangements.[3]

None of Hood's predecessors as U.S. consul at Bangkok had been granted an exequatur, because none, except Aaron J. Westervelt, had been formally appointed by the president and confirmed by the Senate, and so they had only acting status. In the case of Westervelt, the document was withheld because he had offended the Siamese government during his previous stay in Bangkok as a merchant. With this history, the phra khlang was probably hesitant to issue the document without the king's personal consent.

When the interview was over, George Virgin took Captain Hood to the consulate, which the missionary Dr. D.B. Bradley described as being a small building in the back of Virgin's general store and grog shop.[4] Together, they inventoried the records and property of the consulate. These included a long list of archives such as the arrivals and departures book, registers of official letters and dispatches sent and received, records of cases brought before the Consular Court and cases decided, records of relief provided to destitute seamen, a "journal of deceased persons," a register of American citizens, and several others. There were also copies of *Wheaton's Elements of International Law,* the American treaty with Siam, a Bible, and 12 volumes of the *United States Statutes at Large.* The furniture consisted of one boat flag, 2 consular flags, one pennant, and one government desk and press.[5] To these were added the chest of items that Hood had brought with him. When everything was accounted for, Hood legally took over the position from Virgin. Undoubtedly, Virgin briefed Hood on the local issues and politics as well as the details of the day-to-day operation of the consulate.

The history of the U.S. consulate at Bangkok was somewhat checkered. Although a "Treaty of Amity and Commerce" between the United States and Siam had been negotiated by Edmund Roberts in 1833, it did not allow the establishment of an American consulate. A new treaty was negotiated by the American envoy Townsend Harris in 1856, which granted the United States most favored nation status and did provide for the presence of an American consul.[6] When he left the country soon afterwards, Harris appointed a missionary, Stephen Mattoon, as the first acting vice-consul. Mattoon had served as a translator and assistant to Harris during the negotiations and apparently did a good job of getting the consulate up and running. However, Mattoon was never officially appointed to the post of consul by the president. After three years of performing the duties of the office, which he felt interfered with his missionary duties, he resigned and appointed John Hassett Chandler, another missionary, who had become a merchant, as his successor.[7]

Meanwhile, President Buchanan appointed H. Rives Pollard, a politically connected Kansas newspaper publisher, as the official new consul. Unfortunately, Mr. Pollard was not only deep in debt, but he was found to be a bigamist, and he did not gain confirmation from the Senate, so Chandler continued to run the consulate.[8] While doing so, however, he gained a reputation for corruption and vice, and although he did receive a formal commission from the Department of State, it was not confirmed by the Senate. During this time, the consulship became symbolic of a power struggle that was going on between the American merchants and missionaries. The consul, through the Consular Court, decided both civil and criminal matters within the American community. With practically no oversight from Washington, D.C., the opportunities for petty bribery and extortion through unofficial fees were many. The missionaries resented the affluence that the merchants enjoyed as well as their drinking and consorting with Siamese women.[9]

When Chandler's commission expired in 1861, Aaron J. Westervelt, the Brooklyn shipbuilder, became the first U.S. consul at Bangkok to be both formally appointed by the president and confirmed by the Senate in his office. The merchants, who wanted the consulship back, gave him full reign to exploit the office while keeping the missionaries and the Siamese government informed of his actions. He turned out to be no better than Chandler and, after one year, was forced to resign his post due to heightened opposition from the locals. On his departure, Westervelt appointed George Virgin, a leader in the American merchant community, as acting vice-consul. Virgin continued the practices of Chandler and Westervelt, and there the situation stood when Captain Hood arrived.[10]

One of Captain Hood's first concerns was to settle his domestic arrangements. He decided to move in with the Chandlers. John Chandler's house was situated directly on the Menam River, opposite the American Rice Mill, and contained 16 rooms, so it was large enough to accommodate a second couple. It was surrounded by what Bradley described as "perhaps the finest garden of fruit trees in Siam" and had separate houses for the servants, a bath house, and a separate kitchen.[11]

There would be many adjustments for the Hoods to make in Bangkok. One of them was getting used to the food. Siam was a Buddhist

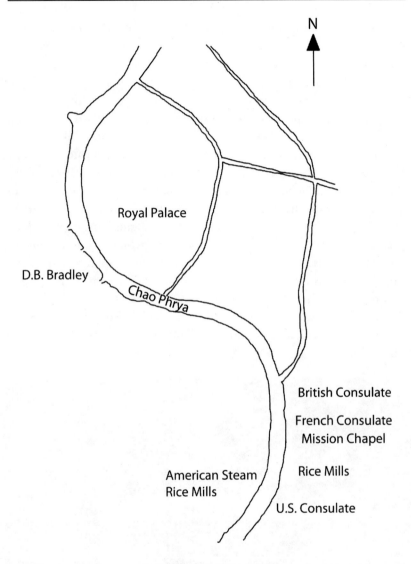

Bangkok, Siam, ca. 1866

country, following the Theravada tradition which came to it from Ceylon in the 14th century.[12] Strict followers of this discipline were vegetarians, so the diet of the country was built around rice and vegetables, with fish providing supplemental protein for those with a looser interpretation of the scriptures. The major meats available were pork and chicken, which were provided by the large Chinese population. Beef was either unob-

tainable or of poor quality. Wheat and European or American delicacies
had to be imported and were extremely expensive. Moreover, the food
was prepared by Siamese or Chinese cooks, so the menus were heavy on
curries of various types.[13] This was about as far from the beef and bread
diet of Midwestern America as it was possible to get in 1865.

In the 1860s, the American community in Bangkok had the makeup
of a town transported from the northeastern United States. Like Captain
Hood, many of the residents had begun life in New England or upstate
New York, and they shared a common culture and some variety of the
Protestant faith. Nonetheless, the foreign community had something of
a wild west feel to it. Aside from the diplomats, missionaries and their
families, the permanent residents were ship captains, engineers, saloon
keepers, and traders, many of whom were single men without families.
To this mix were added sailors on shore leave or temporarily without a
ship and various drifters and women of uncertain character. As long as
they did not disturb the Siamese, the government left them to their own
devices and disputes were settled with fists, knives and guns. According
to Dr. Bradley, a sober Westerner in Bangkok in the afternoon was an
unusual sight.[14]

**House and newspaper office of Dr. Dan Beach Bradley, Bangkok, Siam,
ca. 1865. This house is typical of those occupied by Americans in
Bangkok. Courtesy Oberlin College Archives.**

Captain Hood lost no time in getting things organized. In the next few days, he appointed James McCormick, an American merchant living in Bangkok, to be acting marshal of the Consular Court, the position he had tried to get first Richard Tucker, then William Luther appointed to before he left the U.S. He also rented a building from Chandler to serve as the consular jail. As jailor, he appointed Charles Thomas, a black man who ran Cottage Home, a boarding house and saloon frequented by sailors, in return for a kickback on Thomas' wages. Unfortunately, Thomas died soon afterwards.[15] In a dispatch to the Department of State Hood described these moves as necessary to the dignity of the office, writing:

> It is very desirable that I should have at least one person commissioned by the government associated with me in this consulate, as the Department will bear in mind that external appearances has an important influence with this people, and I am sorry to say that this is to a certain extent true with the foreign officials residing here.
>
> I am informed that the English consul has eight commissioned employees and France, five. I do not of course desire our government to make any such display of her power as this. But I do really think that our proud and noble country should be so represented as not to cause the blush of shame to arise when our countrymen compare the provision which has been made for this consulate and those of the petty states of Europe.[16]

Of course, the representatives of the other treaty powers were diplomatic consuls, taking on the roles of both commercial consul and chargé d'affaires. The French consul, Louis Gabriel Galderic Aubaret, was not only empowered to negotiate treaties with the Siamese government, he was also effectively the French governor of Indochina, and spent little time in Siam when he was not carrying out negotiations. United States consuls, on the other hand, were prohibited by the consular regulations from acting in a diplomatic role, a prohibition that Captain Hood hoped to ignore.[17]

Unstated in his dispatches was the fact that the marshal's salary, the rent for the jail, and the salary of the jailer were expenses that were paid directly by the Department of State and therefore did not come out of his salary. Thus he was able to hand out some patronage and expand his staff at no cost to himself and gain the cooperation of some possibly influential members of the local American community.

There were certainly unofficial financial arrangements between the consul and his appointees. Hood wrote to the Department of State "I have appointed James McCormick temporarily to act as marshal of this Consular Court. Before accepting the appointment I was compelled to give him a guarantee for the payment of his salary. I trust the Department will approve of this arrangement and ... Mr. McCormick will receive his commission as such, dated the 12th of September as he entered upon the duties of the office at that time."[18] McCormick later claimed that he agreed to accept a reduced salary from the consul and told Captain Hood to keep whatever he could manage to get from the Department of State, above what he paid McCormick, because he did not trust the Department to approve his receiving the marshal's salary of $1,000 a year and, in any case, he did not want to wait six months for it to be paid. Hood counter-charged that he had paid McCormick out of his own pocket and when the salary came through, McCormick demanded that money as well.[19]

In another murky arrangement, Chandler charged that Hood was using the consular jail, which rarely held prisoners, for his personal use, and that the rent on the jail included money for the Hoods' board. By Chandler's own admission, however, he had arranged for Virgin to have the consulate pay an inflated rent for the jail building, presumably with a kickback to Virgin, during Virgin's tenure as consul, so Hood was just continuing a practice that Chandler himself had initiated.

By the end of his first few weeks in Siam, Captain Hood seemed to be fitting in well with the American commercial community there. However, his vision for the consulate was very different from theirs. Virgin had viewed the post as a sideline that brought in a few extra dollars and had done little beyond the minimum required to process American ship's papers and adjudicate the occasional dispute. Captain Hood, however, saw himself as more than a mere commercial agent and intended to act as a diplomat. He was very concerned about the dignity and appearances of the consulate, and immediately began to reach out to the Siamese government. This attitude was viewed with skepticism by Virgin and Chandler, who preferred to rely on their own informal relationships with Siamese government officials, while the missionary community watched to see what would develop.

On September 22, just two weeks after his arrival, Captain Hood was granted an audience with King Mongkut, the supreme ruler of Siam.[20] The king, properly Somdetch Phra Paramendr Maha Mongkut, king of Siam, had been called to the throne fourteen years previously at the age of 47 after spending twenty-six years as a Buddhist monk and abbot, a role he had retired to when his half-brother seized the throne on the death of their father in 1825. During his time as a monk, Mongkut laid the groundwork for a thorough reform of Siamese Buddhism, but also studied Western languages, sciences, and history. Upon the death of his elder half-brother on April 2, 1851, Mongkut was elected king and left his temple to assume the throne. When he met Hood, he was almost 61 years old, eleven years older than Hood himself, and well versed in Western culture.[21]

In the late afternoon, Captain Hood, accompanied by McCormick, John Chandler and the missionaries Dr. Dan Beach Bradley and the Rev. William Dean, took a boat up the river to the landing in front of the International Court House. Hood wore his diplomatic uniform for this court appearance, but it is not clear what that uniform was. In 1853, President Franklin Pierce's secretary of state, William L. Marcy, had issued a diplomatic circular which stated that American diplomats were to appear in foreign courts in the simple dress of an American citizen, wherever practical, but left the interpretation of that statement up to the individual consul or minister.[22] Captain Hood was sensitive to the need to reflect the dignity of a representative of a great power, and knew that his clothing was an important part of the impression he would make. Bradley mentions a dark blue coat, so Hood probably adopted the common practice of wearing a modified navy uniform, which differed little from a merchant captain's coat, without any indication of rank, but with a little gold lace and a gold star on either side of his collar. The practice of wearing diplomatic uniforms or costumes would be finally banned by Congress in 1867.[23]

Bradley confided to his diary that just before they started for the palace, Captain Hood "discovered that he had strangely forgotten all the papers he was to have brought together with his written address to read and put into the hands of the king at his audience."[24] Fortunately, there was an hour yet to go before the start of the ceremonies, so he was able to send a boat back for them.

Hood and McCormick were carried to the palace in sedan chairs provided by the king, while the other three followed on foot. The hefty Captain Hood, who weighed more than 200 pounds, proved to be quite a burden to his four Siamese bearers. He described his reception as follows:

A guard of artillery, with two guns was placed at the gate of the wall enclosing the Palace.

Within the first gate we were received by a guard of infantry & the Royal band playing European airs; and were escorted to an open court, where we waited for a few moments, when we were summoned into the presence of His Majesty. We were ushered through two more gates, within each of which were stationed companies of the Royal Guard dressed & drilled in European Style, who went through the usual salute in a creditable manner.

After passing the last gate, we ascended a flight of steps and entered the Hall of Audience, which is a large and magnificent room, partly European and partly oriental in style. The King was seated on a throne immediately in front of the door by which we entered and was surrounded by most of the Princes & Nobles, all in a reclining or kneeling posture. Immediately on the right of the throne were the children of His Majesty & on the left the brothers & nephews of His Majesty & on the right and left of the throne, a little in advance of the other nobles, were the two highest of the Nobility and many of inferior rank in order of precedence.

Between these two ranks of prostrated officials, we were conducted to the centre of the hall in front of the throne where after a formal salutation to His Majesty, we remained standing, while the court speaker announced my name, official title, and the business on which I had waited on his Majesty.[25]

Captain Hood, stating afterwards that "an American kneels to no man," remained standing throughout the audience, in part because he was unsure if he would be able to get up again if he once knelt down.[26] Although this was reported back in the United States as a courageous stand for American honor, the precedent had actually been set by the first American envoy, Edmund Roberts, back in 1833, and by the time of Hood's arrival it was usual for representatives of foreign countries to remain standing in the presence of the king, with the Siamese taking no exception to it.

Hood read a speech to the king expressing his hopes for amicable relationships between their two countries and stating his expectation that he would be treated as the representative of a great power and an equal with the British and French consuls. He put special emphasis on the ability of the United States to project its naval power, now that the Civil War was ended, saying:

The great civil war extending through a period of four years with the history of which your Majesty must be already familiar has not only greatly deranged the commerce of the country but has so absorbed the attention and resources of the government as to make the intercourse with distant though friendly nations less frequent than was desirable and render necessary the apparent temporary neglect of the interests of her citizens residing abroad. I am happy to be able to assure your Majesty of the close of this civil war the government having been everywhere successful in subduing the rebellion.

The conclusion of the war has not only left the United States with undiminished territory and resources but with a large increase of strength in her Army and Navy, the latter being now fully equal in effective strength to that of the first naval powers in the world. The release of a large number of vessels of war from home service by the ending of the rebellion enables the government to greatly increase the strength of her naval squadrons on foreign stations. The squadron on the East India and China stations in which Siam is embraced is to be rendered equal in effective strength to that of any other power. This increase of naval force does not indicate any change in the traditional policy of the government of the U.S. which has ever been against the acquisition of territory in the East. The sole object of this increase is to maintain the honor of the national flag, [and] to protect the commerce and the rights of the citizens of the United States. The government of the United States asks no superior or exclusive privileges; it only claims what as a first class power it has the right to claim — the same honor and privileges for her representatives and citizens as those granted to the representatives and subjects of the most favored nations.

The well known fertility of the soil of Siam and the enlightened and liberal policy which under the beneficent reign of your Majesty has greatly stimulated production and facilitated commercial intercourse, has made the position of consul at your Majesty's capital of such importance in the views of the US government as to lead the President to appoint a consul who is forbidden to trade and who must devote his whole time and energy to his official duties.

It is made my duty as consul and will be my earnest endeavor to maintain [and] strengthen the friendly relations which have existed for so many years without interruption between the government of your Majesty and that of the U.S.

In the promotion of this desirable end I shall trust to the enlightened, liberal and consiliatory spirit which has rendered your Majesty's name and reign illustrious.[27]

This speech is remarkable for its diplomatic content and it clearly indicates that Captain Hood saw his role as encompassing a great deal more than promoting and protecting trade between the U.S. and Siam. He probably meant it as much for the members of the American community who accompanied him as for the king.

King Mongkut replied with a warm welcome and gave Hood his exequatur from his own hand. Following the audience, the Americans were served a lavish banquet in a separate building, during which they were entertained by a Western-style orchestra. A number of Siamese nobles also attended the banquet, but the king did not. Curiously, although a number of curry dishes were served, rice was not, which was a departure from custom.[28]

After the meal, Captain Hood and his entourage were escorted back to the king for a private audience. During this, the king was much more informal and spoke to them both in English and through an interpreter. At this interview, the king promised to send Hood a personal letter of welcome, which he did.

In his letter, King Mongkut described Siam as being a weak nation in treaty relations with several powerful nations, including two "powerful and celebrated ones having adjoining territories," and asked that the U.S. look upon his country with compassion.[29] He was referring to England and France, the first of which held both Burma to the northwest and the Malay peninsula and Singapore to the south of Siam, and the latter of which held Indo-China and had recently entered into a protectorate over Cambodia. Cambodia, which served as a buffer between Siam and Indochina, was a traditional enemy, and recently the tributary, of Siam. The king was hoping that a U.S. presence could counterbalance these two powers and keep his country from being carved up between them.

The French were the most immediate threat. In 1861, only 4 years prior to Hood's arrival, they had invaded Cochin China, today's Vietnam, and the following year forced the king of that country to cede the three southern provinces to them. They followed this by setting up a protectorate over Cambodia in 1864, even though that kingdom was paying tribute to Siam.[30] Only five months before Captain Hood's arrival, King Mongkut had negotiated a treaty with the French consul, M. Gabriel Aubaret, which recognized the protectorate, but also accepted that Cambodia was an independent kingdom and recognized Siamese rights to certain Cambodian provinces, including Angkor and Battambang. However, the government of the French Second Empire did not ratify the treaty and King Mongkut knew that Aubaret would be coming back for more concessions.[31]

Having been accepted by the Siamese government, Hood next proceeded to set the consulate to rights. This required funds which he did not have. Two weeks after his arrival, he wrote to Assistant Secretary of State Frederick W. Seward, who was his contact at the Department of State. Frederick was the son of Secretary of State William Seward, an arrangement that was not considered unusual at the time. The dispatch read:

> I find in looking over the books of this Consular Court that John S. Parker was fined $1000 in March 1863 and that H.L. Westervelt in his account for the 4th quarter applied or rather misapplied that sum to extinguish the indebtedness of this consulate instead of drawing on the proper appropriation devoted by the department for such purposes.
>
> On my arrival I find no proper courtroom and the one I have found without any furniture. Not a table or a chair belonging to it. Only a few days since there was a case of bankruptcy in Court in which there were present over 40 persons all interested in the issue. I conceive that the government never contemplated any revenue from the administration of its judiciary; in fact I find set forth in the act by which this court derives its power and existence in these words "the proceeds shall as far as is necessary be applied to defray the expenses incident to this act." Now I conceive that fixing up an office with the proper conveniences is embraced in this clause, the necessary books, furniture, stationary, etc..
>
> My predecessor has just had published "Laws, Rules & Regulations" which cost about $200. This together with the foregoing I imagine is a proper charge on any funds accruing to the Consular Court. If I am right in my understanding of the law I solicit that you will order the funds in question to be refunded to this Court to meet its wants and that it may be put into an acceptable position.[32]

It appears that Captain Hood wanted the Department of State to transfer the $1,000 from the general appropriation for the consulate to the account of the court, but since the appropriation for consulate expenses was limited to 10 percent of the consul's salary, that is, $200 per year, this was out of the question. This was only the first of many financial disputes between Hood and the Departments of State and Treasury that would endure throughout his tenure in Bangkok and beyond.

On the same day, he wrote a second dispatch enumerating the expenses of running the consulate and demanding a raise in salary. The dispatch clearly lays out Captain Hood's concept of his role and expectations as consul.

> On arriving at this capital I must acknowledge that I find many of the representations I relied on prove unfounded. I will now proceed to point out some of them, and solicit the attention of the department to them. I expected to find living cheap but on the contrary it is high.

Board for self and wife per month	$ 80
4 boatmen absolutely necessary	40
Uniforms for same	12
Servant	12
144 × 12	$1728
To this sum add uniforms for self, being absolutely essential in this country	$ 200
Boat & Fixtures	$ 200
	$2118

You will kindly be pleased to see that these expenses already exceed my salary for the first year without including wearing apparel.

If I take a house I must add $1000 more. This proves that no consul can exist here in a respectable style on a salary less than $3500 per annum. To all the above absolutely necessary there are contingent expenses consequent on my position, for instance I am now receiving the hospitalities of the different consuls which I am of necessity compelled to return if I wish to sustain the character of a gentleman; besides I consider it a duty to cultivate the most friendly relations with those officials as it will enable me the better to execute my various duties.

I find that a salaried consul [here] holds a widely different position from those in Europe. They generally devote their time to commercial affairs only, but it is otherwise here. He is charged with judicial authority and of necessity plays the part of a minister to the court. I find that the people of this country are grossly ignorant of geography and read but little and from these facts are incapable of appreciating correctly our wealth, power, and political institutions and judge us by our appearances and institute disparaging comparisons which place us on a par with petty states.

It is not necessary for me at this time to call your attention to the fact that England, France and other governments represented here have splendid establishments and ample provision for their consulates as this subject has been ably dwelt upon in communication with my predecessor and American citizens residing here.

I trust that the department will see as I do the great necessity for a more liberal provision for this consulate and that all complaints of this character of this letter may not be perfected.[33]

This at a time when $1,000 would purchase a respectable house in the United States. These are very high prices, and echo a similar estimate prepared by Virgin only a few months before Hood's arrival. All of the items listed, except for the boatmen and servant, would, of course, be purchased or rented from local American merchants, primarily Virgin and Chandler, who set the prices. Since Hood was too good a business man to let himself be taken in by them, one can only speculate that these prices were inflated in the hopes of getting more money out of the Department of State and may have involved kickbacks from the suppliers.

This dispatch was followed by a steady stream of requests for authority and funds to hire an interpreter, to purchase a fire-proof safe, and to rent a building for the consulate for $1200 a year. With regard to the interpreter, Hood wrote:

> I have the honor to submit to the department the necessity of having attached to this consulate an interpreter on the same footing as those attached to the consulate in China. It is very difficult to find persons qualified for this position, who have not spent years in acquiring the requisite knowledge of the language, without pay. At present I have to call on anyone that may be at hand; and consequently if there is anything communicated in official correspondence that ought to be kept secret in this office from this promiscuous interpreting it is exposed. Again, in official interviews I am compelled to call on a volunteer to accompany me to act as interpreter in addition I have frequent communications to make to the local judge on account of U.S. citizens.
>
> This service has heretofore been kindly performed by the missionaries but I submit that this is neither just nor proper; it is imposing an onerous duty without profit or benefit on their generosity. Some times letters come from the authorities and require immediate action but delays become necessary from the fact of being compelled to look up a competent person to translate the communication.[34]

Again and again Captain Hood urged the department to ask Congress for a substantial increase in his salary. Of course, none of these requests could be answered in less than six months, so he went ahead with the spending anyway, except for the building rental, borrowing the necessary money in anticipation of congressional approval.

The actual job of U.S. consul turned out to be somewhat less intense than Hood had expected. In all of 1864, only 10 American ships averaging 500 tons each had called at Bangkok, or less than one ship per month. In the last quarter of 1865, the year Hood arrived, only two American ships called there and in the first half of 1866 only five.[35] Hood's major job was to receive the ships' papers on arrival for review and safekeeping and to look after the welfare of the crew. Upon the ships' departure he certified the cargo list and returned the papers to the captain.[36] The Consular Court was fairly active, with 11 cases filed between September 21 and the end of the year. All of these involved debts, ranging, except for William Burdon's suit against John Chandler, discussed in the next chapter, from \$11.70 to \$300. Of these, only 7 went to trial.[37] It is difficult to imagine that the consulship was a full time job.

One of Hood's consular duties was to keep the United States government informed on the state of trade in Siam. In late October, he wrote a report to the Department of State concerning the trade in rice, which was Siam's most important export. The Siamese government had recently issued a proclamation removing a restriction on the export of rice. Such restrictions were routinely imposed in years when the harvest was bad in order to keep internal prices under control and ensure sufficient supplies for the country. In 1865, exports had fallen because the local merchants were holding out for higher prices, but news from the rice growing regions in the interior was good and it was expected that the next harvest was going to be large. In addition, it was reported that the crops of rice in China and Japan were poor. With new supplies coming onto the market, Hood predicted that prices would probably fall and that exports would pick up. He remarked that "this opens to Siam a prospect of a fine market the coming season and employment for vessels."[38]

He also had discovered that the British had a system called closed mail. This was a postal convention between two countries which allowed mail in closed bags from one of them to pass through the territories of the other, free from all fees or examinations. Normal mail was sorted at each stage of its journey and subject to transit fees. In the case of mail from the U.S. to Bangkok, the usual system was for American ships to carry it to Singapore or Hong Kong, either from San Francisco across the Pacific, or from New York around Africa, and then on to Bangkok on whatever ship was going there. These routes took almost twice as long as the British closed mail from London. Captain Hood noted that the British consul had offered to let him use this system by having his mail forwarded through London and he urged the U.S. government to take advantage of this offer, so as to speed up communications.[39] It was a sign of the lower status of the United States that he had to suggest using the British mail system to facilitate American administration, and it seems that he was oblivious to the possibility of having his correspondence examined by the British government before being forwarded to him.

Hood then wrote to Henry B. Anthony, the powerful U.S. senator from Rhode Island, once again requesting that William Luther be appointed as the marshal of the Consular Court at Bangkok. Although another man had been appointed to the post, he had declined it and so it remained vacant. Unknown to Hood, Senator Anthony had had a falling out with President Andrew Johnson and was finding it difficult to influence patronage appointments. For the first time, Hood voiced concern about his temporary appointment of McCormick as marshal, complaining that he had "had good sufficient reason for changing my opinion in regard to him — I find that he speaks disparagingly of the administration, is proslavery from top to toe, justifies the South in the late rebellion, and at times is very dissipated."[40] He also railed against Virgin for recommending McCormick to him.

By November, Hood was asking the Department of State for permission to draw drafts for his salary on the bank of Baring Brothers & Co. before his accounts had been audited in Washington. He noted that he had to wait at least five months for his accounts to be approved and during that time he had to borrow money at a rate of 15 percent to cover his expenses, as the fees collected by the consulate were insufficient to fund them. This indicates that he had little or no personal funds to draw on. He reminded the department that any minor irregularities in his accounts could be reconciled from his salary in a later quarter. At that time, the United States had no central bank and Baring Brothers, a British firm, was the official bank of the United States government, and handled all its payments. They did not have a branch in Bangkok, however, and Hood had to sell his drafts to merchants at a discount. The merchants would then present the drafts for payment at Singapore or Hong Kong. The U.S. Treasury eventually refunded the discounts to Hood, upon presentation of proper receipts, but the entire system was slow and inefficient.

For someone who had spent his entire life as a merchant and businessman, the accounts that Hood submitted to the Treasury Department were surprisingly sloppy and full of errors, so that the auditor was always sending them back with corrections. These errors ranged from failure to credit fees to the expenses of the consulate to failure to provide the proper vouchers and receipts for expenses. A typical dispatch from the Treasury read as follows:

Your account of salary and fees from September 13th to Dec 31st, 1865
has been received per report no. 37,990 and has been found due to you
from the US

a balance of	$492.02
Balance claimed by you	$576.90
Difference	$ 84.88
Thus	
Outstanding difference per Report No.	
36,793 explained in my letter of Jan 31st	$ 39.83
Fees used by you and charged	
but not credited in your salary acct.	$ 45.05
Difference explained	$ 84.88 [41]

It was almost as if Hood was deliberately trying to confuse the accounts.

11

Burdon vs. Chandler

In late November 1865, after only two months in Bangkok, Captain Hood decided to act on the suit that William Burdon of Brooklyn, New York, had filed against John Hassett Chandler of Bangkok. Chandler was a former Baptist lay missionary. Trained as a machinist and mechanic, he had originally been assigned to Burma in the early 1840s, but he had a falling out with the missionaries there and came to Bangkok in 1843. As one of the few skilled mechanics in Siam, he quickly made himself useful, helping Dr. Bradley to set up a printing press and to create matrices, which are molds for type, and cast type in a Siamese font. He also taught Prince Chutamani, who would later become the second king under his brother Mongkut, how to use a machine shop. When the treaty of 1856 opened Siam to American trade, his knowledge of the language and contacts at the court put him in an excellent position to act as a local agent for American and European merchant firms. In this role, he bought rice and other Siamese products for export and sold manufactured goods from the U.S. and Europe. This quickly grew into a profitable business, with Dr. Bradley estimating that Chandler was making about $1,000 a month, six times the consul's salary. The business grew so big that he abandoned his missionary work and devoted himself full time to it, but he remained close to Bradley and served as a bridge between the merchant and missionary communities.[1]

William Burdon was one of the largest manufacturers of steam engines and steam powered machinery in the world. Among his products were steam powered rice mills. He sold them not only in the United States, but exported them to many foreign countries. In 1856, a business directory reported that:

> The name of "Wm. Burdon" as maker is a familiar one wherever engines are familiar machines; and in regions where they are novelties those of

Mr. B.'s manufacture seem to have preceded all others in beginning the
work which they will accomplish, of battering down the dark fortresses
of barbarism and letting in the light of civilization. His engines may be
seen not only in all parts of the United States, including Oregon and
California, and in the neighboring countries of Mexico, Cuba and the
Sandwich Islands, but in Australia, China, Africa, Hindostan. We
recently saw a letter from Mr. Chandler, a missionary of the American
Baptist Missionary Union, at Bankok, the capital of Siam, stating that
several of Mr. Burdon's engines were in use in that city and were highly
appreciated by the king of Siam, who at that time was having a boat
built in front of his palace for the reception of one of them, and that
several more would soon be ordered by the court.[2]

It is clear that Burdon was targeting what we would today call emerging
markets, and was well aware of the credit risks involved in selling expensive machinery over long distances to unknown customers. He was also
familiar with how to pursue claims and was not one to give up on a debt
if he thought he could eventually collect it.

The decision to try the case was a particularly interesting one because
Chandler was Captain Hood's landlord and an influential member of
the American merchant community in Bangkok, while Burdon was a
distant party who was represented by Mr. Miller, one of the engineers
he had sent out to help install his steam engines. The case had been sim-
mering for years, with George Virgin, the acting vice-consul, delaying
and refusing to act on it. Exactly why Hood chose to open this bag of
worms is not clear. As mentioned above, he may well have met with
Burdon in New York prior to his departure for Siam and agreed to look
into the case in return for some consideration, but once in Bangkok, he
must have realized that Chandler's influence in the American community
could cause difficulties if he pressed the suit. In reopening the case, he
may have believed that he could exonerate Chandler, but it is more likely
that he saw Chandler as a rival for leadership of the Americans and was
using this case to both assert his own power and damage Chandler.

The case involved certain steam engines and machinery worth about
$25,000, or about $4,000,000 in today's money, which Chandler had
ordered from Burdon on behalf of the phra khlang and other Siamese
princes. This machinery was intended to be used in Siamese rice mills
and steamships. Having sold such equipment through Chandler previously, as noted above, and relying on Chandler's assurances that the order
was backed by the Siamese government, Burdon shipped them to him,

in 1857 and 1858, without requiring any upfront payment, but this time the deal went sour. Chandler claimed that when the equipment arrived, it did not work properly, in part because it had sat rusting on the docks in Brooklyn for more than a year before beginning its long sea voyage. The Siamese refused to pay for the engines, so Chandler sold the equipment to others and failed to remit payment to Burdon, while insisting that he had sent the money. In 1859, Burdon had the Kings County, New York, Supreme Court send a commissioner to Bangkok to ask Chandler for evidence that the money had been sent to Chandler's agent in New York, Mr. S.T. Smith, so that they could force Smith to disgorge the money, but by that time Chandler had taken over the consulate from Mattoon, and he did not provide them with the evidence they needed. A second commissioner was sent, but he had no better luck. As Hood put it, "Mr. Chandler was consul & only answered as much as he chose. There was no power to enforce him."[3] That is, he was able to ignore the commissioners because he was the senior United States official in Siam and, this being a matter between two U.S. citizens, there was no one else to appeal to.

After the expiration of his term as consul in 1861, Chandler returned to the United States and visited Burdon in Brooklyn where he "amused Mr. Burdon for a time with promises, and at last fled from New York, via Canada to avoid adjusting this business and returned to Bangkok."

When he arrived back in Siam, Chandler announced that he had settled his accounts with Burdon, but before long, yet another commission, this one consisting of three men led by Mr. C. Allen, arrived in Bangkok to serve him with a warrant. Before they could do so, however, Chandler claimed that he was in ill health and took "an excursion outside the bar, not returning before Mr. Allen was compelled to leave on business."

George Virgin, who was a close associate of Chandler, continued to suppress the suit when he took over the consulate. There the matter stood until Hood arrived and took up the case.

The procedure followed in the Consular Court was for the consul to appoint two or more assessors who acted as jurors to evaluate the evidence presented and make a decision as to who had won the case. The consul then certified this decision and handed down a judgment of punishment or damages.[4] In this case, Captain Hood appointed George Virgin and the Rev. William Dean as the assessors to decide the case under his supervision. This choice gave a nod to the two main factions in the American community, the merchants and the missionaries. It also stacked the deck in Chandler's favor, because Virgin was familiar with the case and had not pressed it during his time as consul. Hood officially put the case on the court docket on November 14 and issued summonses to the parties to appear on November 21.

In the interim, Hood tried to mediate between the two parties. On the morning of November 21, before the court convened, Chandler and Burdon's representative, Miller, both signed the following agreement:

> It is mutually agreed between Thomas Miller, attorney for Wm. Burdon of Brooklyn and John Hassett Chandler of Bangkok, Siam, that the claims of the said Wm. Burdon against the said John Hassett Chandler shall be arranged as follows, viz:
>
> 1st The said J.H. Chandler promises to give to Thomas Miller, as said attorney a warrantee deed of his real estate in Siam and a bill of sale of all his personal property of every description in consideration of which Thomas Miller, the said attorney promises to give a receipt in full of all claims of the said Wm. Burdon against the said J.H. Chandler.
>
> 2nd Thomas Miller the said attorney further agrees that if the aforesaid real estate and personal property shall realize on sale any amount above $17,525 and the necessary expenses connected with settlement he will return that amount to the said J.H. Chandler.
>
> 3rd The said J.H. Chandler also agrees to give a receipt in full of all claims against the Said Wm. Burdon.

This agreement was witnessed by Hood and Mattoon.

After signing the document, however, Chandler had second thoughts. He claimed that he had "discovered facts that materially affected his interests and he refused to be bound by this solemn engagement." He demanded that the trial in Consular Court continue.

The court reconvened on November 28 at which point Chandler asked for more time to prepare his case. Captain Hood denied this request on the grounds that the matter was one of long standing, dating back to 1857, and that between dealing with the three commissions and meeting personally with Burdon, Chandler should have all the accounts and other evidence he needed already. Moreover, he had been notified of the trial two weeks previously, and so had already had enough time to gather whatever papers he needed. The court then took up Mr. Burdon's bill and Chandler admitted that he had received the goods in question "with some trifling exceptions."

The court met again on December 4 and Chandler again asked for more time to prepare himself, so it adjourned to December 6. When the trial was reopened, instead of presenting new facts and original vouchers, Chandler produced newly drafted accounts including this one.

Propeller and Machinery shipped per *Oak*, sold for $8,619.45

Charges: Freight from New York per barque *Oak*	$700
Proportion of insurance policy	$274
Commission to S.T. Smith in New York 5%	$353
Cutting beam allowance to ship	$160
Extra expenses getting boiler on board	$ 65
Water color painting for steamer	$ 25
Wood for hull of steamer	$ 25
Overland charges on Moore	$ 15

The court's reaction was sharp.

All of these expenses were paid in New York, as the Court is satisfied by the account current of S.T. Smith, rendered to Wm. Burdon and Mr. Chandler has not produced a shadow of proof that he has ever paid them; but the most extraordinary charge yet to be considered, is in one thousand dollars; "Extra services in collecting bill, together with time & services spent in assisting to explain and aid in arranging and adapting the engine to the boat, making contracts for his engineers to put up the machinery, time and services spent reconciling troubles which were between the prime minister and his son and the engineers; the which services involved a great expenditure of time, efforts and expense which disabled me from attending to important personal duties and causing much personal loss." Mr. Burdon in his instructions to Mr. Chandler ordered him explicitly to sell his machinery for cash or an unquestionable security. Under such circumstances no such charge could be allowed.

Chandler then asked that a commission be sent to New York to take the testimony of Mr. Smith, but this was refused on the grounds that Smith was proved to have committed fraud. The evidence for this was that Smith had arranged passage for four of Burdon's men to Siam for $100 each and charged Burdon $250 per passenger. The court also noted that Chandler claimed to have no books and no vouchers, but relied on his memory to keep his accounts. Miller, on the other hand presented written accounts, copies of Burdon's instructions to Chandler, and signed receipts to support his claims.

Finally, on December 14, Virgin and Dean, the assessors, decided the case unanimously in favor of Burdon.

It becomes the painful duty of this Court to record the conviction forced upon them by the facts elicited during this investigation, that Mr. Chandler has violated the principles of veracity and honesty and therefore forfeited his title to Christian Character.

The assessors ... find that John Hassett Chandler is indebted to the said W. Burdon in the sum of thirteen thousand and 10⁶²⁄₁₀₀ dollars and in addition the costs of Court.

The Bangkok *Recorder* reported:

This is the most difficult case and involving the most money yet tried in Bangkok. It is one too of long standing having been on hand since 1857 and one in which the whole community have been more or less involved. From the character of the Court and the deliberation with which they took up the proofs and vouchers was not any doubt that the judgment is a just one.[5]

This was a somewhat surprising outcome, since Virgin and Chandler were close and often worked together. It is true that the evidence against Chandler was strong, and his signature on the negotiated agreement was effectively an admission that he was in the wrong, but even so, there must have been some falling out between him and Virgin to account for the verdict. However, the final settlement was $4,500 less than the sum in the original agreement, so Chandler did get some benefit from the trial.

Although Captain Hood had appointed James McCormick as acting marshal of the Consular Court, subject to confirmation by the Department of State, in this case he claimed that because it was only an interim appointment, McCormick was not properly appointed. He therefore felt justified in naming himself as receiver for Chandler's property. This was convenient, as he was already living in Chandler's house. As the receiver, he was also in a position to earn significant fees for selling and administering the estate. He sold most of the moveable property at auction on January 13 realizing around $2,000. Chandler's house and the remaining furniture were sold on April 4. The house was bought for $10,100 by the firm of Scott & Co., and the furniture brought in an additional $1,500, for a total of $13,600, or just slightly more than the debt. Hood charged all costs, including his fee as receiver, against the proceeds. Bradley even claims that Hood charged the estate a daily fee for looking after the house, and claims that the trial was the result of a conspiracy between Hood and Burdon.[6] Conspiracy may be too strong a word, but if Hood did meet with Burdon and come to some sort of agreement in New York before departing for Bangkok, as conjectured in chapter 10, it would help explain why he decided to re-open this long dormant case so quickly after his arrival. In spite of this loss, Chandler continued to live and do business in Bangkok, so it would seem that his financial position was better than he had claimed. He was given a position as a translator and interpreter in the Siamese court and a comfortable residence. After the departure of Anna Leonowens, he replaced her as the tutor to Prince Chulalongkorn, the designated successor to King Mongkut.[7]

Having sold Chandler's house, Captain Hood moved his residence to a brick house belonging to the firm of Messrs. Pickenpack, Thies & Co., a Dutch trading company, that was closer to the center of Bangkok.[8]

This trial instilled a deep hatred of Captain Hood in Chandler. He wrote to a United States senator complaining about Captain Hood's conduct of the trial and the subsequent liquidation of his assets. The senator, who was not named, wrote to Hood, demanding an explanation. It was in response to this letter, as well as to information received from "private sources ... of reports being circulated impugning the honesty of my proceedings" that he wrote his Dispatch #31 to the Department of State in May 1866, defending his actions and giving a transcript of the trial.[9] From this point on, Chandler began to scheme with Virgin to find a way to get Hood recalled for real or cooked up financial improprieties. They may have thought that this would be easy, because they had both become familiar with ways to manipulate the consular accounts during their own turns as vice-consul, but their efforts were complicated by the distance to Washington and the fact that they were just as guilty as Hood of making side profits from the position of consul. However, they hoped that, as they had done with Aaron Westervelt, they could pressure Captain Hood into resigning and take back the consulship for themselves. But they did not reckon with the stubbornness and resolve of J.M. Hood, who never forgot that he was the captain in charge of his fate.

12

The First Year in Bangkok

Captain Hood was proud of his developing relationship with King Mongkut. While he was preparing to try Burdon's suit against Chandler in November 1865, he was invited by the king to attend the annual elephant festival and noted that he was the only consul so invited. This festival was an important Buddhist event and continues today on the third Saturday in November.[1] In Buddhism, the Precious Elephant, one of the Seven Jewels of Royal Power, is a symbol for serenity and strength of mind and there are numerous sayings of the Buddha which invoke the elephant as an example. One of the most well-known is the story of how a wild elephant was put in a harness with a tame one in order to domesticate it. This, the Buddha explained, meant that a Buddhist novice should form a close relationship with an older monk so as to better learn the message of Buddhism from him. The novice should avoid taking initiative until he was well grounded in the principles of the Way.[2] If the king meant the invitation to the festival to be a hint to the new American consul to take this advice and learn the ways of the country before taking action, it did not seem to have been effective.

Besides its religious overtones, the festival was also a great holiday for the people and the court, as well as an opportunity for King Mongkut to display his wealth and power as represented by his many richly caparisoned war elephants. There were demonstrations of the strength of the beasts and a simulated charge by the elephant corps. It was the equivalent of a military review on Pennsylvania Avenue back home, meant to make the point that Siam was a strong and independent country. As King Mongkut had intended, Captain Hood was very impressed by it all, writing:

> The elephants were equipped with royal howdahs, their trunks were ornamented with massive gold rings, their necks and bodies with

gorgeous trappings and as they passed along were sprinkled with holy water. The royal stud numbering one hundred and upwards were in the procession richly decked with golden ornaments. These too made a grand appearance. His majesty closed the fete by throwing to the assembled crowd limes in which were pieces of money.[3]

Soon after the festival, Captain Hood was invited to dine with the king and, after dinner, he was escorted by the king on a tour of his private Buddhist chapel and shown "the many interesting objects in it." According to Hood,

> I was informed that I am the first foreigner that had been honored with admittance into the temple. His Majesty repeatedly expressed his gratification that my government had been pleased to appoint a consul who is not engaged in and consequently cannot be fettered by commercial pursuits. His Majesty assigns as a reason that he can more readily consult and expect more candid advice from such and intimated that he will always distinguish between them and those who act in the double capacity of consul and merchant.[4]

Clearly, Captain Hood was trying to improve his reputation at the Department of State.

The difficulties of communicating with his superiors began to become clearer to the consul. On Christmas Eve 1865, Hood wrote a dispatch acknowledging the receipt of one from the Department of State which had been sent on August 22, before he had even arrived in Bangkok. This dispatch had taken four months to make the journey from Washington. It would not be until six months later on June 16, 1866, that Captain Hood would receive the first reply from the Department to his initial dispatches of September 1865.

The year-end festivities in the American community must have been subdued, because on New Year's Eve, Captain Hood wrote a long dispatch that included a twelve page annual report on the people, climate, and economy of Siam. His opinion of the country is interesting. In spite of the king's favorable treatment of him, Hood wrote:

> The nation is barely semi-civilized, has but recently come into treaty relations with the great powers of the World and it is impossible from the disorganized system in the national affairs to acquire reliable information upon topics that are matters of much interest to all well regulated governments. Even those who have long resided in the country can give but impressions approximating corrections upon such topics.[5]

This attitude was typical of westerners when confronted with a civilization that was older than that of Northern Europe. He described the climate as comparatively mild, with sea breezes moderating the heat on the coast and the mountainous interior being cool. He was of the opinion that "the peculiarity of the government, the want of system in its administration and of principle in the officials keeps the masses of the people in abject poverty."[6]

In describing the government of Siam, Hood wrote:

> The Government is in its essential features an absolute despotism. The first King is the supreme head. On the demise of the sovereign, the rule is that the Sinabodi[7] see that the eldest prince, whose father was the King and whose mother was a Queen is quietly put in possession of the throne. If there are no such princes, the Sinabodi select one of the King's sons, though not the son of a queen, who in their judgment possesses the best qualifications and place him upon the throne. There is a rule, but to it there are many exceptions and interregnums are sometimes the causes of anarchy and wreckless bloodshed. "Might makes right" seems to be the practical rule. The King and each of his nobles is a despot in his way.
>
> The Second King is a rank peculiar to Siam. A King in every respect, subordinate only to the first King. He is addressed and treated by all the officers of state as a King. Has his retinue of nobles, his court, and his palace, inferior only to the Supreme King. He has his proportion of the revenues of the Kingdom and is usually successor to the throne on the demise of the First King. The present incumbent of the office has a deserved reputation for intelligence. He is now very ill and is not expected to live. The First King is a ripe scholar and is one of the most intelligent, and probably the worthiest Sovereigns that has ruled in Siam.[8]

The first king was Mongkut. The second king, Chutamani, would in fact die early in January 1866. Captain Hood's remarks on the Siamese judicial system were particularly scathing, and reflected the difficulties he had already experienced in dealing with it.

> There are courts and there are judges. There are codes of law. There are no lawyers, no pleaders, as in civilized and Christian countries. Most of the noblemen have, to a certain extent, judicial powers. Owing to the treaties now in existence, with civilized and Christian powers, the Siamese have found it necessary to create a new court; a court of equity, which they style the "International Court." The chief judge of this court is an intelligent man, who visited England as principal interpreter of the Siamese Embassy, which recently was sent to that country. He has

considerable knowledge of the English language. In this court Siamese are tried against whom foreigners lodge complaints. In all native courts there is very little real justice. Bribery rules the decisions. The Siamese government has complete power over its people, and generally can effectively carry out its wishes instantaneously.[9]

Eighteen sixty-six would be the most successful year of Captain Hood's term as consul, but also the year in which his world began to come apart. As a consequence of his verdict against Chandler and his disapproval of McCormick, he had alienated the American merchant community in Bangkok and they started to circulate rumors about him, alleging financial misdemeanors and misuse of his office, but at the same time, he was growing closer to King Mongkut and raising the profile of the United States in Siam.

New Year's Day signaled the beginning of an extraordinary royal festival for the tonsure of the topknot of the crown prince, Somet Chowfa Chulalongkorn. This was a coming of age ceremony and confirmed the prince's status as the designated successor to the throne. It continued for seven days, and on the last day of the ceremony, January 7, Captain Hood invited Dr. Bradley and his family to join him in attending the exhibitions in the courtyard of the royal palace.[10]

This joyful ceremony was also coupled with a tragedy. On January 7, the same day that Hood was enjoying the celebrations in the palace, the second king of Siam, Chutamani, died. He was a younger brother of King Mongkut and was 59 years old at the time of his death. This event plunged the court into mourning. As soon as he heard of the death, Captain Hood sent the following letter to King Mongkut, expressing condolences of the government of the United States.

> To His Majesty the Supreme King of Siam
> This morning I received the first notice of the sad event announced by your Majesty's circular of yesterday.
> Altho it is not usual to reply to notices given in this manner, yet I feel that I should be wanting in duty to allow a mere point of etiquette to prevent me from expressing the honest emotions of my heart. and at the same time I should do great injustice to my country if I withheld from paying that respect due to his late Majesty, your brother, on this solemn occasion.
> One of the noblest of Siam's Kings has paid the last debt of nature but history has already recorded much that was noble and great in his character. When the reign of your Majesty was inaugurated it marked an era

of progress in Siam. She then burst the shackles of exclusiveness and stood forth the peer of nations socially and from that day the motto of Siam has been "upward and onward!" At that time your lamented brother was known to the western world as a young prince of great promise and he has more than met the expectations they formed of him.

He has nobly seconded your Majesty in introducing the arts of civilization that have adorned and blessed Siam through his generation; he adopted the western idea of commerce and led the way — his monuments are to be found now in every port in the east and some in Europe. He encouraged agriculture and trade — abandoning the old idea on this subject — The advantages of the new system are too obvious to need comment and the glory of your Majesty's reign is the adoption of these new ideas and having so wise and noble a brother to assist in the gigantic work will afford some consolation in your Majesty's grief— and I tender you the condolences of one who admired and esteemed the character of your brother the late second King of Siam and I know that many in my country will sorrow in your Majesty's bereavement.[11]

He also asked Seward at the Department of State to request that President Andrew Johnson send a personal letter to the King expressing his sympathy. The Second King was responsible for the creation of a modern shipbuilding industry in Siam, and, with the assistance of John Chandler, had built the first Siamese steamship from scratch, so Captain Hood, himself a shipbuilder, related to him well. In his letter, he ascribes much of the recent progress of the country to the second king, including reforms in agriculture and trade that are often attributed to King Mongkut himself. The amount of detail in the letter indicates that Hood had assistance in writing it from someone with more experience in the country, possibly Chandler or Bradley. This letter helped cement the relationship between Hood and the king.

At the end of January, Captain Hood followed his year-end report with a more detailed discussion of foreign trade in Siam. After mentioning prices and volumes for the export of teak and sugar he wrote:

Rice, the principal article of trade and the great staple of Siam — it is mostly shipped to China and Singapore where it generally has a steady and remunerative market. The total export in 1864 reached 2.300.000 piculs and 38.000 piculs paddy and in 1865 just ended the crop was a failure the export was only 36.718 piculs & paddy 10.324 piculs, but this year there is a prospect of a great export. Prices vary according to advices from ports above referenced and frequently when a great number of vessels are here (which is the case now, more than 50 foreign vessels and about the same number of Siamese) are waiting for cargo the crop is coming in slowly and much yet remains in the fields under such circumstances competition becomes excited and prices advance. Vessels seldom come here seeking and for that reason are generally chartered to come here for rice in which case consignees are forced into the market to provide the vessel with a full cargo of this staple in a certain number of days specified in the charter. Hasty forced purchases become necessary to prevent overlay days and when the quantity of this article is moderate in the market; and from a ready combination on the part of holders who are soon made acquainted with the demand & the necessity of the merchant buying & soon the price upwards.

Rice is purchased her by the coyan, and should yield according to the quality from 20 to 22 piculs to the coyan. The coyan is 100 buckets ... and of food rice a bucket should weigh about 27 lbs. It is brought to market the whole year round but from January to April is the most abundant.[12]

Paddy refers to rice that had not been milled. The milling of rice was done at steam driven mills in Bangkok some of which were owned by European or American companies, such as the American Steam Mill Company, and others of which were owned by the government. Hood also gave an explanation of how foreign exchange worked in that corner of the globe, showing that he had not lost his grasp of the intricacies of the subject.

In former years when there was no opportunity to dispose of bills in China or Singapore funds accompanied or preceded the vessel. Gold leaf or clean Mexican dollars (the word "clean" signifies dollars not defaced by the chop & stamps) was used. Gold leaf is worth from 15 to 20 times its weight in ticals and the Mexican dollars were taken to the mint & exchanged for ticals at the rate of $1000 for 1666⅔ ticals but when the mint was unable to supply the market, the ticals, being the one money that the native traders know the value of, they frequently advanced so high as 5 percent premium. This premium was unjust to the foreign purchasers and upon being represented to the King that the value was justly $^{60}/_{100}$ of a dollar His Majesty ordered the dollar to be received in trade at that value. Besides the Siamese mint was on a limited scale & unable to supply the demand of the trade. At the present time no inconvenience is experienced. For the last four or five years funds are remitted in an easier and more economical manner, viz. contacts are opened from China or Singapore either with substantial mercantile houses of note or banking corporations. Little is required for China. The import trade has much increased of late so that exchange is sought at about the extent of $60.000 per the semi-monthly steamer for remittance. The exchange varies according to the amount to be disposed of from 2 pr. ct. discount to 3 pr. ct. premium — this is a general rule. But in last September and for some mails previous reached as high as 6 percent premium: this was however owing to the troubles in the banks, consequent upon the heavy failures in India & the high price of specie in Singapore.[13]

The most important import was cloth, especially cotton cloth, which came from England and America. The majority of this was imported via Singapore. The second most important import was currency in the form of gold leaf and silver coins, received in exchange for the rice and wood exports. The standard international currency in Siam was the Mexican silver dollar, or peso. This was a de facto international monetary standard throughout Asia and the Americas during the time after the Civil War when the United States was awash in paper currency and U.S. gold coins were scarce.

Soon after the death of the second king, Captain Hood was called upon to explain certain financial transactions to the Department of State. It seemed that a Mr. Marsh, a sailor and citizen of the U.S., had died in Bangkok in the fall of 1865, and Hood had appointed his wife, Mary Thomas Marsh, who was also there, as the executor of his estate. He paid her for her services out of consulate funds, and noted that he received a voucher from her for the money. The department questioned whether this was an appropriate use of public funds. This system of vouchers was open to abuse, because, if a recipient of funds signed a voucher for the full amount, but received a lesser sum, there was no way to prove it, especially since the consul kept the books himself and there was no local audit of the original records. This practice was the center of later allegations that Hood demanded kickbacks for his services.

On a happier note, Hood served as a witness at the marriage of George G. Graham, of New York, and Elizabeth Franks, of Edinburgh, Scotland, which was conducted by Dr. Dan Beach Bradley, a Congregational missionary.[14] It is interesting that this marriage was carried out by an American clergyman and witnessed by the American consul, given that the bride was a subject of Britain, but George Graham was also a missionary and was an assistant to Dr. Bradley at the *Recorder*. The American Protestant missionaries were strong believers in marriage and were quick to find new wives in the Western community if they were widowed by the diseases which were endemic in Siam. Two years later, in 1868, Graham would begin to publish his own newspaper, the *Bangkok Daily*

Advertiser. By that time he had turned against Captain Hood and used the paper's columns to attack him.

Dr. Dan Beach Bradley was a missionary physician who had worked for the American Board of Commissioners for Foreign Missions when he first came to Bangkok in 1833, but in 1847, during a visit to the United States, he was forced to resign over a doctrinal matter to avoid being fired for heresy. He had been converted to the doctrine of Christian Perfectionism, a doctrine promulgated by Charles Finney, the founder of Oberlin College in Ohio. Finnney held that a man could be redeemed from his innate sinfulness during his earthly existence through personal communion with Christ. This went against the Congregationalist belief in pre-destination. Bradley therefore transferred to the American Missionary Association, which had no such strictures. He returned to Siam and supported himself as a missionary by running a printing press that published both English and Siamese language newspapers, almanacs, and other printing jobs.[15]

Captain Hood kept in communication with the palace, and the Siamese government began to turn to him for independent opinions on United States foreign policy. In one confidential note, the Siamese foreign minister, the phra khlang, asked him about the potential for war breaking out between the United States and France over the issue of the Emperor Maximillian, under whom the French had set up a puppet government in Mexico, or for hostilities between the United States and Great Britain over British aid to the Confederacy during the Civil War. The minister wrote:

> I would like to ask you a few things privately in regard to a certain matter. I have lately heard news which came from Singapore saying the U.S. and France have a difficulty of a troublesome nature between them in regard to Mexico or something else which I don't exactly know. If this be so when will it be settled? If it is not settled I think it will lead to a great war between the U.S. and France. Whether the nations adjoining France will enter into it and assist France or not, I don't know exactly. Some people say the U.S. and England have also a difficulty between them to settle. This news they say came by telegraph and is late. What do you know in regard to this matter? Is it so or not? If the U.S. and France actually came to war the French have established themselves strongly close to Siam and will come and give the Siamese much trouble for they the Siamese have already favored the publication by American newspapers and they also speak reproachfully of the French. When it comes to

this what do you think of it and how can the Siamese escape trouble?
You will do me the favor of replying privately and not let it be generally
known.[16]

Captain Hood replied:

It is true that there are matters of controversy between the French and
English governments and the United States; but it is my firm belief that
war is far from imminent and will only be resorted to where every other
means has failed. War between powerful nations with widespread commerce is too awful an alternative. Under these circumstances we may
safely expect that every means will be exhausted that diplomacy affords
for an amicable settlement. From the peculiar position of the treaty powers in Siam, from their extraterritorial jurisdiction, the Siamese government can not be held responsible for the acts of one foreigner against
another. All the representatives above referred to have their courts for
trial & determination of all grievances that may occur; and this will continue till the Siamese government makes a municipal law regulating the
press — but I do not find any thing in the papers published in Siam that
angers or offers any cause of offense. Compare their manner with those
of Singapore or Hong Kong and if I mistake not they will be found more
temperate.

You ask me what the matter of controversy is between French and the
U.S. The French, in the year 1863 by their military power established an
Empire in Mexico and with the concurrence of the other nations
appointed an Emperor to rule the Mexican people & agreed to sustain
this Emperor — it is the opinion of the U.S. that the majority of the people of Mexico are unfriendly & patriotically opposed to this order of
things; and as the U.S. is opposed to any government being established
& sustained by European powers on the continent of America, are bound
to do all they can to prevent any permanent sovereign ruling in Mexico
in opposition to the wishes of the people & sustained by foreign bayo-
nets — so it is the wish of the U.S. that the people of Mexico should be
permitted to establish their own government by themselves.

Your second question in regard to the matter between the U.S. and
Great Britain — During the rebellion certain vessels were built, equipped
and manned & sailed from the ports of England & as the same arma-
ments were despatched to a common rendezvous, where the armament
was received — the flag of rebels is hoisted & cruising inaugurated by
these vessels who had no home & never had been in any port of the
rebels. The U.S. maintains that it was the duty of England to have
restrained and to have prevented the building, fitting &c. by her citizens
& therefore seek indemnity for losses by their action in this matter.

In my last advice from home every thing indicated present prosperity.
The telegrams you refer to & certain newspapers employ themselves in

disturbing the public by speculation & agitating questions generally for their own benefit but disturb few people.[17]

After advising the phra khlang about relations between the United States, France and Britain, Captain Hood received two confidential messages from the king asking many questions concerning politics and municipal law in the United States. He replied to the first one, but was reluctant to encourage the king by replying to the second because of the time taken up in researching and writing an answer. Instead, he wrote to the department of State, asking if he should reply to these requests and any subsequent ones. He also asked if the Department wanted copies of the messages and his replies, mentioning that both were very long and that copying them would be a great burden and sending them to Washington would add greatly to his postage bill. At that time, postage between the United States and Bangkok, by way of Southampton, England, was $0.45 for a half ounce letter, but Hood leaves the impression that he would rather not share what he had written to the king.[18]

A typical Consular Court case, which developed in April, illustrates the conditions under which merchant seamen served at the time. Capt. John A. Dawes preferred charges of mutiny and revolt against John Long, Isaac Hayes, and Thomas Cam, American crew members on the *Jacmel Packet,* a 150-ton British schooner named for a city in Haiti, which was lying in the river at Bangkok. The schooner had been in Bangkok in February and after sailing to Singapore, returned to the city. The complaint read:

> That on the 27th day of April 1866 the crew collectively refused duty and requested to see the U.S. consul. I accordingly landed and accompanied them to the consulate. Their complaint was then that they had insufficient provisions & that the schooner "Jacmel Packet" was going back to Singapore a port not legally in their shipping articles as the port of Singapore was not a port on the China Station.
>
> They were on that occasion admonished by the consul & the complaint of not providing their provisions was found to have been accidental, the provisions not having reached the ship in time for breakfast. The crew then turned to and discharged the vessel. On the 11th inst they refused duty and disobeyed all the lawful orders of myself and mate. I again had recourse to the consulate. It was decided that Singapore was a port on the China Station; they then refused to go on board together. I forced to do so. I ask that the Record of the consulate be introduced as evidence in the case & exhibiting the basis of the charge. I request that inquiry be made & justice done in the premises.[19]

As a former merchant ship master, Hood was more sympathetic to Capt. Dawes than to the sailors. According to Capt. Dawes, at the end of the month, the crew members came on board drunk and refused to work. The captain then discovered that several barrels of beer in the hold of the ship had been drained since leaving Singapore and he put the men in irons on a diet of bread and water. After a week and a half of this, he attempted to put them back to work, but they again refused duty and disobeyed his orders and those of the mate, at which point the captain brought the miscreants back to the consulate. The crew insisted that they would not go to Singapore. Captain Hood decided that Singapore was a port on the China Station, which was what their shipping orders specified, and that they had to obey the captain. Captain and crew went back to the ship, but the crew refused to board. The captain forced them to so, but they still refused to sail, so the captain swore out the formal complaint against them. Trial was held in the Consular Court on May 18, and the court found the three men guilty of insubordination. They were given a choice of sentence. They could either go on board and proceed to Singapore or they could serve three months of hard labor in the consular jail in Bangkok. The men chose the jail over the ship, which indicates something about the true conditions of serving under Capt. Dawes.

In mid–June, Hood received notice that George B. Bosworth of New York City had been appointed as his marshal, but that the temporary appointment of McCormick had also been approved, pending Bosworth's arrival. As it happened, Bosworth refused the assignment and Hood never did get an officially commissioned marshal.[20]

In his reply, Hood complained that the latest dispatches from the Department of State had taken 146 days to reach him, while the first set of dispatches he had received from them had taken 120 days. He was obviously keeping up with his contacts at home, because he noted that a private letter from a U.S. senator, presumably his sponsor, Lyman Trumbull, had reached him in 62 days and one from Cincinnati in 72 days from their mailing. It is important to note that the rhythm of Hood's dispatches was dictated by the arrival and departure of the mail steamer from Singapore, and that he was rarely able to post them more than once or twice a month. In many cases it is obvious that he was writing in haste to reply to a question from the Department of State before the mail steamer left on its return voyage. Bad weather or mechanical breakdown could delay the mail for an indeterminate amount of time.

Hood also informed the department that he had taken a lease on the house formerly used by consul Westervelt to use as his consulate. The lease was for more than $1200 a year, including upkeep of the grounds and building. This is a vast sum when one considers that, in 1866, it would buy a moderately good house in the United States, and that Dr. Bradley was living in a large, two-story house that would have rented for less than $200 a year,[21] but he justified himself as follows:

> I have from absolute necessity to sustain the respectable position of US consul and I need not in this despatch more than hint at what has been repeatedly mentioned to the Department that the necessity of a consul having an imposing establishment this will go far, very far with this people in estimating the importance of my Government & in fixing the estimation of the consul...
>
> The position [of the house] is peculiarly fine being on the river & in a central part of the foreign community. The building is large, commodious and of imposing appearance surrounded by one of the finest garden plots in the city & has every requisite for a consulate. It may appear singular to the Department that I dwell so particularly on this subject. It must be imputed to a national feeling & the desire to see my government represented on the footing with other representatives of great powers, and the Siamese look for my position being proportionally enlarged as I am the only consul that had ever been here who was exclusively confined to official duties, all the others having other avocations to attend to & their time. They was considered mere traders & held by this government in small estimation seldom consulted on any matter of importance. It is entirely different with my position. I am taxed to a great extent by both His Majesty and his ministers within the last few weeks. I have received from them of translated exceeding forty sheets of cap paper — putting questions to me on International Law and again on Municipal Law. The Siamese Government appear to wish to establish a municipal law in accordance with those of the civilized world and anxious in doing so to avoid all international difficulties.[22]

As the rainy season progressed, the conflict between Captain Hood and his marshal, James McCormick, came to a head. Hood accursed McCormick of habitual drunkenness and of being absent without permission for three weeks. To avoid further difficulties, George Virgin, who had originally recommended McCormick for the job, persuaded him to resign rather than be fired. Hood then appointed Simon H. Cordier as temporary acting marshal, still expecting Bosworth to arrive from the United States in a few months.[23]

He asked the Department of State to authorize him to appoint an interpreter in place of the marshal and to set the salary of this interpreter at $1500 a year, half again as much as the marshal got. He intended for the interpreter to also act as a consular clerk. He recommended the Rev. Noah A. McDonald for the post and suggested that he had already approached him and that he would accept it.[24]

In a dispatch dated July 26, Hood for the first time explicitly came out against the American merchants, who he asserted were led by Virgin. He wrote:

> I am truly sorry to trouble the Department with complaints but my duty compels me to say that since Mr. Mattoon left the consulate there has not been one of his successors who has commanded the least personal respect from the Siamese government or from the foreign officials here and as a consequence of this great neglect on the part of our government at home. I found that about a month previous to my arrival here the Supreme King of Siam had entered the field as one of our nation's defamers and proclaimed abroad that the high position which had been heretofore assigned the government of the U.S. was not warranted and to prove his position he adduced the fact that U.S. vessels of war seldom if ever visited these waters and that the character of the representatives of that nation at his court had not been such as to have him believe it a great nation. That portion of American citizens who have resided here for a number of years admit that the evidence of our greatness as a nation which has been presented to this people justifies His Majesty in thus expressing himself. We may call to assist the fact that Mr. Chandler has since proved himself to be a consummate scoundrel and was so considered at the time of his appointment. Again, Mr. Westervelt had not the least respectability to uphold him in his official position. In fact he was what may be called a "raister" and his reputation was so low that he could not receive an exequatur from the Siamese government under any consideration. His successor, G.W. Virgin had been employed as chief mate for a time on board of a Siamese vessel which position is about as respectable as that of cook on a first class American ship. Afterwards, he started a line of row boats to carry mail and passengers from the city to the mouth of the river and eventually became a ship chandler. In any of the above named positions he could not be considered a good representative of such a nation as the U.S. I am also sorry to say that Mr. Virgin is the leader of a degraded class of American citizens which was formerly rather numerous here.
>
> Those now remaining of that class are mostly rum sellers and pimps, but although Mr. Virgin is not a man given to drink himself he manages to control this class most thoroughly. We have here principally but two classes of American citizens, viz. the missionaries and their families,

some mechanics and seamen and the class already alluded to. The former are principled, intelligent and high minded. The latter class all see nothing good in these devoted missionaries or their labors and whoever looks upon them as worthy of respect is at once denounced as a supporter of the "D — d hypocritical missionaries" and this kind of "billingsgate" has frequently been heard from the likes of Mr. Westervelt and Mr. Virgin. I find that the majority of the missionaries are all that I have represented them to be, intelligent and worthy and with them I have taken my stand. The consequence is I am denounced (quietly) as not better than one of them and as unworthy to represent the government of the U.S. I found soon after appointing Mr. McCormick that he belonged to the anti-missionary class and I wrote to Senator Anthony of RI that I desired his displacement. Of course I could not communicate these facts to the Department while Mr. McCormick was in the consulate as he had access to my despatch book.[25]

Hood related the story of how he persuaded a Siamese noble, Krom Luang Womsa, who was a half-brother to King Mongkut, to pay a long-standing debt of $1,000 to the American captain William J. Higgins. Higgins was a longtime resident of Bangkok, but he had gotten on the wrong side of the Siamese government by attempting to defraud it of a large sum of money by forging a nobleman's seal, so he had no hopes of recovering his money in a Siamese court. Hood negotiated the settlement with the inspector of customs, J.C. Campbell, acting for the government.[26] Although he recovered almost the full amount for Higgins, Hood charged a large fee for his services, an act that would later cause him some difficulties.[27]

Money matters again surfaced at the beginning of August. Hood complained that the Treasury Department had denied his claim for wages for an assistant jailor, and he could not afford to pay this essential individual out of his own salary. The dispatch contains two telling quotations. The first, "where one man is required at home to do a certain duty, five is required here" reflects both his frustration with the performance of the Americans available for hire and his desire to increase his staff so as to increase his dignity. The second, "I am to more than three times the expense of living here as any one who has preceded me in office" reinforces Hood's sense that he must maintain an establishment that expresses the power and dignity of a representative of a first class world power. He followed this up with another request for an increase in salary, a theme that he harped on again and again.[28]

Of course, the Department of State had no intention of going to Congress with a request to raise the salary of a consul at an obscure Asian port, and it continually replied to Hood's pleas with instructions to either limit his expenses to those allowed by the consular instructions or to pay any additional expenses out of his own pocket.

Later in August, Hood received a dispatch from the Department of State in response to his request for instructions on how to deal with the Siamese government. The assistant secretary of state, Frederick W. Seward, tersely reminded him that his duties were limited to trade and that he was forbidden from acting in any diplomatic capacity.[29] This sent Hood over the edge. He felt that he was doing everything he could to represent the United States as a world power on the same level as England and France and here was his own government putting him in his place and telling him to back off. On August 20, he replied with a dispatch that departed sharply from his normal respectful tone and dripped with sarcasm. It is worth quoting it in full.

> Sir,
>
> I have the honor to acknowledge the receipt of despatches from the Department numbered 19, 20 and 22. In No. 22 you are pleased to call my attention to section 15 of the consular manual in answer to my despatch No. 30. I am gratified that the Department has seen fit to circumscribe my duties to the protection of the revenue, the commerce and the citizens of the US. This will save me much time and labor as both His Majesty and Ministers have frequently addressed me on matters pertaining to their kingdom solely. I seem to have been mistaken in supposing that when His Majesty or any of his Ministers addressed me on a political matter or any other subject that I was in duty bound to reply and give my views in answer to such communications there being no superior functionary in the kingdom representing our country to whom his majesty or his ministers could address themselves in case of emergency — So I have already informed the dept. That consuls not engaged in trade are looked upon by the authorities here as occupying a much higher position than those residing in countries where they are subordinate to higher officials of this our govt. and are treated in every respect as ambassadors are treated in Eastern countries. His Majesty has been pleased to write to me quite often since my arrival and always addresses me as Hon. J.M. Hood, diplomatic consul for the U.S. to Siam — Dr. Knox the English — Mr. Aubaret the French consul in the same style. I have been somewhat ambitious for our nation to stand on the same footing with this people as that of England and France.
>
> The course I have pursued places us as a nation in that position —

Under these circumstances will the Department permit me to suggest the propriety of the President giving me permission as indicated in Section 30 of the consular Manual to correspond with His Majesty. I am confident that his majesty desires it.[30]

The Department of State never bothered to reply to this request.

Enclosed with this dispatch was a note from Simon Visconti, another of the merchants, denouncing Hood. It read:

> I have the honor to forward for the action of the Department my personal account against J.M. Hood, Esq., U.S. consul. The Department must be perfectly aware of the position of citizens of the U.S. are placed in relation to consuls; there is no way of reaching him by any legal process, he is above all law within his consular jurisdiction; and should the Department have no remedy to apply to redress grievances our situation is indeed to be commiserated; and at the same time, I feel it to be my duty to prefer charges against Mr. Hood of the gravest character, accusing him of malpractice, peculation and extortion.
>
> I will in the first place begin with my own affair. Enclosed (No. 1) is my authenticated account. It will be seen that it consists of my personal services and the fees due me for official and other services. Enclosed (No. 2) will be found copies of the notes that passed between us on the subject of his pretense to account which I am unable to procure from him. I must go into a detailed narrative of the connection.
>
> I undersigned Simon Visconti do make the following statements. That J.M. Hood agreed with me to serve him as jailor for the sum of twenty-five dollars per calendar month and when the month was completed I sent to him for my wages to JMHUSC for $25 twenty five dollars which he said was inconvenient & that he would make out a form and when he done so I seen I had signed for $40 forty dollars per calendar month and that it had to go to the US Government for him to receive. And I received only $25 per month as Mr. J.M. Hood's consular jailor for the calendar month and not the sum of $50 which I ought to receive per month for making a verbal agreement. On that I had to live as I could not get my wages. Blasphemy and insubordination so I poor being had to live without wages, which I could get no redress from JMHUSC since which I know that he has received from the U.S. Govt. $120 which would leave J.H. Hood splendid profit in a poor labor. The treatment which I received from him was awful bad.[31]

Captain Hood did not offer any defense or rebuttal to this charge, probably assuming that the rambling nature of the note was evidence enough of Visconti's lack of honesty.

In October, Hood wrote complaining about his difficulties in deal-

ing with the Siamese authorities with regards to Americans who had
claims against Siamese, echoing the concerns about the Siamese judiciary
that he had raised earlier in the year. He pointed out that there was no
English translation of the Siamese municipal laws, so Americans were at
the mercy of the Siamese judges and justice could not be obtained. He
was referring to three cases which he had appealed to the king to settle.
The first was a theft of $2,463 from George Virgin which had occurred
three years earlier. Hood asked the king to compel the masters of the
thieves to compensate Virgin for the loss, in accordance with Siamese
law. The second was an assault in which one of Hood's servants had been
stabbed just outside the consulate, and he asked for $240 in damages.
The third was a case involving goods that a certain Chew-Hong had
purchased from Virgin several years earlier and never paid for. Hood
denounced the Siamese as "monstrously depraved" and asked that a vessel
of war call regularly at Bangkok to awe the Siamese into being more
agreeable to negotiations with him.[32]

In spite of these denunciations of the Siamese government, Hood
attended a birthday celebration for the king on October 18 at the palace.
This was a dinner for the foreign consuls and other officials, and was a
departure from previous practice. As Bradley recorded in his diary:

> 18th The king had a birthday party of the Foreign Officials this pm at his
> palace departing from the long established custom of having the mission-
> aries & merchants with the consuls. He had the former invited to Break-
> fast at his palace on the morrow. This King has made this change
> because the English & French consuls last year had the occasion of a
> great disturbance of pleasure of the King's birthday party because they
> insisted that the consuls of the treaty powers should have a table by
> themselves. It appears hard that this new plan would make State matters
> worse rather than better. The 2nd table and that not on the birthday but
> on day after appears a little too [undignified] in relation to these officials.
> 19th I have heard that there were but very few Foreigners who break-
> fasted at the royal palace today. I should have gone had I found the time
> that I could spare and would not have stood much upon my dignity in
> the matter of the consuls — though I abominate such mean acts as that
> which the two consuls became evident.[33]

Towards the end of the year, Hood wrote to the Department of
State that in the third quarter of 1866 only one American vessel had
arrived at Bangkok and that it had not yet departed. He attributed this
to American vessels being too deep in draught to cross the bar of the

river, which was no more than 14 feet deep at the highest of tides and was normally much more shallow. He mentioned the high freight rates to be obtained at Bangkok and suggested that shallow draught American vessels should be encouraged to call there. He also sent letters to American ship captains in Hong Kong, touting the trade to be had at Bangkok and inviting them to come there.[34]

Captain Hood closed out the year by summarizing the trade at Bangkok in the fourth quarter, noting that the number of American ships arriving had increased to seven, all of them sailing ships, so perhaps his letters to American ships at Hong Kong had paid off.

He remarked on the makeup of the Siamese population, noting that the Siamese themselves appeared to be descendants of the Karens, Laos, and other mountain tribes, but that the population included Chinese, Cambodians, Cochin Chinese, Malays, Peguans (a people in Burma on the border of Siam), and Burmans, the largest non–Siamese element being the Chinese. He estimated the population as consisting of four million Siamese and other Southeast Asians, three million Chinese, and three thousand foreigners claiming treaty protection, that is, Europeans and Americans, for a total of a little over seven million people. This was obviously a rough estimate, as no accurate census of the country had ever been taken.

He noted that the king had recently granted a charter to an English company to construct the first telegraph line in the country. It was planned to connect it to the existing line which ran down the Malay Peninsula from Rangoon, Burma, to Singapore. Through Rangoon, it would connect to Calcutta and then on to Europe. Unfortunately, this project was not completed before Hood's departure in 1868.[35]

He again reminded the Department that he had the need to maintain a boat with four boatmen and asked that he be allowed to charge these to the consulate as a miscellaneous expense instead of paying for them himself. For the first time he conceded that if the department would pay for the boat, he could get along on his present salary very well.[36] This admission indicates that Captain Hood had discovered other sources of income than just his salary. Some of these would come to light during the following year. But before he had to deal with that, he would find himself thrust into the center of an international incident that threatened to explode into a conflict between Siam and France.

13

Aubaret vs. Bradley

The enmity between Dr. Dan Beach Bradley, the American missionary physician and publisher of the *Bangkok Recorder*, and Monsieur Gabriel Aubaret, the consul representing the government of Emperor Napoleon III of France, began even before Captain Hood arrived on the scene in Bangkok. Although he was an American, Dr. Bradley became close friends with both the British consul, Thomas Knox, and the English royal governess, Anna Leonowens, who also served as personal secretary to King Mongkut, especially for correspondence in English and French. This may have been a result of Bradley's isolation from the American merchant community, and his doctrinal differences with some of the other missionaries, but whatever the reason, he began to side with the British against the French as early as the beginning of 1865. In this, he was probably encouraged by consul Knox, who could use Bradley as a neutral mouthpiece, while distancing himself from any controversy that might arise.

M. Gabriel Aubaret was both the French consul at Bangkok and the chief inspector of native affairs in Cochin China (Vietnam), a post which put him in control of that country. He spent most of his time at the Vietnamese capital, Hue, and came to Bangkok only when necessary. The French had begun seizing territory in Cochin China in 1858 and in 1862 officially incorporated several provinces into their empire. They were concerned that the British, who were already ensconced in Burma and Singapore, would use Siam to threaten their western flank. In fact, although he held the title of consul, Aubaret had the powers of an ambassador or minister in residence and was charged with negotiating a treaty that would guarantee the neutrality of Siam in any conflict between France and Britain, as well as neutralizing Cambodia. This was to replace the previous treaty of 1863.[1]

By the spring of 1865, Aubaret had succeeded in negotiating such a treaty, and it was signed on April 14. It included ambiguous clauses in which Siam acknowledged a French protectorate over Cambodia, and France accepted that Cambodia was an independent kingdom. The treaty also recognized Siamese rights to certain Cambodian provinces, including Angkor and Battambang. The treaty was supposed to remain secret until it was ratified by the French government in Paris. Somehow, Bradley obtained a copy of the treaty and published its terms in his newspaper, the *Bangkok Recorder*, on May 1.[2] Bradley never revealed his source, even in his private diary, but it most likely came from a pro–British official of the royal court, possibly passing through Knox's hands. The king was infuriated, and asked George Virgin, in his role as the American acting vice-consul, to shut the paper down, but he declined, stating that, since Bradley was acting in a private capacity, any problems were strictly a matter between the Siamese government and Bradley. These demands were published in the *Recorder* on May 16,[3] and again on June 1,[4] with Bradley defiantly defending his right to publish what he pleased, irrespective of the desires of either the Siamese or French governments.

The feud simmered over the summer, with Bradley trying to dig up incriminating information on Aubaret, and Aubaret becoming increasingly frustrated in his dealings with the Siamese government and making threats to the king of what his government would do if no action was taken against Bradley. Aubaret was scheduled to return to France with the treaty at the beginning of September, when a French ship of war was expected to pick him up. Bradley reported that Aubaret had threatened to use the ship to bombard Bangkok if his demands were not met.

On September 1, Bradley recorded in his diary that Aubaret's assistant, M. Lamache, had insulted Mom Rachotai, the international judge, when he arrived bearing a message from the king. According to Bradley, Lamache grabbed him "by the tuft of his head and led him out of his house and kicked him and threw his betel box out of the house. It would seem that the man must be crazy or knows that he will be supported by the French consul."[5] If true, this was a serious action, because the tuft of hair was an indicator of the messenger's noble status, and the betel box was a symbol of his office. However, the king took no action against the French, so it is possible that the story that Bradley recorded was nothing more than palace gossip.

The next day, Saturday, September 2, Bradley wrote: "The French Man of War arrived yesterday. She has not yet made her first shot in the war which the French consul has threatened. We are all glad to hear that the Man of War is going to take the French consul out of the country, probably for good."

Aubaret finally did depart on September 5, without further incident. No sooner had his ship sailed over the horizon, than Bradley struck back. On September 6, he "Issued My 13th no. of My Siamese paper [in] which a full statement of the late arrogance and insolence of the French consul and Lamache in their addresses to the king. The patience and forbearance of His Majesty seem to border on pusillamity and the conduct of the other two Frenchmen on madness. The Fr. consul took his leave yesterday for Paris via Saigon, intending to stir up the Emperor of the French to send his troops against Siam."

Two days later, Captain Hood arrived.

With Aubaret out of the country, the pressure on Dr. Bradley was reduced but did not disappear completely. Bradley continued to rail against the French consul and French efforts to increase their influence in Southeast Asia. At first, Hood took no notice of this, but in March 1866, he began to become concerned with the difficulties caused by the *Recorder*. The trigger was the letter written to him by the Siamese minister of foreign affairs which pointed out that if the United States and France went to war against each other over Mexico, the French might use the Siamese government's tolerance of the American Bradley's tirades against France as an excuse to invade Siam.[6] Unlikely as this may seem, it was a real danger at the time. France had invaded Indo-China just a few years before on a similarly flimsy pretext.[7] Hood considered this letter a prelude to another demand to shut down the *Recorder* and asked the Department of State for advice on his course of action.

> The great cause of annoyance complained of is a newspaper published by a citizen of the U.S. called the "Recorder" This paper at different times has [commented] on the various aggressions of the French in these parts & on their encroachments on Siam also on their impertinent bearing towards this helpless government. It is the interest of all the treaty powers to preserve this government intact to prevent its becoming a colony of France — the late French consul before leaving this capital by his measures and conduct rendered himself odious to the people of Siam; and it is now reported that he is to return with the power of the French government to not only humble the king but to exact three southern

provinces of Siam — the paper before mentioned is made one of the great causes of complaint that it has insulted his Supreme Majesty the Emperor of the Great French Nation — the French consul demanded that it should be silenced. The Siamese authorities requested my predecessor to silence the paper (for there were then two). This he declined to do; asserting that he had no power to do so, but if it could be shown that [the editor] had infringed any laws that he would try the matter & should it appear that they had done any injury the injured party should be indemnified and the causing party punished.

I now apprehend that this correspondence is the precursor of again demanding the suppression of the paper. The paper has never been violent and to my understanding temperate and moderate in its discussions and that nothing in its conduct has been reprehensible; under the circumstances I hope I may be instructed as to what course to pursue. First in case of suppression and 2nd for indemnification to the publisher if no case be made out against him.[8]

This was another of the skirmishes which would lead Aubaret to sue Bradley in the Consular Court the following year.

In April 1866, an anonymous article appeared in the Singapore *Daily Times* newspaper which claimed that Dr. Dan Beach Bradley opposed the continuation of the Siamese dynasty. It accused him of not supporting the succession of the crown prince, the Chowfa Chulalongkorn, and of predicting that the northern province of Chang Mai would rebel and transfer its allegiance to Burma.[9] This prompted the king to threaten to stop the publication of the *Bangkok Recorder*, which Bradley had taken over as the editor, as well as publisher, in January. In a letter to the king that was by turns both obsequious and defiant, Bradley affirmed his friendship with the king and the royal family and his approval of the crown prince, but reserved the right to continue criticizing them.

While I have ventured to criticize your Majesty sometimes and may do so again, be assured that it is as a friend and by no means an enemy that I have done it or shall do it. I hold that such criticisms are among the best witnesses of real friendship even as a husband and wife who faithfully criticize each other.

I think that Siam has never before had so promising a Prince Chowfa educating for the throne of the Prabats as now and that if his life be spared and his education continued increasing in thoroughness as he has begun, he will become a most illustrious prince and a most worthy heir to the Siamese throne. My eyes and my heart fix upon him as the future King of Siam.[10]

However, he then went on to threaten the king by saying:

Should your Majesty succeed in stopping the *Recorder* it would not stop people from writing for Singapore & China papers and you would most certainly find that Foreign community here would be so aroused by the Government suppressing the paper that they would pour in their communications for the Singapore and China papers in opposition to your Majesty's government ten times more than they ever have thought it possible to do through the *Bangkok Recorder*. I beg to give in this my opinion beforehand as a real friend. There will be no peace to your Majesty's reign if your Majesty use his influence to stop the *Recorder* and succeed in doing it. But I must be frank and say that in my opinion the paper will not and cannot be stopped any more than the work of printing the Bible & Christian tracts can be stopped. It is quite too late in the day to think for a moment of doing such a thing by virtue of any Treaty relation already done. The Treaty must first be changed or broken. Shall either be done?

Having said that, Bradley became obsequious again, thanking the king profusely for the many favors the king had bestowed on him, including providing him with a the rent free use of a large house worth 320 ticals, or $191, a year for the last 10 years. He also apologized to the king for billing him for subscriptions to the *Bangkok Recorder* and blamed the bill on his fellow missionary, Noah MacDonald, who had been the editor and publisher at the time, although he was using Bradley's printing press and the two were close collaborators. Bradley promised to provide the paper to the king for free in the future.

Bradley also promised to provide him with a free copy of his printed edition of the Thai translation of the Chinese classic *The Romance of the Three Kingdoms*, or in Thai, *Samkok*. This was a series of stories about the Three Kingdoms period of Chinese history, a period of turbulence extending from the end of the Han Dynasty in 169 C.E. to the reunification of the country in 280.[11] The *Romance* had been translated into Thai under the direction of King Rama I around 1830 but had existed only in manuscript form. Bradley's was the first printed edition of the work.[12] Although the *Romance* is one of the great Chinese classics and contains stories that became the basis of much Chinese folklore and tradition, it also is about a time of dynastic overthrow and change. This resonated with Rama I, who founded the Prabat dynasty of which Mongkut was the fourth king, but its publication may have had less salutary connotations at a time when Mongkut felt his kingdom was under pressure from the British and French through their puppets, the Burmese and Cambodians. This may well have triggered the king's accusation that Bradley was stirring up opposition to the current dynasty.

While documenting Bradley's deteriorating relationship with the king, this letter speaks in a surprisingly familiar tone. Bradley, a missionary who was in the country at the pleasure of and partially supported by an absolute monarch, compared their friendship to that of a husband and wife, an indication of Bradley's arrogant streak and of his sense of superiority over all Asians, even kings.

This conciliatory letter did not mollify the king, especially as Bradley continued to publish articles that criticized the ongoing negotiations between the Siamese government and the French consul, Aubaret, especially after Aubaret's return.

On June 30, 1866, Hood noted the arrival of the French consul in the city.

> I have the honor to inform the dept. of the arrival of G. Aubaret, French consul at this place, and that he entered upon the discharge of his duties of the consulate. This is the gentleman who gave so great offence to this Government just previous to my arrival here and who would never have had permission to return if the Siamese government were not in great fear of the French nation's appropriating the whole of Siam to their own use. Mr. Aubaret has brought with him an autograph letter from the French Emperor and a present of a magnificent sword for the King, also one from the Prince Imperial of France to the heir to the Siamese throne. All this looks friendly but it seems as I am confidentially informed by Mr. Knox, the English consul, that behind all these friendly demonstrations lies a grand plot to transfer the Siamese territory to a French Protectorate.
>
> I have every reason for believing that Mr. Knox is correct and the French will continue to make encroachments upon this territory until they finally get possession of the whole Kingdom of Siam. I would respectfully request the Department to give me such instructions for my future course of action as the importance of the subject demands as I am satisfied that I shall be called upon by His Majesty for advice and for cooperation with the English consul in shaping the course of events as they may occur in this country.[13]

It is clear, however, that Aubaret's purpose was to try to renegotiate the treaty he had made with the king early in 1865, because the French government had refused to ratify it. The French did not want to establish a protectorate over Siam, but simply to confirm the protectorate they had established over Cambodia and to include in it the Cambodian provinces that were still under the control of Bangkok. The original treaty had created a joint protectorate with Cambodia still acknowledging the suzerainty of Siam and had allowed Siam to retain the provinces in question. Now Aubaret had the unenviable task of trying to regain what he had bargained away. Knox worked hard to turn both Captain Hood and Dr. Bradley against Aubaret so as to reinforce British policy with American support, and he appears to have succeeded.

In August, the king demanded that Bradley start paying rent for his house, in part because Bradley was no longer treating the sick in the royal palace and in part because he was under the impression that Bradley was making a good living from his printing press. The king apparently felt that if he cut off his subsidy to Bradley, the missionary would have to cease printing his newspaper, which was a money losing proposition. In his reply, Bradley again defended himself as being a friend of the king. He wrote:

> I would beg leave to say that myself and family and the American Missionary Association feel very grateful to your Majesty for the free occupancy of this beautiful place these many years and for the several other valuable gifts which your Majesty has been pleased to grant our mission and more than all, the high regard which your Majesty has ever condescended to show me as your Majesty's old and personal friend. These favors are truly great and worthy of much praise from me and mine and the Board under whose auspices I remain in Siam and I may add have been continually spoken of to your Majesty's praise these many years by myself and my family and the Board, and by many good people in the United States of America. In return for this your Majesty's beneficence I have continually desired to render your Majesty some suitable return. And I have flattered myself that though I have not latterly been called to take charge of the sick in your Majesty's family as formerly, that I am in some other respects of some service to your Majesty's people and kingdom though not the half of what I have a heart to be. The two newspapers which I publish, the one in the Siamese language, the other in the English have for their grand object only the good of your Majesty's people and government and they both come far short of [enabling] in the income they bring me of paying the expenses of publishing them.[14]

Bradley then again apologized for billing the king for the first volume of the newspaper, a mistake that was apparently a sore point for Mongkut, pushing the blame once more onto McDonald, and promising to provide 8 subscriptions of both the English and Siamese versions of his paper to the palace for free.

In fact, Bradley's printing operation was quite profitable. His accounts for the period April 1, 1865, to April 1, 1866, show that he took in a little over $4,000 from the newspaper, job printing, and sales of printed copies of the Siamese Laws, a book of Siamese History, and the *Samkok*. His expenses for printing paper, printers, and a Siamese writer amounted to only about $2,400, leaving, after another $300 for the expenses of the mission, about $1,300 for the support of his own family.[15] Given that he lived rent-free and that his lifestyle was much simpler than that of Captain Hood, this should have been sufficient.

Also in August, Captain Hood sent a dispatch to the Department of State, again warning them about the growing conflict between Dr. Bradley and the Siamese government over his treatment of Aubaret in the *Recorder*.

> Siam has no law regulating newspapers. The publisher of the Bangkok Recorder is an American citizen entitled to the protection of the American Government in the lawful pursuit of any business he may engage in. Article 1st, 2nd of our treaty with Siam. Whereas the government is about to make laws for the regulation of newspapers the Editor of the Bangkok Recorder will no doubt strictly comply with them provided the said enactments are not in violation of our treaty.[16]

By taking this position, Hood distanced himself from Bradley and his actions, perhaps to make sure that he did not give the impression that the American government endorsed Bradley's views.

In December, the bad relations between Dr. Dan Beach Bradley and M. Gabriel Aubaret came to a head. Aubaret's lack of progress in his negotiations with the Siamese government on a new treaty regarding French and Siamese interests in Cambodia frustrated him and he became more brusque and subject to angry outbursts. Finally, he demanded that the prime minister, the Kralahom Sri Suriyawongse, be removed from the negotiations and that they be carried out directly with King Mongkut. This resulted in an ugly incident, the details of which were never clarified. On December 20, Bradley published an account of this incident drawn from information he had received from persons who had been present at it, in particular the son of Anna Leonowens. [17] In the article Bradley alleged that Aubaret had physically threatened the king and demanded that the prime minister be removed from his premiership.

The published report outraged Aubaret and he demanded an apology from Bradley. Bradley took this demand extremely personally, to the point of wondering if he had offended God. He wrote in his diary on December 21:

> [I have with] occasional shame fallen into sad doubt about it and feel that my labor has been all for naught. Today I had such confidence that the Lord has defended my paper & that he has not [disapproved] the work I have pursued for him on the papers. I too trust it is my duty as well as privilege to believe always that he does direct my steps when I ask him to do so.

On December 22, Bradley sent a correction, but not an apology, to Aubaret, which he later published in the *Bangkok Recorder*.

> The following is a copy (or as nearly so in a rough draft of the original and our own memory enables us to give) of an apology which we sent to M. Aubaret, the French Consul, for the reports we had heard and published under date of Dec 20th concerning his interview with His Majesty the King of Siam on the 16th or the 14th ultimo.
>
> Monsieur Aubaret, French Consul
>
> Sir,
>
> I pray you will allow me through J.M. Hood, Esq., U.S. Consul, to come in this way before you for the purpose of offering some explanation and proposing some amicable settlement of the affair in which you feel that I have aggrieved you. After further and careful inquiry I am now inclined to think that the reports which I made in the Bangkok Recorder of the 20th ultimo were based on some misunderstanding of the true sense of that part of your conversation with His Majesty the King of Siam relating to H.E. the Prime Minister.
>
> The Siamese Government affirms that there was a great mistake made in this matter, and there seems to be collateral evidence that what it affirms in regard to that point is true — to wit — that you did not demand or even request that H.E. should be removed from his place as Premier, but only that he should be removed from his post of Chief Commissioner in reference to the Cambodian Treaty.
>
> For any expressions in the article with which you feel aggrieved, and which may not be true, and in regard to which I have been misinformed, I am willing to make all reasonable apologies and corrections.
>
> Allow me to declare unto you that my only object in writing that article was to perform faithfully what I regarded my duty as a public recorder. [18]

In response, Aubaret sued him for libel in the U.S. Consular Court, demanding $1,500 in damages. This was more than a simple case of a newspaper publishing an exaggerated story. It threatened to become a full blown international incident. Bradley had clearly been won over to the British side by their consul, Thomas Knox, and was strongly opposed to French expansion in Southeast Asia. The Siamese government, in the person of King Mongkut, had to maintain a more neutral position. Although the king had pro–British leanings, to the extent that he appointed Sir John Bowring, the man who had negotiated the British-Siamese treaty, as his special envoy to the French court, he could ill afford to provoke the French. They had troops and a naval squadron in Cochin China and a treaty with Cambodia which would allow them to use that country as a staging area for an invasion of Siam. If the king ignored Bradley's article, which was only the latest in a series of attacks against Aubaret, his inaction might be seen as implicit approval of it and provide an excuse for such an invasion. Bradley heard about the filing of the suit on Christmas Eve and expressed the hope that God would stand by him at his trial.

On January 1, 1867, Bradley called on Captain Hood with several of his supporters among the missionaries, including Noah McDonald, to begin making arrangements for the trial.

Tellingly, the next day, he called on the English consul, Thomas Knox, who "gave me good cheer in regard to my trial & agreed to be my mediator. I had written a letter of apology to consul Aubaret yesterday which Mr. Knox [thought] will greatly abate the damages but added that the case on trial should by no means go against me."

Bradley's reliance on the support and legal advice of Knox is among the strongest indicators that, in attacking Aubaret, he was carrying out the British agenda. Unfortunately, by relying on the Englishman's advice, he was looking at the case through the lens of British law while the trial was to be carried out under American law, which differed in some respects with regard to the subject of libel.

Bradley's journals for the next few days give the best description of how things proceeded.

> Jan 3 — Met my prosecutor at the U.S. consulate at 10 a.m. having Br. McDonald with me as a counsel. M. Aubaret will not listen to any apology — is determined to get hold of the names of my Siamese witnesses. I am determined not to give up the names be the consequences what they may. Court was adjourned to the 21st inst.

This passage is telling, because it shows that, for Aubaret, this case was not simply about an insult to him, but it was a means of identifying

Bradley's sources of information. If Aubaret could not get the newspaper shut down, he at least intended to stop the leaks from the palace.

> Jan 4 — Called on Mr. Knox who gave me much hope concerning my case with Mons. Aubaret. He thinks that he ought to lose his case. He read from an English law book showing that an editor has a right to criticize a public man in his public acts as much as he pleases provided he do not touch his private character. Then surely I have not transgressed the lawful bounds of editorial privileges for I had not written a word against him in his private life nor against his morality.

The suit plunged Bradley into a morass of self-doubt, especially with regard to his spiritual life. He seemed to feel that the suit was a result of his imperfections as a Christian, and not of his dabbling in political affairs that were beyond his understanding. On January 7, 1867, he confided in his diary:

> Have had unusually strong exercises of mind many days in searching after the full assurance of hope. I perceive an important distinction between this grace and that of the full assurance faith. It seems to me that by the grace of God I am in the possession of the latter already but not of the former. I have been latterly greatly concerned with fears about my own spiritual state with God. The truth is I have not to this day made my calling and election sure. I feel that I grieve the spirit of God by remaining in this state and must not continue in it. I trust the Lord Jesus is with me this evening enabling me to believe in the efficacy of his blood to cleanse me of all sin and to rely on his promise that he that believeth on the son hath everlasting life. Having been brought to this point why should I ever doubt again? Lord Jesus help me to hold on to this thy word without wavering for my own strength is utter weakness. Let thy strength now be made perfect in my very weakness.

Yet, the very next day, he had recovered his spirits and wrote:

> Enjoyed sweet peace of mind much of the day in believing on the efficacy of Jesus blood to cleanse me from all sin by simple reliance on his promises that such is God's righteousness imputed to me by faith which he himself had given me. Suffered from a little bewilderment of mind after dinner which I trust has been an invaluable lesson to impress upon me my utter helplessness by myself to do a good deed or even think a rational thought without divine mercy and aid.
>
> Called on Mr. K[nox] in the p.m. to read his law books and consult with him on the subject of my suit with the French consul. By his advice I went to inquire of [Aubaret's assistant] what the French consul would have me say in the way of an apology more than I have already done. I

accordingly called upon him. It appears that he would have me say not only that I am inclined to think that I was misinformed on that point — but positively that I know I was misinformed and that consequently that part of my article on which he has framed his indictment is false — but this I cannot say for I do not certainly know that it is so, just I did not indubitably know that what I reported of was not true. I could only say that it is quite credible.

In spite of his precarious position, Bradley continued to attack the Siamese government. On January 9, he published an article in the Siamese language edition of his paper attacking idolatry, that is, Buddhism, the fundamental religion of Siam, and reprimanding the king for not taking steps to abolish it. At this point, he was playing with fire.

On January 10, Bradley called on Captain Hood to make some arrangements for the trial, and discovered that the Siamese government has also made a complaint against him for having written in his second article that among the witnesses to the incident were members of the Siamese nobility. The king was trying desperately to downplay the importance of the incident and did not want any of his officials called as witnesses at the trial.

The next day, Bradley called on the phra khlang to see if he could get the government to withdraw its complaint against him. He found "the old man quite angry with me for having published a Siamese article written by a native reflecting somewhat upon himself. It was the first that I had heard of it, [indeed] the first of my knowing that there was any allusion to Siam in the article. He says I must give up the name of the author as well as the Princes & Nobles to whom I refer as witnesses of the French consul's outbreak." But Bradley had no intention of revealing his sources.

Bradley continued to prepare for his trial spiritually. On January 12, he wrote: "By the grace of the Lord I am quite calm in view of my approaching trial — I am enabled to cast my cares concerning it all on the Lord believing that he will overrule it all for the good of his cause and my own personal growth in grace."

In the midst of the preparations for the trial, a momentous event occurred that raised Captain Hood's spirits, but also distracted him from Bradley's case. The U.S.S. *Shenandoah*, an American ship of war under the command of Capt. John R. Goldsborough, arrived at Bangkok on January 15, 1867. This was the first American warship to call there since before the Civil War and it had arrived in response to Hood's request. Not only did the visit provide a show of force to convince the Siamese government that the United States was really a first class power, it reinforced Hood's status as someone who could influence the actions of the American government. The *Shenandoah* was a three-masted, screw-propelled, steam-powered sloop. She was armed with 10 heavy guns and displaced almost 1,400 tons. Her crew consisted of 175 officers and men. She had sailed from Philadelphia on November 20, 1865, and had come via Brazil, South Africa, India, Penang and Singapore.[19] Because of her deep draft of 15 feet, 10 inches and also in deference to the sovereignty of the Siamese government, the *Shenandoah* anchored outside the bar and did not ascend the river to the city of Bangkok.

The ship and its crew were warmly received by the Siamese government. Captain Goldsborough and his officers were entertained at the palace with theatrical exhibitions, torchlight processions, and fireworks, and were put up at the U.S. consulate when they stayed ashore. The arrival of the *Shenandoah* at this critical point in the French-Siamese treaty negotiations probably had a greater impact on weakening Aubaret's bargaining position than any revelations that Bradley had printed.

Thursday, January 17, was a busy day for Bradley. In a last ditch effort to forestall the trial he published another apology to the French consul and stated that Aubaret had sued him for libel. He then wrote in his diary:

> To the praise of the grace of my dear Redeemer I will record it that he enables me to hope cheerfully in him for wisdom and counsel and sufficiency in preparing myself for my approaching trial five days hence. I believe he will stand by me in it and however may be the apparent result he will cause it to work together for my own good and the glory of his own name.

That same afternoon, he called on the English consul, Knox, to consult with him again about the case. Knox advised him that he had little to do now but to keep still, and told Bradley that he thought that the French consul would probably withdraw the suit.

Bradley then went to the American consulate where he was introduced to Capt. Goldsborough and two of his officers, who were staying there. He suggested to Captain Hood that it might be well to have some of the American officers appointed as assessors in the libel case, but Hood refused to commit to that.

Bradley then visited the Rev. McDonald, who had just returned from a trip into the interior of the country, and took dinner with him. McDonald offered to assist him as a counselor at the trial.

At Hood's request, on his way home, Bradley called again at the American consulate, where he had a long chat with Capt. Goldsborough and the officers, and received a letter from Captain Hood for him to deliver to the prime minister. These two visits on the same day show that, at this point, Bradley and Hood were still on cordial, if not friendly, terms. Hood still appeared to be neutral in the case, and Bradley had hopes that he would give preference to an American over a Frenchman in any decisions he would have to make.

On the morning of Friday, January 18, Bradley visited Anna Leonowens. He wrote:

> I learned from her still more startling revelations concerning the outrages which M. Aubaret the French consul has been guilty of since those which I reported. It now appears that what I reported is not the half of his abominable conduct — that the gov't have now got thoroughly awake to the importance of resisting his aggression and have sent long complaints by today's mail to the French gov't and say in substance that he is most outrageous in his treatment of the Siamese gov't in regard to the Cambodian Treaty and absolutely unendurable.

This passage from his diary is the most direct indication that Anna was one of his primary sources of information about the negotiations going on at court. Mrs. Leonowens was much more than a governess. She was a personal secretary to King Mongkut and regularly wrote or translated his correspondence in English and French. If she was revealing the juiciest incidents of the supposedly secret talks to Bradley, she was surely also keeping the English consul, Knox, informed of the substance of the discussions as well. In fact, she was acting as an English mole in the heart of the Siamese government. What is not clear is if King Mongkut knew what she was doing and deliberately used her to leak information to weaken the French position.

Later that day, Bradley called on Mom Rachotai, the international court judge and an old friend of his, to "see if I could arrange by him to get hold of some of the names of the persons who heard M. Aubaret insult the king on the occasion which I had reported and for which he has sued me. He frankly said to me that they would not tell the truth, even under their terrible oath, because of fear of the king."

The next morning, Saturday, January 19, Bradley visited Mr. Bateman, the prime minister's secretary,

> to see if he would not be willing to witness for me before Court touching the fact of an outbreak between the king and the French consul which it would appear the latter denied. Mr. B. was willing to do it provided the Prime Minister would not be displeased with it and requested that I should go to His Excellency and speak to him about it. I did so but found him unwilling to allow Mr. Bateman [to] testify lest it should involve the government in some troubles with the French consul. He expressed a warm sympathy for me in my troubles and said he hoped I would get the case. He knows perfectly well that I shall have the truth on my side.

From the prime minister's, Bradley went again to see Anna Leonowens. She told him that she had seen the king the day before and that

> she said to him that her son (who heard all that the French consul said to His M. on the occasion of the outbreak) would probably be subpoenaed as a witness for Dr. B. and that he would then speak the truth.
> His Majesty was struck with alarm at the thought and said in much anger that he should do not such thing. Mrs. L. left him in a rage and became more fully determined than ever to render me all the help she could by the testimony of her son. She determined that she would take the counsel of Mr. K[nox] the Eng[lish] consul and would inform me in the evening.

Later that day, Captain Hood sent word to Bradley that the trial was going to be postponed. He did not give any reason for this, but the events of the next few days show that it was because he was occupied with entertaining the captain and officers of the *Shenandoah*.

Early the next morning, Anna Leonowens sent Bradley a note asking him to come to her house. This was a highly unusual, because it was Sunday morning and Bradley would normally be preoccupied with preaching. However, he went to see her, fearing that she might have gotten into some trouble on his account. When he got there, she delivered perhaps the greatest shock to his pre-trial preparations. Bradley wrote:

> The king had the evening before sent in a message to her delivered in the hearing of the H[on]. Eng[lish] consul that she must by no means allow her son to testify in the case [and] if [he] did he will inflict a heavy fine upon her. It was quite providential that the Eng. consul who is my counsel heard that message which proves most conclusively that there

was an occurrence on the day of the fracas which will, if brought out, disprove the assertion of His M. & the gov't that there was no great offense committed by the Fr. consul at the time. It will show that –instead of my reports a falsehood and desiring to be called a liar as the king published it was he himself was the liar for the purpose of purifying the consul at the expense of my good name as a man of truthfulness. I start praising God my savior for this intervention in my behalf.

The following week was filled with activities to honor and entertain the officers of the *Shenandoah*. On Monday, Captain Hood arranged an American style picnic at Temple Pratomawan at which breakfast and lunch were served. The guests included the *Shenandoah*'s skipper, Captain John R. Goldsborough, Lieutenant Commander Smith, Lieutenant S. Cotton, Chief Engineer Richard M. Bartleman, Surgeon Archibald C. Rhoerdy, Marine lieutenant Robert L. Meade, First Assistant Engineer Edward Farmer, and Midshipmen M.R. Buford and C.M. Thomas. The resident Americans present, besides Hood and his wife, were Rev. Stephen House, John Campbell, M. Seavy and Dr. Bradley, all of whom brought their wives along. Neither Virgin nor Chandler attended. That evening, King Mongkut gave an audience to Capt. Goldsborough and his officers. The next day the first group of officers returned to the *Shenandoah* and a second company came ashore, to be similarly entertained.[20]

On Thursday, January 24, however, the ongoing tensions between the palace and foreign community again raised their heads. As Bradley reported,

Capt. Goldsborough with Mr. Consul Hood and Lady called on us in the morning. I went with them to see the Royal Mint but found the gates to the outer courts of the royal palace closed and no importunity or diplomacy could prevail upon anyone low or high to use his influence to carry our word within to the Chief of the Mint. This extraordinary [situation] was doubtless one of the results of the French consul's outrages for the report of which he has sued for $1500 damages. We were obliged to give it up and turn our attention another way. We went to some elephant stalls and saw eight elephants which was a pleasing sight to the Captain. From this we returned to our boats in front of the royal palace and went up the river as far as the lime kiln and turned about. The Captain together with Mr. & Mrs. Hood took tiffin with us.

On Saturday, Capt. Goldsborough invited the American residents of the city to come aboard the *Shenandoah*. King Mongkut supplied two steamers to provide transportation to the ship, which was lying in the Gulf of Siam, beyond the bar of the river. As an indication of the distance involved, the party left Bangkok at 8 a.m. and did not reach the ship until 12:30 in the afternoon. The residents returned in the evening after a lavish entertainment aboard, and the *Shenandoah* sailed down the gulf, heading for Japan, while Hood basked in the reflected glory of America's naval strength.[21]

Bradley's trial finally opened on the following Saturday, February 2. Captain Hood presided and the assessors were the missionaries, Dr. Samuel House and Rev. William Dean, and an American rice-mill proprietor, Michael Gurvey. Austin Mattingly, another missionary, was appointed clerk of the court for the trial. House and Dean were both colleagues and friends of Bradley's and should have been sympathetic to him, but Bradley's public interference with Siamese governmental affairs may have put them off, given that they knew that their missionary work was being done by the forbearance of the king.[22]

Bradley opened his defense by claiming that it was up to Aubaret to prove that what Bradley had reported was false. McDonald and his other supporters voiced agreement with this, but after he had argued this point for more than half an hour, the court, that is, Captain Hood, ruled that it was not necessary for Aubaret to deny the truth of the report, but that it was Bradley's duty to disprove the charge of libel.

Afterwards, Bradley wrote:

> I sense the onus probandi was thrown upon me and I saw no way to cast it off. Mr. Alabaster, the Interpreter to the Brit[ish] consulate, was then to serve me as a witness and he counseled me strongly to persist in claiming that M.A. should first try to prove his charge. But nothing would do. His bare charge that my words were a libel to his damage must be taken on his honor and I must disprove them or lose my case. I had come to the trial trusting from what I had heard from the U.S. consul that all the labor of proof might fall upon me and had consequently penned down an argument in self-justification.
>
> And having been called on by Mr. Hood to answer for myself I had read a part of my plea. The object of my argument was to show that according to English and American law the case was not at all libelous —
>
> 1st because the report I made of M. A[ubaret] was not made with any malicious feelings or spite or pique or revenge towards him and that to constitute libel in law it is necessary not only that the statement on which the charge is made be false but also that it shall have been made maliciously, and that mere false reports of a public man in his public acts

not intentionally false and consequently not made with any personal spite or pique or revenge against him at whom it aims.

2nd That if this case was libelous then all the papers in Asia & Europe & Am[erica] are committing such libels continually. Cannot be libelous & That there is no evidence of any malice or spite or pique or revenge.

3rd The reason why I copied the article against him in the London and China Telegraph was [that it was] sent to me from good authority [with] consent for copying the paper.

4th My silence about M.A. from Oct to Dec 13th in the face of much that was rumored against him in Bangkok.

5th The reasons why I published the first article of the outbreak and a week after the second as showing I thought clearly that there was no malice in all that I wrote, and

6th That the apology I made in the paper in good faith to the full extent that my conscience would allow me to go should be seen as good evidence that I had no malicious intent in what I wrote.

Before I had closed my plea the court ruled that if I had any witnesses it was now time to have them testify. In reply I stated in substance that I would be wished to prove only one thing by witnesses — and that was, that there was an outbreak at the time specified and that His Majesty the king was alarmed by it, and that M.A. was the cause of it.

Mr. Alabaster was first sworn who testified that but a little before the time he was at the royal palace and found no difficulty to access the outer court but that on the day after he went there in company with two or more of the officers of H.B.M.'s gunboat the Pearl and found the outer doors closed and barred so that it was impossible to gain admission that usually easy and that by some effort he succeeded in getting into the outer court by another gate quite unusual and that he heard the cause of the change was the alarm which Mr. A. had caused the day before.

Bradley then proceeded to call his witnesses. Unfortunately for him, whatever had actually happened in the palace, the king had no desire to admit that Aubaret had in any way insulted him, and prevented any of his nobles from testifying. Bradley was reduced to calling some westerners who were minor officials and who were reluctant to say anything that could alienate their employer, the king. All he was really able to establish, was that after the alleged incident, the palace gates were closed to foreigners for a period of time. He recorded the result in his account of the trial.

Mr. Fisher, foreman in the King's printing office was next sworn who testified not as clearly to the same point but substantially the same though with the most studied caution that he might displease his employer and loose his place.

The next witness was the deputy mayor of the city with the consent of both parties whose testimony was taken without an oath. He testified that there was an outbreak created by M.A. on that day.

Simean Ta, the keeper of the king's seals was next called as a witness to the same point who testified to the same point (not under oath) that the outer gate, the usual way of access to the outer court of the palace was shut against all foreigners from that day.

And finally M.A. acknowledged before court that he had troubles on that day with the King and that he did complain of the Prime Minister's proceedings in the Cambodian Treaty matter and did say that he ought to be exchanged for another man as he could not get along with the business while he remained commissioner in that matter. Having made this remarkable acknowledgement it was thought that the trial was over [and] need not proceed any further since I had in my apology confessed that I had made a mistake in at first supposing that M.A. meant to demand that the Prime Minister should be removed from the Premiership.

When Bradley's defense was complete, the court was dismissed and Hood announced that his decision would be made on February 5. The court would meet on that day at 10 a.m. to sum up the evidence in the case in open court and the verdict would be announced at 2 o'clock the same day.

After the fact, Bradley wrote that

there were many persons Eng. Am. & Siamese whom I could have called who would have testified that all who heard M.A. speak on the occasion understood him to demand that the Prime Minister's degradation from the Premiership that he really menaced the king so that he felt himself to be greatly insulted and that he was so alarmed that he abruptly retired from M.A. into his palace & had the gates barred against him. But these persons were so situated, holding stations in the government that I had from the first determined that I would rather suffer all the claimed damages of $1500 than to trouble them with the matter. Hence I did not call them. Had I called them, there could not have remained a shadow of doubt that I was fully justified in making the report I did of the matter.

On Sunday, February 3, while awaiting the verdict, Bradley preached at the Protestant Chapel, taking as his text Romans, chapter 8, verse 35: "Who shall separate us from the love of Christ?" But his mind was probably more set on verse 33, "Who will bring any charge against those whom God has chosen? It is God who justifies."[23]

Tuesday, February 5, was the day that the verdict was to be handed down. Bradley did not attend the court, pleading illness and having heard the day before that "I had probably lost my case for the want of the witness of _____ whom I persisted in not calling." The blank space was Bradley's. He refused, even in his personal diary, to name the person who he considered to be his key witness for fear of retaliation.

When Bradley did receive the verdict, he was humiliated. Not only was he found guilty of libel, he discovered that he was to be treated as a charity case. He wrote in his diary:

> Still I felt calm about it but when near midnight the papers came to me from the U.S. consul announcing that judgment had been rendered against me for $100 with damages amounting to $107.75 that in consideration of my being a poor man the U.S. consul had ordered the $100 to be remanded to me and that the assessors & other agents of the court for similar reasons of commiseration had given me credit on the Bill of cost for $69.00 leaving only $38.75 for me to pay. I felt exceedingly embarrassed. I must confess that I was tempted to feel that it was adding insult to injury.

Captain Hood's conduct of the trial has been assailed by supporters of Dr. Bradley. In particular, his ruling that Bradley must prove that his article was truthful has been questioned as a violation of the American legal principle that the accused is innocent until proven guilty, but Hood was perfectly correct. Although he was not a lawyer, Hood was acquainted with the laws of libel and perjury through the case his nephew William Perry Hood brought against his accusers after he was acquitted of arson in the 1854 shipyard fire. Under United States law it is up to the person accused of libel to prove the veracity of his allegations.[24]

The trial also had the effect of finalizing a growing rift between Anna Leonowens and King Mongkut. It began when the king asked her, in her role as his amanuensis in English, to compose a letter to Sir John Bowring, whom he had appointed as his special envoy to the French government, revoking that status. This was done under pressure from Aubaret. Anna refused to write the letter in the way that the king wanted, because she felt that the statements he asked her to include were false. This enraged the king and he exiled her from his presence. When the trial occurred soon afterwards, he forbade her and her son from testifying against Aubaret, and sent men to threaten her in her home. At that point, she asked to be allowed to go back to England, but permission was withheld for six months, and she was unable to leave until July 5, 1867.[25]

The trial may have been over, but its consequences were just beginning. Among other things, as a convert to the doctrine of Christian Perfectionism, Bradley felt that if his conviction was justified, it would be a sign that he had not done enough to perfect himself. He therefore decided that Captain Hood had betrayed him and he started to gather material that he could use against the consul, while continually trying to justify his own actions in his diary.

On February 9, soon after the trial had closed, he confided to this diary:

> I hear from many quarters that the judgment of the U.S. Consular Court against me in favor of the French consul has provided a great indignation among all the English residents almost unendurable. It now has come out as an unquestioned fact that the king hearing of the fact that M.A. had in court acknowledged that he had trouble with his M[ajesty] on that day directed Mrs. L[eonowens] to say to the court before it should meet on the 5th that it would not be right to have Dr. B[radley] suffer by any verdict of the court. And that he gave Mrs. L. permission to write to the assessors what she heard & saw of the outbreak hoping that would be good evidence in good time in proof of the truthfulness of Dr. Bradley's report of the matter. Consequently Mrs. L. wrote to Dr. House & Dr. Dean which letter was read by them on evening of the 4th the day before the case was decided. That letter declared substantially that Mrs. L was herself a witness of the outbreak and alarm it produced in the mind of the king and of all his attendants — that she herself was so alarmed by it & that she could scarcely sleep that night. Mrs. L. had express instructions from the king that she must not say anything in her letter to the assessors that would be at likely to embarrass the Siamese government in its relations to the French nation and hence she studiously omitted to say in the letter what insulting words her own son Louis heard fall at that time from the lips of the Fr. consul.

A week later, Bradley learned that the sum of 300 ticals had been placed in the hands of the Borneo Company Limited on his account.

> This sum I understand has been raised by sundry contributions from among the European residents of this city whose sympathy has been with me in the suit brought against me by the French consul and decided against me by U.S. Consular Court. It is designed as I am informed as a quiet as well as real indignation that the court should have rendered the verdict as they did.
>   I feel devoutly thankful to my heavenly father for this verification of his faithfulness to bless those who put their trust in him. I feel a clear conviction of my own conscience that I prayerfully and even tearfully

endeavored to do his will my part as well in reporting what I did about the French consul and that I have trusted in him ever since that he would cause that trust to work together for my good.

It is interesting that Bradley states that the sum had come from the European, not the American, community. The only substantial European contingents in Bangkok were the British and the French, so this statement implies that the money came from the British, and probably from consul Knox, as an under-the-table payment for his troubles.

Bradley's fixation on justifying himself caused him to quarrel with the Rev. Noah McDonald, when the latter expressed the opinion that the trial had seen justice served. Bradley became indignant and harsh words were exchanged between the former friends in front of their wives.

Bradley began to see a conspiracy and reported rumors that Hood had proposed to the Siamese government to arraign him and force him to give up the names of his sources. He wrote in his diary:

> Now I have had a little comfort about it because a wicked man in a place of such power can do much damage to any one against whom his ire is kindled. But I was enabled by divine grace to commit this case generally to the Lord so that my mind has for the most part been peaceful about it. And now I feel quite happy to hear that the Lord has indeed take good care of this matter for my good. Oh how constantly is My Father proving to me his loving kindness and tender mercy! And how shameful in me ever to indulge in even to a murmuring & distrustful spirit in the future!

Captain Hood had succeeded in silencing Bradley's attacks against the French consul, and the *Bangkok Recorder* stopped publication, but it was succeeded by other newspapers with other editors, who now turned their investigative sights on the American consul.

14

The Last Year in Bangkok

As 1867 opened, even as he was dealing with the case against Dr. Dan Beach Bradley, Captain Hood found it necessary to defend himself from accusations which had been lodged with the Department of State. The department had requested a full transcript of the trial of the Burdon vs. Chandler case, which Hood had conducted in the Consular Court early in the previous year.[1] This was an unusual request, prompted by political pressure brought to bear by Chandler's friends in the United States. Although Chandler had probably sent letters giving his side of the story as soon as possible after the trial, the year-long delay in Washington's response was due to the slow communications of the day. Hood tried to sidestep the request by writing to the department that making a copy would take too much time as the record was over 200 pages long. Instead of the requested transcript, he summarized the facts of the case, emphasizing that prior to the trial Chandler had first negotiated then repudiated an agreement with Burdon's agent. Thus it was Chandler's actions which forced the case to go to a trial which he lost. In the course of this explanation, Hood admitted that he received fees both for mediating the initial agreement and for presiding at the Consular Court. These fees were his to keep and were probably substantial given the size of the judgment.[2]

In the same dispatch, Captain Hood answered a complaint from Capt. Higgins, a resident of Bangkok. Hood had helped Higgins to recover a debt of $947.80 from a member of the royal family. As mentioned earlier, Hood had pointed to this as an example of his effectiveness in dealing with the Siamese. Higgins, having received his money, and encouraged by Chandler and Virgin, complained that Hood had charged exorbitant and illegal fees. Hood asserted that the department should not become involved because the case never came before the Consular Court. The dispute was between an American citizen and a Siamese national and the court had no jurisdiction. Instead, Hood claimed that he acted as a private arbitrator and that his fees, which totaled $230, almost 25 percent of the judgment, were perfectly legal and proper. He further asserted that Capt. Higgins had been encouraged to complain against him by Virgin and Chandler because of his refusal to rent the building behind Virgin's store for the consulate. He warned the department that he expected more charges from those two because of their antipathy towards him. In fact, their campaign against him was largely the result of his diligence in conducting the Chandler vs. Burdon trial, which had turned what Chandler expected to be a quick judgment in his favor into an expensive defeat. Hood's repeated use of the story relating to the location of the consulate seems calculated to avoid any accusation of bias during the trial itself.

In February, the bones of the second king, who had died at the start of 1866, were brought down from the temple where his body had been kept and placed in front of the palace in which he was born, in preparation for his funeral. Captain Hood served as the official representative of the United Stated at the ceremonies. The rites lasted a full week and took on a festive nature, including a fireworks display. Bradley attended and recorded:

> His majesty the king graciously called me up to him and gave me five limes containing silver or gold as it might chance to be and two tickets concealed in a wooden lime to draw from the royal lottery of sundry dry goods, hardware, and matting pillows the which had been provided for the occasion. To each of my children the king gave each a real and a wooden lime enriched as usual by silver, gold and tickets.
> Having secured the limes we went to the lottery office to have our wooden limes opened by the proper officer and found that we had drawn small pieces of woolen, silk and cotton cloth, small mats & pillow the worth of all of them perhaps 6 or 8 ticals and our real limes which we had opened ourselves were found to contain each a new [coin]. We remained after that still an hour or two and had a fine view of the fireworks and other amusements almost indescribable.[3]

With the trial and the funeral out of the way, Captain Hood left Bangkok and went to the coast for a few weeks to escape the heat and recover his health. He was even more anxious to get away from the political heat in the American community.[4] By trying two separate, significant cases a year apart, he had managed to alienate some of the most influential Americans in Bangkok. The Burdon trial had turned Virgin and Chandler against him. Now the Aubaret trial had turned Bradley, the editor of the most prominent English language newspaper in the country, against him as well. From this point on he would be fighting a rearguard action to maintain his position.

Soon after this vacation, Hood addressed a long dispatch to the Department of State again complaining about the Siamese courts and system of justice. He wrote that the Siamese had a well-developed code of civil and criminal law, but the judiciary was fragmented and corrupt. In Bangkok itself, the principle criminal courts were the lord mayor's and the sub-mayor's, while civil cases were heard by several courts within the palace, presided over by various ministers of state. There was also an international court, established by King Mongkut and presided over by a judge appointed by him, for cases involving both Siamese and subjects of the treaty powers. In addition to these, all Siamese nobles above a certain rank were also vested with judicial powers and could hold court within their own palaces.

Hood cited two cases in which U.S. citizens residing in Bangkok were unable to recover funds stolen from them and one in which his jailer and one of his boatmen were injured by Siamese subjects. In all three cases the Siamese courts decided against the Americans. Hood had then appealed to the king who sent the cases back to the same judges who merely confirmed their earlier decisions. Hood stated that the British and French got better treatment than that and that, even after the visit of the *Shenandoah*, the Americans were being treated as subjects of a second-class power, on a par with "Denmark and the German States." He informed the department that he was again appealing to the king and asked the secretary of state to formally instruct him to inform the Siamese that the United States government was demanding payment of the sums in question and damages. Such instructions, if issued, could be taken as a threat to U.S.—Siamese relations. He accused the Siamese judges of taking bribes and called the government "uncivilized."[5]

Around this time, Captain Hood entered into another money making scheme. Following the lead of the European consuls, he began to issue papers stating that the person named on them was "under the protection of the United States consulate" to Chinese ship captains and merchants, for a fee. This practice arose from the fact that the Chinese did not have the same extraterritorial rights that the Americans and Europeans had been granted by their favorable treaties with the Siamese government. The protection certificate supposedly gave the Chinese the same rights as citizens of the country of the issuing consulate in Siam. In general the Siamese accepted these, and both the consul and the merchant benefited. Under U.S. consular regulations this was illegal, but this objection was usually ignored and the practice flourished.[6]

In June, Hood wrote a dispatch that laid out for the first time the kind of shady financial dealings he had become involved in. Virgin, Chandler and McCormick had written to the Department of State accusing Hood of embezzling government funds. In response, Hood stated that when he arrived in Bangkok he felt the immediate need for an assistant in the consulate. Virgin recommended his friend James McCormick. Since Hood could not afford to pay him out of his own salary, he proposed to appoint McCormick as acting marshal, which would entitle McCormick to draw the marshal's salary of $1,000 a year. McCormick declined, because he did not believe that the government would pay him. Instead, he proposed that Hood pay him a small amount out of his own pocket and allow him to keep the fees received by the marshal's office. In return, if Hood did succeed in getting the marshal's salary paid, Hood could keep it for himself. When the salary did come through, however, McCormick tried to claim it in addition to the money he had already received. Since this was a verbal agreement, it was impossible to confirm whose version was correct.

In addition, Chandler accused Hood of using the rent he was supposed to be paying for a prison to pay for room and board for himself and his wife. It appears that when the Hoods arrived, the consulate had no jail. Chandler offered to rent Hood a building he owned that he had previously rented to Virgin as a jail, and charge him $50 a month for it. Hood thought that this was exorbitant, but Chandler refused to take less, because that was what he had charged Virgin and he was afraid of being accused of overcharging the government for the previous lease. So, Hood agreed to this and got Chandler to give him a receipt showing that the $50 a month was only for rental of the jail. Hood did not deny that Chandler also provided him with room and board, but claimed that that was separate, although he refused to provide receipts for it because he considered it to be a private expense. In this case it seems that Hood was simply continuing an arrangement that Virgin and Chandler had set up previously, when each had served as acting vice-consul. It was only because he had alienated them that they brought the complaints now.[7]

Hood also condemned McCormick as a drunk and a tool of Virgin, while he defamed the character of Virgin as well. He enclosed a letter of support from six members of the American community in Bangkok, from which the name of Dr. Bradley was conspicuously absent. The letter praised Captain Hood's honesty and integrity, and actually asked that he be appointed a "consul general."[8] That request indicated a lack of understanding of the consular service. A consul general was a consul who had authority over other consuls in a country, such as China, with more than one major port. As Hood was the only consul in Siam, he was in no position to claim such a title.[9]

Enclosed with the above was the following letter from Noah A. McDonald, Hood's interpreter and the man whom he would name as acting vice-consul upon his departure.

> I have the honor at the request of J.M. Hood, Esq. US consul at this place to address the Department in reference to certain charges which have been preferred by certain parties here against Mr. Hood and which if true would be highly derogatory to his character as representative of the US Government at the Court of Siam. I therefore deem it my duty as well as my privilege to lay before the Department any facts of which I may be cognizant in regard to those charges.
>
> The nature of the charges themselves is such I think that if the Department were fully acquainted with the character of the persons making them they could not for a moment entertain them.
>
> Very soon after the arrival of Mr. Hood at this place Mr. Virgin, late US vice consul conceived a very strong antipathy against him and since that time has done all in his power to effect the removal of Mr. Hood from the position which he now occupies. The only plausible reason which can be assigned for this antipathy is the fact that Mr. Hood refused to let the consulate remain in a small office belonging to Mr. Virgin and situated directly in the rear of his ship chandlery or in other words situated in his back yard. Mr. Hood did not think it a suitable place for the consulate and had it removed to another place.
>
> It is scarcely necessary for me to refer to Mr. McCormick who was the principle thinker in getting up these charges and who it is believed is still engaged in the same business. Suffice it to say that he was formerly a man of some mind and held an honorable position in the US Navy but he is now a confirmed inebriate and little more than a wreck of what he was formerly. When Mr. Hood entered on his official duties as consul he wanted someone to assist him and upon the recommendation of Mr.

Virgin appointed Mr. McCormick acting US marshal. He did very little for several months and finally left on a drunken spree and was absent for some weeks so that Mr. Hood was obliged to address a note to him telling him if he did not return to duty he would be dismissed. Upon the accepting of that note, Mr. McCormick at the instigation of Mr. Virgin sent in his resignation which was accepted. Since then at the instigation of Mr. Virgin and others inimical to Mr. Hood he has employed most of his sober moments in concocting schemes through which if possible to have Mr. Hood removed from office.

Mr. J.H. Chandler who it appears was also one of the party is already so well known to the Department that he needs no comments from me.

Fortunately Mr. Hood is also able to furnish testimony to confute most of the charges brought against him. I have only to say that Henry Bush the young man whose testimony has been forwarded to the Department was brought up in the school in connection with the Presbyterian mission. I have known him well for the last six years and have always found him to be truthful and honest. I firmly believe that his statement is correct. The other person whose testimony has been forwarded to the Department also I believe sustains a good reputation for honesty in the community.

Mr. Hood has also forwarded to the Department a document which should silence for all future time the calumnies of that particular party. That document is headed by Rev. W. Dean, D.D. a veteran missionary of the American Baptist Mission of nearly thirty years standing. His veracity no one here would think of doubting. The next is Rev. D.R. House, M.D. a missionary of the Pres. Board of Foreign Missions of nearly twenty years standing. Michael Gurney, supt. of the American Steam Rice Mills in this place and has superintended them for the last seven years. He stands at the head of the mechanical portion of the American community. Mr. J.C. Campbell has been employed for about seven years by the Siamese government as Inspector of Customs and in consideration of the faithful discharge of his duties His Majesty the King has lately conferred on him a title of nobility in connection with a vast quantity of rice land.

I therefore trust that my statement may have some weight with the Department in defeating the object of the calumnies concocted by the parties already referred to.[10]

Sorting through the charges and countercharges, it appears that, with a wink and a nod, Hood was in fact doing some dubious accounting to allow him to use government funds for purposes that were not strictly allowed in the consular regulations. Given the distance in both space and time between Bangkok and Washington, and Hood's skillful avoidance of a paper trail, the charges did not stick, although they did chill relations between him and the merchants and began to sow seeds of doubt in the Department of State.

On July 2, in the midst of the rainy season, Captain Hood with his wife and two of the missionary daughters, Miss Dean and Miss Field, left in the evening for the coast of the province of Petchaburi (Phetch-aburi), which is southwest of Bangkok.[11] Bradley saw this as way for Hood to escape the attacks against him and to avoid any embarrassing confrontations on the upcoming American Independence Day. He wrote:

> The consul goes as an invalid in quest of health. As he is manifestly not very ill and the cause not at all urgent for a change it does not seem quite right that he should leave so near the 4th of July when, according to good old custom the U.S. consul has led in the usual festivities of the day.

On July 4, Bradley continued:

> The anniversary of our country's Independence seemed very likely in the morning to be slight as the Americans had no Am. Official to lead them in the usual festivities of the occasion. But after it appears that His Majesty the King was specially and uncommonly gracious to Mrs. Bradley taking her about and showing her many things which he did for no one else. This was thought to be done to make some atonement for the sullenness which he had treated Mrs. B. and myself in the affair of M. Aubaret.[12]

The next day, July 5, Mrs. Anna Leonowens, the governess of the royal children and confidential secretary to the king, left Bangkok to return to England, having finally received permission from the king.[13] With her departure, both Captain Hood and Dr. Bradley lost an ally in the palace.

In September, the feud between Hood and Bradley broke out into the open. Bradley had stopped issuing the *Recorder*, but his campaign against Hood was being carried on by Mr. D'Encourt, the editor and publisher of a new paper, the *Siam Weekly Monitor,* which Bradley printed on his press. Bradley relates the subsequent events as follows:

> Sept 23 Rec'd a very extraordinary letter from consul Hood endeavoring to make me see and feel that the US laws will hold me responsible for any thing that may be libelous in the issues of the "Monitor" although the paper had an independent editor and the libelous article appears over the name of its author another independent man. He said in his letter,

that because he feared I might be ignorant of this law he felt it to be his duty as my consul to warn me of the danger I was in on being the printer of the Monitor which he stigmatized as "a very scurrilous and demoralizing paper."

In my reply to him this evening I frankly confessed my utter ignorance of such a law and begged that he would show me the statute in which it was contained. I also expressed much surprise that he should pronounce so severely on the paper and its editor, that I could not yet see any sufficient reason for such a denunciation and that no one could be more ready to exert his influence to change the paper from such a character than myself.

Sept 24 The consul received my letter today at noon and forthwith returned the following

Sir, Your communication of last evening's date was not rec. at this consulate until 12 O'clock meridian today. I take no other notice of this missive than to return it to its author whose hands it should never have left.

Knowing the character of the man I could more easily bear this insult than if it had come from one whom I highly respected.

It appears but too plainly that the consul having heard that Mr. D'Encourt the editor is contemplating publishing a long list of grave charges against him over the name of Capt. Higgins whom he has lately, without any law or precedent or reason attempted to expel from his privileges as an Am. Citizen, has taken the course to gag our press by intimidating me if he can so that I will not dare to publish any thing against himself. Common sense is enough to show me that no law can take hold of a simple printer for printing a decent paper for a meritable editor who has not been publicly proved to be "devoid of moral character and a wholly irresponsible person." And the same ordinary amount of sense teaches me that if I print libelous articles without any other man for author or editor the law will hold me alone liable. And I have the satisfaction of knowing that such is the view of an eminent English lawyer now in town with whom I have consulted.

Sept 28 Having some business at the U.S. consulate I called there and had a free talk with Mr. Hood. It is of but little use however to talk to such a man when his temper is stirred up. He seems to be exerting his utmost to put down the Monitor. He is trying now is to intimidate me so that I will [refuse] to print the paper for Mr. D'Encourt. He is greatly enraged now because of an article in the last issue concerning his selling protections [to the Chinese].[14]

Captain Hood was definitely feeling the heat from the attacks and in this case could not expect any help from the palace, as this was a strictly American affair. With Chandler continuing to put political pressure on in Washington, Captain Hood caved in. Less than two weeks after his confrontation with Bradley, Hood abruptly wrote to the Department of State asking for a leave of absence to return home in February 1868. He gave his reasons as the state of his health and his desire for a personal interview with the secretary of state to answer the charges against him. He also mentioned the hardship of the post and the need to consult with the government on changes he felt needed to be made to the U.S.-Siamese treaty. He stated that his two assistants, McDonald, who was his interpreter and Mattingly, who was now his acting marshal, could handle the business of the consulate in his absence.[15] He attached a note from Dr. Campbell attesting to his health problems.

> I here certify that since Mr. Consul Hood's arrival at this port I have been often consulted by him for sickness incidental to the climate and that during part of last hot season it became incumbent on him to leave his post for a few weeks and proceed to the sea coast for change of air. I consider that Mr. Hood would be endangering himself by remaining in Bangkok during the next hot season and strongly advise him to seek change of climate by proceeding to a colder country.[16]

The trip to the coast referred to was the July 4 vacation to Petchaburi that Bradley had complained of in his diary.

Soon afterwards, Captain Hood sent a preemptory dispatch to the Department of State in an attempt to head off another scandal. In this, he responded to an article that Capt. Higgins had published in D'Encourt's new Bangkok newspaper, the *Siam Weekly Monitor*, about the protection papers Hood had been issuing. Higgins' article was a part of the larger campaign against Hood involving Virgin, Chandler and Bradley. Hood admitted that he had issued the protections in question, stating that he had been pressured into it by the demands of the Chinese merchants, and noting that some of the European consuls, including the French consul, Aubaret, were doing the same thing. In all, Hood had issued some 143 certificates of protection in 1867, at an average fee of about $3.00 each. His total income from this, after allowing for some bad currency, was $346, a fairly substantial sum. It was only after the article was published that Hood credited this amount to the consulate account, where he recorded it as being used it to help defray the costs of operating the consulate.[17]

There was little more correspondence until the end of the year, when Hood reported that the king had ordered a change in the treaty regulations. Instead of requiring foreign ships entering the river to remove all their guns and leave them at the customs house before ascending to Bangkok, in the future they would only have to leave their gunpowder there. This was a significant concession in the tightly controlled Siamese state, and it cut a full day out of the voyage to and from Bangkok by eliminating both the removal and the reinstallation of the ordnance.[18]

In early December, as Captain Hood prepared to leave Bangkok, apparently without making his preparations known, Bradley was again conspiring against him. As Bradley records in his diary for December 3:

> A very singular paper was given to Mrs. B[radley], this p.m. by Mrs. G[urvey] written by the request of consul Hood with the view that Mrs. Gurvey further it and send it to Mr. Burdon of Brooklyn N.Y. evidently with the hope that in case any damaging reports against Mr. Hood's character shall come out in the States Mr. Burdon will publish this letter to counteract their tendency. This paper extols Mr. Hood very highly and sets forth the party who are against him in Bangkok as being vindictive, unreasonable & false in all they have reported against him and the most prominent among these so called false reporters it represents the former editor of the Bangkok Recorder and the printer of the Siam Weekly Monitor. It appears that the person who wrote this paper is not willing to have it appear who he is — nor is Mrs. Gurvey willing to do this dirty work for Mr. Hood — Hence it is not probable that the paper has been sent in any one's name. Mr. Gurvey and his wife have both been up to my house this evening and had a long talk with myself & wife on the subject and they give us every reason to believe that the paper is one of the evil machinations of Mr. Hood and that he has signally failed in his designs. They who have been the consul's staunchest friends have become thoroughly disgusted with him and came up to let us know it.
>
> Mr. Chandler has also informed me this evening that Mr. Hood has within two or three days written to the Prime Minister with the aim to set in operation a plan intended to seriously injure my character and that H[is] E[xcellency] has given him a confidential answer by which the consul can get no advantage over me by that plan. I look to my almighty savior for help. I believe that he will shield me so that the roaring lion shall not be able to hurt me. The 1st part of the 37th Psalm of David I feel to be his teaching appropriate to my present circumstance.[19]

In the King James Bible, Psalm 37 begins:

> Fret not thyself because of evildoers, For they shall soon be cut down like the grass, and wither as the green herb.[20]

The letter described above was actually sent to Burdon by Dr. Samuel House, who was one of the American missionaries, and forwarded by Burdon to the Department of State. After casting aspersions on Bradley and the new newspaper, the *Siam Weekly Monitor*, it concludes with praise of Captain Hood.

> As to Mr. Hood, I can say that he is regarded by the American community here (with the exceptions specified above) with much sincere respect. He is evidently desirous of maintaining the honor of his country and the best interests of its citizens here and has labored hard, almost offending the authorities in endeavoring to secure from loss some of those thankless ones who are now his bitterest enemies. In purity of moral character, Mr. Hood is a gentleman, who will compare most favorably with any of his predecessors, and whatever his enemies may allege, he has doubtless secured the respect of the King and his Ministers, from whom he has received even more consideration than any former Consul.
>
> I will make no apology for writing to you so fully on this subject as you yourself were unwittingly by reason of the verdict given in your favor, the beginning of this war waged so vindictively against our Consul, and cannot but be interested in the history of it throughout.[21]

On Christmas Day, Bradley further recorded:

> The Weekly Monitor is filled with a terrible disclosure of consul Hood's conduct while he [was] occupying the station of Am. consul in Bangkok. The author of the article comes out most boldly and affixes his name to it. The disclosure is probably nearly all true. But the spirit of the writer is too bitter. But that may claim as an apology — the "oppressing makes a wise man mad." There can be but little doubt that Mr. Hood will have to succumb to the terrible blow he has seen — While I am sorry for the fallen man I am glad to have iniquity in the high place he has occupied brought out to light that it may be a good lesson to others in power and to their successors. I am glad can speak and speak boldly though it is too often guilty of folly — Mr. Hood has latterly exerted himself to his utmost to gag our press by trying to put me, the mere printer of the Monitor, in fear of being made responsible for all that issues by it. I could not so understand American laws and consequently have not tried to circumscribe the editor & proprietor and publisher in any way but to hold him to his promise that he will not allow anything scurrilous or blasphemous to have a place in his columns nor any thing that will be calculated to defame Christianity. As his paper has not done this to my knowledge I make no objections to its weekly issues. Though I think the paper is [far] from what it ought to be and one in which I cannot possibly take any pride in owning an American Newspaper.[22]

On December 30, Captain Hood held an auction to sell those of his possessions that were not easily transportable.[23] Then, on New Year's Day 1868, having finally received approval for his leave of absence,[24] Captain Hood wrote to the Department of State that he was leaving for the United States the next day and had appointed the Rev. Dr. Noah A. McDonald as the acting vice-consul in his absence. He noted that he had authorized McDonald to draw money only for the rental of the jail, the salary of the jail keeper, and the expenses of the office. McDonald was to move the location of the consulate from the house that Hood had been renting to the grounds of the Presbyterian Mission, thereby removing the expense of the lease of the larger house on the river. McDonald would be paying himself out of the fees generated by the consulate, as Hood intended to keep receiving the consul's salary of $2,000 a year during his leave.[25]

Captain Hood's time in Bangkok had come to an end.

15

Home to Illinois

On the evening of January 1, 1868, Captain and Mrs. Hood went on board the Prussian schooner *Danzic* and the next day sailed away from Bangkok, never to return.[1] This time, they sailed first to Hong Kong. The voyage took less than two weeks. In Hong Kong, they arranged passage with Captain Gibbons on the American ship *King Fisher*.[2] The *King Fisher* was an extreme clipper, 217 feet long and 37 feet wide. She had been built in 1853 in Medford, Massachusetts, by the yard of Hayden and Cudworth, and was described as an extremely comfortable ship for passengers.[3] She made good time, crossing the Pacific Ocean to San Francisco in only 50 days, arriving on March 7.[4] The Hoods entered the city quietly. They did not register at either of the two big hotels, The Brooklyn Hotel or the Russ House, but probably stayed with Captain Hood's nephew Alfred H. Hood, who was living in the city at the time.[5]

They were in the city when Samuel Langhorne Clemens, better known as Mark Twain, arrived from Washington, D.C., on April 2, after the Mediterranean tour that provided the material for his book, *The Innocents Abroad*. Clemens had come back to San Francisco to assert his rights to the articles he had penned during that trip for the San Francisco *Alta*, a newspaper which was proposing to publish them in a compendium without further compensating him. Whether or not Captain Hood met the famous author, who had been a complete unknown when Hood left for Bangkok in 1865, is not known, but Clemens' arrival was greeted with such public acclaim that the Hoods would have heard of it.[6]

After a brief stay in San Francisco, the Hoods boarded the steamer S.S. *Sacramento* for the relatively short trip to Panama City.[7] The *Sacramento* was a wooden side-wheel steamer of 2,686 tons which was built by William H. Webb in Greenpoint, Long Island, in 1863 and sailed for the Pacific Mail Steamship Company.[8] From there, they crossed the isthmus on the Panama Railroad to Aspinwall (present day Colon). In Aspinwall, they boarded the S.S. *Henry Chauncey*, bound for New York.[9] This was another side-wheel steamship of 2,657 tons launched in 1864 and capable of carrying up to 800 passengers, although there were only a little over 200 on the voyage with the Hoods. She also sailed for the Pacific Mail Steamship Company and was named for one of its principal shareowners.[10]

The Hoods finally arrived in New York on April 28, 1868, having completed a circumnavigation of the globe in almost exactly 3 years.[11]

Captain Hood did not immediately return to Illinois. Instead, he took up temporary residence in Somerset and on May 13 filed for bankruptcy in the United States District Court, District of Massachusetts.[12] Interestingly, the notice of the filing was published only in the *Taunton Daily Gazette* and the Boston *Daily Advertiser*, and was not published anywhere in Illinois. The first meeting of the creditors was held on June 12 and Henry J. Fuller of Taunton was appointed as the assignee in the case.

The only claim to be proved at that first meeting was one from Captain Hood's relative and former neighbor, Joseph Marble, who claimed a debt of $3,058.08. This may have been money he lent Hood to finance his travel to Siam. This was also the only new claim. The rest of the $74,690.28 in claims were debts that had supposedly been paid off at the rate of $0.198 on the dollar by Captain Hood's declaration of insolvency in 1855 following the last fire in his shipyard, leaving $59,901.60 unpaid. However, that insolvency had been declared under Massachusetts law, which did not actually discharge the debts, but merely arranged for a distribution of assets to the creditors, leaving the unpaid portion still collectable. It appears that this bankruptcy filing was designed to take advantage of the Act to Establish a Uniform System of Bankruptcy throughout the United States, which had been passed into law on March 2, 1867, to finally discharge all these debts and leave Hood with a clean slate.

There are several odd things about the bankruptcy filing, however. To begin with, Hood chose to establish residency and file his petition in Massachusetts, even though he had been living in Illinois since 1855. Furthermore, there are no claims for debts in Illinois, although, given Captain Hood's lifestyle and his past history, he probably had some debts out there, raising the possibility that he was trying to preserve his credit in that state by not notifying creditors about the filing, notice of which was only published in the two Massachusetts newspapers. This echoed his behavior when divorcing his first wife, Anna, in Illinois without notifying her in Massachusetts.

It is also interesting that Captain Hood claimed to have no assets at all, no land, no cash, and no personal possessions of any kind. This while he was still receiving his consul's salary of $2,000 a year and owned a farm in Illinois. Thus it appears that he was once again hiding assets, possibly by having transferred them to his wife, whom he had married after incurring the debts.

The second and third creditors' meetings were originally scheduled for October 26 in Canton, Massachusetts, but were adjourned to Taunton on November 30 for the convenience of the creditors. This was also a friendlier venue for Captain Hood, because of his extensive business and family connections in the area. At the conclusion of the meetings, Mr. Fuller recommended that the debts be discharged by the court. Some of the creditors were not satisfied with this and sent a telegram to Canton asking for a delay in the discharge to allow them more time for investigation. In spite of this, the case was closed and Captain Hood's debts discharged on November 10, 1868.[13]

In July, with the bankruptcy still pending, the Hoods returned to Sycamore.[14] It is interesting that at this stage of his life Captain Hood should choose to return to Illinois, rather than remaining in Somerset where he had family and where he was still involved with a number of business ventures, including the Boston Stove Foundry. It is possible that he felt that he had a stronger political base in Illinois and that it would be a better venue from which to fight any charges against him.

Captain Hood made at least two trips to Washington to defend himself against the charges that had been made by Bradley and the Bangkok merchants, the first in December 1868 and the second in March 1869, when his health had deteriorated badly. There is no record that any attempt was made by the Department of State to prosecute or otherwise reprimand him for any of his actions. There did ensue a lively correspondence as Hood attempted to get the government to continue paying his consul's salary.[15]

On July 16, 1868, seven months after starting his six month leave of absence, Captain Hood wrote to the Department of State asking for an extension.[16] The department replied that they would approve a six month extension of the leave, but could not continue to pay his salary, because he had already been paid for sixty days after leaving his post. Hood wrote back arguing for continued payment, without result. He even considered returning to Bangkok, and about this time the Department of State informed the acting vice consul, Rev. N.A. MacDonald, that Hood would be coming back within three months aboard a warship.[17] This prompted Bradley to dash off a letter to the secretary of state opposing Hood's return.

> We have long had the conviction that Mr. Hood has done a sad work in this metropolis to the injury alike of American citizens and American interests generally. And we are satisfied that the Siamese government not only feel much displeased with his official intercourse but [that it] sometimes has felt insulted by his acts and has entertained the hope that after all which the United States government must have learned of the disturbances he created amongst us, that it would never allow him to return as its diplomatic agent.
>
> And now as these views have been corroborated by remarks which his Ex[cellency] the Prime Minister and Minister of War (at present the head of the government of Siam) made concerning Mr. Hood to one of our number in the presence of Hon. W.J. Shaw, Senator from California on the 14th inst. And as also H[is]. E[xcellency]. clearly signified that the Siamese government would feel itself insulted by the return of Mr. Hood as a diplomatic representative, we feel that it is a duty we owe both to ourselves and to our country, to inform your Excellency of these facts with the least possible delay most earnestly hoping that our peace and quietness may not again be disturbed nor our American interests be jeopardized merely in order to gratify the wishes of Mr. Hood.
>
> We also beg to represent that we do not recommend any person for appointment as consul, but are anxious that our Government shall send to us some person of sufficient standing, good judgment, and ability who will earnestly labor to bring back Americans and American interests to at least that excellent position which they held with the authorities of this country in former times and which now we regret to say is fast becoming secondary in consequence in great part of the course pursued by Mr. Hood.[18]

Finally, on December 16, 1868, while he was visiting Washington, D.C., to meet with Representative Farnsworth, Captain Hood asked the Department of State for another sixty day extension, citing his poor health. The handwriting on the December dispatch is very shaky, not at all like his normal firm script, so he was probably already very ill.[19]

As it became apparent that the Department of State was not going to continue to pay his salary as the United States consul at Bangkok as long as he remained in Sycamore, Captain Hood appealed to his political allies for help. In December, as Hood was asking for his second extension of leave, Congressman Farnsworth of Illinois introduced a bill, HR 1532, for financial relief for him. The congressman did not, however, put a lot of support behind it. The bill was referred to the Committee on Foreign Affairs and died there without ever coming to the floor of the House.[20]

Meanwhile, the attacks against Hood's reputation continued in the form of a letter from George Graham, one of Dr. Bradley's assistants in Bangkok, to John Chandler, who had returned to the United States. This was the same George Graham for whom Captain Hood had stood as a witness at his wedding in 1866. In this letter, Graham reported that there were rumors in Bangkok that Captain Hood was planning to return to his post as consul, as conveyed by California state senator W.J. Shaw, who was visiting Siam. Given the timing, it is likely that Hood had visited Shaw when he passed through San Francisco in the spring. While Hood had been away, the scandal machine had been at work in Bangkok, and Graham reported that the Siamese prime minister, the kralahom, was sending a letter to the Department of State saying that if he returned, Hood would not be allowed to act as consul. In rather coarse language, Graham attributed the falling out between Hood and Chandler to the verdict against Chandler in the Burdon case, which was tried a few months after Hood's arrival. He finished by saying that a petition to the secretary of state had been gotten up by the American community in Bangkok "that Mr. Hood be sent to the east of Nuck o' Fife or some other outlandish place but not to Bangkok."[21]

Chandler forwarded this letter to the Department of State, along with one of his own also attacking Hood. To these he attached a note: "Private letters generally give a better idea of the real state of things than formal despatches and petitions, and hence the forwarding of the above."[22]

King Mongkut had died on October 18, 1868, from malaria that he contracted while observing a solar eclipse in August.[23] Upon his death, the prime minister, the kralahom, Si Suriyawongse, took control of the government until Prince Chulalongkorn, who was only 15 years old at the time, could recover from his own bout of malaria. The kralahom then continued as regent until 1873, when the new supreme king, now known as Rama V, was finally crowned.[24] The kralahom was apparently not as favorably inclined towards Captain Hood as King Mongkut had been and did not want him back in the country.

Captain Hood probably heard about these letters soon after their arrival at the Department of State in late February. With his salary stopped, and fearing to return to Bangkok for reasons of health, finances, and his problems with the American community, Captain Hood finally wrote a letter resigning his commission as consul on March 4, 1869.[25] Thus ended a four year saga of political and financial intrigue, diplomatic triumph, and exotic travel.

During that time, he had maintained the dignity of the United States in Bangkok with little support from Washington and laid the groundwork for increased trade with Siam. He had made careful observations of the country and its potential and cultivated cordial relations with King Mongkut. On the other hand, he had managed to alienate the merchant community, especially the trio of Chandler, Virgin and McCormick, by not supporting their schemes. While he had generally good relations with the missionaries, Dr. Bradley never forgave him for the judgment against him and in favor of the French consul, Aubaret. Since Bradley was the most prolific English language writer on this period in Siam, both with his newspapers and his memoirs, he managed to create a one-sided portrayal of Captain Hood as a somewhat shady character. Given the difficulty of the post, isolated as it was and cut off from meaningful communication with home, Hood managed to navigate the minefield of the British and French face-off in Southeast Asia, and to support a dignified consular establishment, even if his accounting was sometimes a little shaky.

In spite of his difficulties with the Department of State, Captain Hood quickly reconnected with the business and social leadership in Sycamore. Within a year of his return, he became a resident stockholder of the Lamar Insurance Company in the town[26] and was selected to serve as a grand juror.[27]

Towards the end of 1869, Captain Hood experienced a religious enlightenment and formally declared his faith in Jesus Christ, most likely in the Baptist Church.[28] Although he was a life-long Baptist, prior to this he had not taken religion seriously, and this personal conversion may indicate that he felt that he was nearing the end of his life.

One of Hood's most significant business ventures was his service as a director of the Sycamore Marsh Harvester Manufacturing Company.[29] This company produced the most successful mechanical harvester of its day. It was pulled by two horses driven by a man seated at the back of the machine and carried two more men who sat on a platform built out from the side and who bound the sheaves of grain as they came up a belt. The company eventually built five factories to keep up with the demand. It had been founded by two brothers, Charles and William Marsh, in 1857, and moved its manufacturing operation from Plano, Illinois, to Sycamore in 1865. Although it would go through bankruptcy at least once, the Marsh Harvester Company was one of the predecessor companies to the International Harvester Corporation.[30]

Captain Hood also served as an officer and director of the Sycamore Woolen Manufacturing Company. This company was founded in September 1868, with Hood as a founding shareholder and its first chairman. It started production in 1869, but quickly ran into financial difficulties. Captain Hood helped direct its liquidation as vice-president of the company in 1870.[31]

In the summer of 1870, Captain Hood convinced another of his nephews, Capt. John Hood Luther, the son of his sister Mary Luther, to move to Sycamore. Together with William Loomis they purchased the Sycamore flax mill from Bryan Ellwood. This was located east of the town on the East Branch of the Kishwaukee River, just north of where the Sycamore Golf Club is today. They paid $6,650 for the three parcels which made up the mill and its grounds.[32] Flax was an important crop in the area, grown chiefly for the oil that could be extracted from its seeds. Hood's mill processed the left over flax straw, which had been allowed to decompose first, to extract flax fiber. The fiber was sold to another company which produced linen thread and fabric. Hood not only bought the "well rotted flax straw" but sold flax seed at low prices to encourage farmers to plant this crop.[33]

Captain Hood also remained active in politics. On his return from Bangkok, he retained his reputation as a drinker, with the local paper publishing the following story about him many years later.

> One fourth of July, a day of all others that raised the spirit of the captain to the heights above, he gathered his friends around him and celebrated the day like a regular Kentucky Colonel.
> The afternoon wore away and it was evident to his friends, that the captain's sense of equilibrium was so impaired that he might not be able

to negotiate Somonauk street. Casting about for assistance, they spied Billy Burdett, his white horse and two wheeled dray. They drafted him in the service.

The captain required careful handling as he was attired in a palm beach suit, spotless and attractive.... All went well until the corner of Ottawa and Somonauk was reached, when one wheel of the dray dropped suddenly into a deep mud hole and the captain ... rolled off into the mud ... and then the captain cast all diplomatic language aside and told Billy in his most emphatic English and choicest Siamese expletives just what he thought of all draymen and Billy in particular.[34]

Whether it was this incident or his failing health that reformed him, Captain Hood went on the wagon and became affiliated with the Temperance Party in Sycamore, where he quickly rose in its leadership ranks. He claimed to practice total abstinence and was encouraged to run as a Temperance candidate for mayor of Sycamore in the March 1870 municipal elections, but he declined the honor.[35] Instead, he arranged to be appointed chairman of the local nominating convention of the Temperance Party on March 11, and engineered the nomination of Moses Dean to the mayoralty, which Dean went on to win.[36] The Sycamore *True Republican*, which was the local newspaper, then backed Hood for the office of state representative.

For the lower House, Hon. J.M. Hood of Sycamore is the leading candidate in this portion of the County. We know of no other aspirant for the position who will fill it so creditably. He has extensive experience in Legislative bodies.... Since that time he has served three years as U.S. consul to Siam, from which post he retired with the warmest commendations of the State Department for his zeal and efficiency. These opportunities have served to give him not only considerable experience in state craft but also extensive acquaintance and friendship with the leading men of the State and Nation ... Captain Hood has always been an earnest Radical Republican and has taken an active interest in public enterprises. DeKalb County will find in him an efficient and influential Representative.[37]

Captain Hood seriously considered running, but eventually backed out of the race with the following announcement.

Some two months since, at the request of friends, I consented to allow the use of my name in connection with the office of Representative from this County. Since then, having made business arrangements that will require my whole attention, I take this method of stating to those who have expressed a willingness to support me for that position, and to the people generally, that I have decided not to be a candidate. I desire to thank those who have given me the assurance of their support and trust they will be able to secure the election of some other man, who will discharge the duties of the position honestly and faithfully.[38]

Although he was not an active opponent of the nascent women's rights movement, Hood was not a supporter of it either. In the early spring of 1870, he attended the Illinois Constitutional Convention as a spectator. While there, he listened to a speech by Lucy Stone, an early feminist who was one of the founders of the American Woman Suffrage Association. She had previously addressed the Massachusetts Constitutional Convention of 1853, which Hood may have also attended as a spectator. After hearing her speak in Illinois, he remarked to a newspaper reporter,

> Why, Lucy Stone has been a perfect terror to me for twenty years. I had imagined her to be a regular virago, and expected to hear a such a scolding as I never listened to. Wasn't I taken aback when that gentle, quiet, ladylike woman began to talk! I wanted to agree with her before she had spoken ten minutes and was only sorry when I couldn't.[39]

Captain Hood took great interest in civic activities as well. During the winter of 1870, he headed the committee that put on the fifth annual convention of the Musical Union, an association of amateur musicians that was attended by over 150 members from all over northwestern Illinois.[40] Later that year, he helped organize the first annual DeKalb County Fair. At the fair he was the superintendent of Floral Hall, and his wife, Sarah, was a judge for both the flower show and the household arts and textile fabrics competition.[41] At this fair, the Exhibitors Hall was decorated with paintings loaned by local residents, including Hood. One of these paintings, which was owned by Hood's nephew John Luther, was described as depicting the 2000-ton ship *Monarch* under full sail. This ship was reported to have been built by Captain Hood.[42] Unfortunately, the only American built clipper ship with a similar name, *The Monarch of the Seas*, 1971 tons, was built by Roosevelt & Joyce in New York City.[43] It has been described as a sister ship of the largest known ship built by Hood, the clipper *Governor Morton*, which was only 1400 tons, because they both were once owned by the same firm.[44] Nonetheless, the painting was representative of Captain Hood's past accomplishments.

Hood resumed his real estate activities as well, purchasing a "cottage house containing 6 rooms" which he advertised for rent. It was located

Home of Captain Hood, 614 Somonauk Street, Sycamore, Illinois. Photograph by G. Kingston.

opposite Paine's Hotel, one of the major businesses in Sycamore.[45] Soon afterwards, he purchased the Townsend house.[46] This was a large and elegant residence on Somonauk Street, the most fashionable street in Sycamore, just south of the DeKalb County courthouse. It had at least 5 chimneys and was situated on a large, well landscaped lot with a carriage house in the rear. It still stands today at 614 Somonauk Street, where it is known as the P.M. Alden House from a later prominent resident.[47]

Hood remained litigious. He became enmeshed in a lawsuit over a contract with General Frederick W. Partridge, another resident of Sycamore, who would eventually succeed him as U.S. consul at Bangkok.[48] Partridge received his title when he had served as a brigadier general with the 13th Illinois Infantry Regiment during the Civil War.[49]

Later, Hood successfully sued the Chicago and Northwestern Railroad Company for "injuries done to his horses and carriage by an engineer blowing his whistle ... unnecessarily and maliciously with intent to frighten his horse."[50] He was awarded $500 in damages.

Hood became heavily involved in a different railroad issue that was causing significant controversy in Sycamore at the time. The city was not located on a main railroad line, the Chicago and Iowa having been built through the town of Courtland, about five miles south of Sycamore. Although a spur called the Courtland and Sycamore Railroad was built, Sycamore was still at a commercial disadvantage. In 1870, the Belvedere and Illinois River Railroad proposed to construct its main line through Sycamore, connecting the Courtland and Sycamore to the Chicago and Dubuque at Rockford, some 30 miles to the northwest. This would give the city direct connections with two east-west railroads, the Chicago and Iowa, and the Chicago and Dubuque. The construction of the new railroad was to be financed by the Chicago and Iowa by selling stock to the cities and towns along the route, which would issue bonds to pay for it.

Grave of Captain Hood, Elmwood Cemetery, Sycamore, Illinois. Photograph by G. Kingston.

The bonding issue divided the town. The supporters of the project saw it as a boost to the local economy and a potential source of personal profit. The detractors were concerned that the railroad company would take the money and then not finish building the line, a not unusual occurrence in those times. Captain Hood, who was among the opponents of the measure, stepped into the middle of this fray and brokered a compromise. He and other prominent opponents would vote in favor of the tax to fund the bonds, to the extent of $60,000, but only if the bonds were not actually issued until the line was built all the way to Rockford. In the end, the measure passed, but the other towns along the route did not go along with the scheme, so the railroad was never built.[51]

At the end of March 1871, upon his return from Washington, D.C., Captain Hood came down with "a congestion of the lungs." This was probably flu augmented by pneumonia. After a month of this he began to recover, but developed complications, including congestive heart failure. At last, he succumbed to these multiple problems and died on May 20, 1871, in Sycamore, Illinois, at the age of 56.[52]

His obituary read in part:

> No one of all our people took a more active interest in all matters pertaining to the general advancement of the interests of the town. Always liberal and public spirited, ready to co-operate promptly and generously in every enterprise for its benefit: and in this respect his loss will be sensibly felt by the entire community. In the social circles of this city his departure will leave a sad vacancy. His natural vivacity banished awkwardness and silence and his entrance into company brought with it a breeze of cheerful life. His cheery spirit acted like a tonic and will be more appreciated as we shall mark its loss.[53]

Captain Hood is buried in Elmwood Cemetery, in Sycamore, Illinois, in the same plot as his nephew John Hood Luther and his grandnephew John Hood Luther, Jr.

16

Epilogue

In his will, dated August 1, 1870, Captain Hood bequeathed all of his estate to his second wife, Sarah Alexandra Hood, and named her his executrix, cutting his first wife, Anna, out entirely.[1] One year before his death, he claimed to own real estate worth $7,000 and an additional personal estate of $800, a considerable reduction from what he claimed in 1860, indicating the extent of his losses in the job of consul.[2] The DeKalb County Probate Court appraised the value of the estate, primarily the house on Somonauk Street, at only $1,682.50 with an additional $801.50 in personal property. Captain Hood's interest in the flax mill did not have any significant value. The land that he still owned in Loda was heavily mortgaged, and his widow and executrix, Sarah eventually conveyed it to Levi S. Wood, the holder of the mortgage, for $1.[3]

In May 1872, one year after Captain Hood's death, Sarah sold their house in Sycamore to Mr. Philander Alden, the cashier of the Sycamore National Bank, for $3,650.[4] A few days later, she auctioned off all her furniture and other household goods in the basement of J.C. Waterman's dry goods store. The auction was very popular, as the Hoods were known to have had many luxurious possessions. The *Sycamore True Republican* carried a notice about the sale on its front page.

> Don't forget the great Auction Sale of Mrs. Hood's Household goods, next Saturday, consisting of Parlor, Chamber and Dining-Room Furniture, Carpets, Mirrors, Pictures, Crockery, Glassware, etc. This will be a rare chance for getting something nice.[5]

After selling her home and possessions, Sarah went to live with her brother in Waukegan, Illinois, northeast of Sycamore on Lake Michigan. She kept up her Sycamore connections, however, and in 1872 was again listed as a judge at the county fair. On October 22, 1872, a year and a half after Captain Hood's death, she married Henry D. Brown and moved back to his home in Sycamore. Henry Brown was a merchant who had been born in Herkimer, New York, and came to Sycamore when he was only 18. He had served with the 105th Illinois Volunteer Infantry during the Civil War and achieved the rank of major.[6] After he returned from the war, he had married Libbie Bennett, with whom he had four children, all of whom died young. Soon after she died, he courted and married Sarah.[7]

Sarah would live to the age of 76, dying on December 27, 1926. Her obituary did not mention either her marriage to Captain Hood or the two and one-half years she spent in Siam with him. Apparently, that was an episode that she wished to forget.[8]

In October 1871, five months after Captain Hood's death, his first wife, Anna M. Hood, filed a writ of dower in Bristol County Court, alleging that she was the widow of Captain Hood, and asking that the land they had bought in 1847, using her mother's legacy, be returned to her and not included in his estate. This land was a fishing camp on the Taunton River. The defendants in the case were William Perry Hood, Captain Hood's nephew and business associate, and another man who had acquired the land as a result of Captain Hood's insolvency in 1855. William was one of the assignees in that case and he had con-

Grave of Anna Moison Hood, Center Street cemetery, Dighton, Massachusetts. Photograph by G. Kingston. Kingston — The U.S. Consul at the Court of Siam: James Madison Hood.

veyed the land to himself, presumably to settle a debt. Anna claimed, as she had in 1866, that the Illinois divorce was invalid and the result of fraud, and that she remained Captain Hood's wife until the end of his life. William argued that the divorce was valid, and that therefore Anna was not Hood's widow and had no standing to claim the land. The Bristol County Circuit Court decided in Anna's favor, ruling that she was Captain Hood's widow and was entitled to the land. William appealed the decision and the Bristol County Superior Court overturned the verdict, confirming the earlier ruling that the divorce was valid and concluding that Anna could not recover the land.[9]

Anna continued to live in Fall River, and died there on March 1, 1874. She is buried next to the grave of her mother in the cemetery on Center Street in Dighton, Massachusetts, under the name of Anna Moison.[10]

Notes on Sources

Specific references are given in the end notes, but because Captain James Madison Hood left few writings of his own, other than his consular correspondence and legal documents, I feel that it is necessary to comment on the major sources used in this book. I am therefore providing here a list of my most important sources, with brief notes about their reliability and bias, where appropriate.

James E. Bradbury, *Seafarers of Somerset*, Somerset, MA: privately published, 1996. This little book is full of anecdotes about the many merchant masters and shipbuilders of Somerset, but does not give references and I have had to independently verify specific facts, some of which differ from the recollections related by Mr. Bradbury.

The Dr. Dan Beach Bradley Archive at the Oberlin College Archives, Oberlin, Ohio (Record Group 30/5), preserves the original diaries of Dr. Bradley, his correspondence, some photographs, and some copies of the *Bangkok Recorder* and the *Bangkok Calendar*. These are original documents and, while they are reliable as to facts, they naturally reflect the views, opinions and biases of Dr. Bradley.

William L. Bradley, *Siam Then*, Pasadena, CA: William Carey Library, 1981. William L. Bradley was a descendant of Dr. Dan Beach Bradley and he chose to write the book as a memoir, as if it were written by Dr. Bradley himself. It draws extensively on the diaries and correspondence in the Oberlin College Archives, but it is selective and designed to present the best possible portrait of Dr. Bradley. I have used it as a guide but have gone back to the original diaries and publications of Dr. Bradley wherever possible.

William L. Crothers, *The American-Built Clipper Ship: 1850–1856,*

Camden, ME: International Marine, 1996. This is an invaluable reference on clipper ship construction and contains extensive information on almost every clipper built in America during the years it covers.

Octavious T. Howe and Frederick C. Matthews, *American Clipper Ships: 1833–1858*, originally published in 1926 and reprinted, New York: Argosy Antiquarian Ltd., 1967. This is the original definitive compilation of all American clipper ships built during the period covered and includes information on their builders, dimensions, and careers, based on original information and extensive newspaper research.

I have made extensive use of contemporary newspapers, mostly through online reading of scanned copies available through two Newsbank sources, America's Historical Newspapers (infoweb.newsbank.com. ezproxy.bpl.org) accessed through the Boston Public Library, and Genealogy Bank (www.genealogybank.com). These include *The Daily Atlas*, Boston and the *Springfield Republican*. The *Sycamore True Republican* was accessed through the Illinois Newspaper Project at the University of Illinois (http://www.library.illinois.edu/hpnl/) and clippings preserved by the Joiner Historical Room at the Sycamore Public Library. The *Taunton Gazette* was reviewed at the Old Colony Historical Society in Taunton, Massachusetts. The *Iroquois Republican* was accessed on microfilm at the Lincoln Library in Springfield, Illinois. Contemporary newspapers must be used with care, as they were often reporting with a political bias and are prone to typographic errors, but they are a wonderful window into the culture, language, and opinions of the times.

Anna Leonowens, *The English Governess at the Siamese Court*, Boston: Fields, Osgood, 1870; and Margaret Landon, *Anna and the King of Siam*, New York: John Day Company, 1944. Anna Leonowens' book is her personal memoir of her experiences at the court of Siam and is more accurate than Margaret Landon's later retelling of the story, which took some liberties to improve its commercial potential. *The King and I*, in its many incarnations, is loosely based on the Landon book and must be considered fictional.

Noah A. McDonald, *A Missionary in Siam*, Bangkok, Siam: White Lotus, 1999, originally published in 1871. This book should be looked at as a companion to William Bradley's *Siam Then*. It concentrates more on the geography, customs, and culture of the country than on specific events, and is useful for understanding the background against which the events involving Captain Hood unfolded.

U.S. Department of State records, including Despatches from U.S. Consuls in Bangkok, Siam 1856–1906, M448; and Instructions to the U.S. Consul at Bangkok, Siam, 1857–1912, T403, both in Record Group 84, published on microfilm by the National Archives and Records Administration (NARA). These sources contain the correspondence between Captain Hood and the Departments of State and Treasury, before, during, and after his time in Bangkok. While they are original sources, Captain Hood was always writing to portray himself and his actions in a favorable light, while Frederick Seward, the assistant secretary of state attempted to maintain a formal, noncommittal tone. These dispatches are the largest extant body of Captain Hood's own writing and provide valuable insight into his personality and character.

Where possible, I have used material from both the Bradley and Hood papers to provide their different perspectives on a given event.

Chapter Notes

Preface

1. Margaret Landon, *Anna and the King of Siam* (New York: John Day, 1944).
2. William L. Crothers, *The American Built Clipper Ship: 1850–1856* (Camden, ME: International Marine, 1996), p. xv.
3. *Ibid.*, p. xi.
4. John S. Morgan, *Robert Fulton* (New York: Mason/Charter, 1977), p. 138.
5. Richard Woodman, *The History of the Ship* (New York: Lyons, 1997), p. 148.
6. Roger W. McAdam, *Salts of the Sound* (New York: Stephen Daye, 1957), p. 48.
7. *Bangkok Recorder*, shipping news, 1865–1867.
8. http://www.measuringworth.com.
9. J.M. Hood, report accompanying Despatch No. 24, Despatches from U.S. Consuls in Bangkok, Siam 1856–1906, RG 84, M448, National Archives and Records Administration (NARA).

Chapter 1

1. J.M. Hood, Despatch No. 11, Despatches from U.S. Consuls.
2. *Treaty Between the United States and the First and Second Kings of Siam*, 1856.
3. Landon.
4. *United States Consul's Manual*, 2d Ed. (Washington, D.C.: Hudson Taylor, 1863), Sec.30, p. 16.
5. J.M. Hood, Despatch No. 11, Despatches from U.S. Consuls.
6. *United States Consul's Manual*, Sec. 9, p. 7.
7. Article reprinted in the *Sycamore*

True Republican, December 20, 1905; *Bangkok Recorder*, September 1865; and diary of Dr. Dan Beach Bradley, RG 30/5, Oberlin College Archives.
8. J.M. Hood, Despatch No. 11, Despatches from U.S. Consuls.
9. William L. Bradley, *Siam Then* (Pasadena: William Carey Library, 1981), p. 45.
10. R. Stanley Thomson, "The Diplomacy of Imperialism: France and Spain in Cochin China, 1858–63," *The Journal of Modern History*, Vol. 12, No. 3 (Sep. 1940), pp. 334–356.
11. J.M. Hood, Despatch No. 12, Despatches from U.S. Consuls.
12. Abbott Low Moffat, *Mongkut, the King of Siam* (Ithaca: Cornell University Press, 1961), p. 75.
13. Bradley, p. 96.

Chapter 2

1. Massachusetts State Library, legislator biographies.
2. Beers & Co., *Representative Men and Old Families of Southeastern Massachusetts* (Chicago: J.H. Beers, 1912), p. 591.
3. Donald R. Hickey, "American Trade Restrictions During the War of 1812," *The Journal of American History*, Vol. 68, No. 3 (Dec. 1981), pp. 517–538.
4. George Howe, *Mount Hope: A New England Chronicle* (New York: Viking Press, 1959), p. 198.
5. D. Hamilton Hurd, *History of Bristol County, Massachusetts* (Philadelphia: J.W. Lewis, 1883), p. 635.

6. Mary Jane (Jennie) Hood Bosson, *John Hood of Lynn, Massachusetts and Some of His Descendants* (Salem, MA: Essex Institute, 1909), pp. 1–5.

7. U.S. Census, 1790, series M637, roll 4, pp. 620–621.

8. Beers & Co., p. 591.

9. *Massachusetts Soldiers and Sailors in the Revolution* (Boston: Wright and Potter Printing Co., State Printers, 1896–1908), Vol. III, p. 216.

10. Revolutionary War Pension Application, Mary Peck, widow of Peleg Peck, RG 21, NARA, Waltham, Massachusetts.

11. *Providence Gazette*, January 11, 1772.

12. Beers & Co., p. 591.

13. *Vital Records of Swansea Massachusetts to 1850*, trans. H.L. Peter Rounds (Boston: New England Historic Genealogical Society, 1992), p. 362.

14. U.S. Census, 1810 and 1820.

15. Bristol County, MA, Registry of Deeds, Book 104, p. 376.

16. William A. Hart, *History of the Town of Somerset* (Somerset, MA: Town of Somerset, 1940), p. 77.

17. *New Bedford Mercury*, January 5, 1816.

18. Hurd, p. 637.

19. James N. Arnold, *Vital Record of Rhode Island*, First Series (Providence, RI: Narragansett Historical Publishing Company, 1896), p. 545.

20. Passenger manifest of the Brig *James*, May 10, 1823.

21. *Providence Patriot*, June 27, 1827.

22. Linda K. Salvucci, "Atlantic Intersections: Early American Commerce and the Rise of the Spanish West Indies," *The Business History Review*, Vol. 79, No. 4 (Winter 2005), pp. 781–809.

23. *Gazette*, Edenton, North Carolina, Friday, Oct. 20, 1809.

24. *Boston Commercial Gazette*, July 22, 1824.

25. Joseph Blunt, *The Shipmaster's Assistant and Commercial Digest* (New York: E. & G.W. Blunt, 1837), p. 10.

Chapter 3

1. James E. Bradbury, *Seafarers of Somerset* (Somerset, MA: privately published, 1996), p. 8.

2. Charles Everett Ranlett, *Master Mariner of Maine* (Portland, ME: The Southworth-Anthoensen Press, 1942).

3. *Rhode Island American and Gazette*, Providence, Rhode Island, Sept. 11, 1832.

4. Ralph D. Paine, *The Old Merchant Marine: A Chronicle of American Ships and Sailors* (New Haven: Yale University Press, 1919), pp. 137.

5. Ship manifests, Fall River Customs District, RG 36, NARA, Waltham, Massachusetts.

6. *Ibid.*

7. NOAA Chart 13226.

8. Henry V. Poor, *History of the Railroads and Canals of the United States of America* (New York: John H. Schultz, 1860), Vol. 1, p. 154.

9. Records of the Fall River Customs District, RG 36, NARA, Waltham, Massachusetts.

10. *Rhode-Island American and Providence Gazette*, Providence, Rhode Island, January 24, 1826.

11. *Rhode-Island American and Providence Gazette*, Providence, Rhode Island, February 7, 1826.

12. *Providence Patriot*, February 24, 1826; *Boston Commercial Gazette*, July 20, 1826; *Rhode-Island American*, July 21, 1826; *Providence Patriot*, Aug. 5, 1826; *Baltimore Patriot*, September 21, 1826.

13. James E. Bradbury, p. 9.

14. Bristol County Court, MA, 1854, and U.S. District Court, District of Massachusetts, Case No. 918, 1868.

15. Bristol County, MA Registry of Deeds, Book 153, pp. 487–489.

16. Reginald C. McGrane, *The Panic of 1837: Some Financial Problems of the Jacksonian Era* (New York: Russell & Russell, 1965).

17. Records of the Fall River Customs District, RG 36, NARA, Waltham, Massachusetts.

18. *Ibid.*

19. Bradbury, p. 9.

20. *Newport Mercury*, Newport, Rhode Island, October 14, 1837.

21. Elizabeth Standish (Moison) Gravestone, Center Street Cemetery, Dighton, MA.

22. *Columbian Centinel*, Boston, May 4, 1816.

23. Bristol County, MA, Court Records, Taunton, Massachusetts.

24. *The Albion*, New York, June 10, 1826.

25. Anna M. Hood vs. James M. Hood, Bristol County Circuit Court, MA, October Term, 1865.

26. Records of the Federal District Court of Rhode Island, 1842.

27. Bristol County, MA, Registry of Deeds, Book 167, p. 467.

28. *Boston Courier*, January 15, 1844.

29. Hood vs. Hood, Bristol County Superior Court, October Term, 1872.

30. Anna M. Hood vs. James M. Hood, 1865.

31. Gravestones, Center Street Cemetery, Dighton, MA, and Elmwood Cemetery, Sycamore, IL.

32. Bristol County, MA, Registry of Deeds, Book 177, p. 433.

33. Justin H. Smith, *The War with Mexico* (New York: Macmillan, 1919), vol. 1, p. 142.

34. *Ibid.*, pp. 156ff.

35. Military Sea Transportation and Shipping Control, Bureau of Naval Personnel, Navpers 10829-A, Washington, D.C., 1954.

36. Records of the Fall River Customs District, RG 36, NARA, Waltham, Massachusetts.

37. U.S. House of Representatives Document No. 46, January 19, 1847.

38. *Pensacola Democrat*, Pensacola, Florida, May 6, 1846.

39. *Ohio Statesman*, Columbus, Ohio, May 18, 1846.

40. *Times-Picayune*, New Orleans, June 2, 1846.

41. *The Daily Atlas*, Boston, July 7 to September 18, 1846.

42. K. Jack Bauer, *Surfboats and Horse Marines: U.S. Naval Operations in the Mexican War, 1846–1848* (Annapolis, MD: United States Naval Institute, 1969), pp. 37–47.

43. Bristol County Registry of Deeds, Book 184, page 261.

44. Records of the Fall River Customs District, RG 36, NARA, Waltham, Massachusetts.

45. *Newport Mercury*, Newport, Rhode Island, November 7, 1846.

46. Quartermaster Corps list of ship leases, Ex. Doc. 29, 1847.

47. Bauer, p. 72.

48. Somerset Town Records; Leslie Luther, *The Luther Family in America* (Moravia, NY: privately printed, 1976), p. 414; and Bradbury, pp. 9–10.

49. Bradbury, p. 10.

50. Bauer, pp. 75–82.

51. *Ibid.*, p. 230.

Chapter 4

1. Beers & Co., p. 591.

2. Hurd, pp. 228–229.

3. Many books have been published on the history of clipper ships. For further reading on the subject, I recommend *The American Built Clipper Ship: 1850–1856* by William L. Crothers (Camden, ME: International Marine, 1996); *Greyhounds of the Sea* by Carl Cutler (New York: G.P. Putnam's Sons, 1930); *The Tea Clippers* by David MacGregor (London: Conway Maritime Press, 1983); *Clipper Ships of America and Great Britain, 1833–1869* by Helen and Jacques La Grange (New York: G.P. Putnam's Sons, 1936).

4. Octavious T. Howe and Frederick C. Matthews, *American Clipper Ships: 1833–1858* (New York: Argosy Antiquarian, 1967), p. 501.

5. Woodman, p. 149.

6. Helen Lagrange, *Clipper Ships of America and Great Britain: 1833–1869*, New York: G. P. Putnam's Sons, 1936, p. 54.

7. Bristol County, MA, Registry of Deeds, Book 177, p. 433.

8. Bristol County, MA, Registry of Deeds, Book 184, p. 261.

9. This account of Lincoln's visit to Massachusetts is compiled from contemporary newspaper accounts in several newspapers, including the *Springfield Republican* and *The Daily Atlas* of Boston, and from *Abraham Lincoln Visits The Old Colony* by Jordan Fiore; *The Crockers of Taunton* by Edward F. Kennedy, Jr.; and *Abraham Among the Yankees* by William Hanna, all published by the Old Colony Historical Society, Taunton, MA.

10. *The Daily Atlas*, Boston, May 26, 1848.

11. *Springfield Republican*, Springfield, Massachusetts, October 19, 1849.

12. The details of the ships built by the

Hood shipyard have been compiled from a number of sources, primarily *Ship Registers of Dighton-Fall River 1783–1938*, The National Archives Project, 1939, published by NARA with additional details on some ships from *American Clipper Ships: 1833–1858* by Octavious T. Howe and Frederick C. Matthews (New York: Argosy Antiquarian, 1967) and *The American Built Clipper Ship: 1850–1856* by William L. Crothers (Camden, ME: International Marine, 1996).

13. Personal communication, Diane Goodwin, Somerset Historical Society.

14. John W. Griffiths, *The Ship-Builder's Manual and Nautical Referee* (New York: J.W. Griffiths, 1853).

15. Crothers, pp. 20–30.

16. Edward F. Kennedy, *The Crockers of Taunton* (Taunton, MA: The Old Colony Historical Society, 1988), pp. 10–11.

17. Hurd; see the accounts of industries in the chapters devoted to these towns.

18. David MacGregor, *The Tea Clippers* (London: Conway Maritime Press, 1983), p 84.

19. *The Daily Atlas*, Boston, October 18, 1949.

20. Edward H. Bennett, *Fire Insurance Cases* (New York: Hurd and Houghton, 1874); Hood vs. The Manhattan Fire Insurance Company, 11 N.Y. 532, p. 53.

21. *Boston Courier*, March 28, 1850.

22. William F. Sprague, *Barnstaple and Yarmouth Sea Captains and Ship Owners* (Boston: privately printed, 1913), pp. 17–18.

23. *Ship Registers of Dighton-Fall River 1783–1938*, NARA, 1939, p. 44.

24. *The Daily Atlas*, Boston, April 4, 1850.

25. *New York Times*, July 8, 1865.

26. Records of the Fall River Customs District, RG 36, NARA, Waltham, Massachusetts.

27. Bradbury, p. 12.

28. MacGregor, pp. 79–80.

29. Christopher Blossom, personal communication.

30. Bradbury, p. 115.

31. Lagrange, p. 192.

32. Howe and Matthews, p. 400.

33. The Maritime History Virtual Archives, http://www.bruzelius.info/Nautica/Nautica.html.

34. *Ship Registers of Dighton-Fall River 1783–1938*, p. 54.

35. Arthur H. Clark, *The Clipper Ship Era* (New York: G.P. Putnam's Sons, 1920), p. 254.

36. Bradbury, p. 96.

37. Howe and Matthews, p. 247.

38. *Ibid.*, p. 581.

39. J.W. Griffiths, *Treatise on Marine and Naval Architecture* (New York: D. Appleton, 1854); *The Ship-Builder's Manual and Nautical Referee* (New York: J.W. Griffiths, 1853).

40. Bradbury, p. 118.

41. *The Daily Atlas*, Boston, March 17, 1851.

42. *The Times*, London, July 5, 1852.

43. *Hunt's Mercants' Magazine and Commercial Review*, Vol. 26, 1852, p. 135.

44. *Argus*, Melbourne, Australia, November 12, 1852.

45. Howe and Matthews, p. 507.

46. Paine, pp. 172–173.

47. Crothers, p. 496.

48. Bristol County, MA Registry of Deeds, Book 203, page 3.

49. Bradbury, p. 123.

50. Cutter History File, Coast Guard Historian's Office, USCG HQ.

51. Lightship History File, Coast Guard Historian's Office, USCG HQ.

52. *The Sun*, Baltimore, May 6, 1854.

53. *Milwaukee Sentinel*, May 13, 1854.

54. Lightship History File, Coast Guard Historian's Office, USCG HQ.

55. Records of the Fall River Customs District, RG 36, NARA, Waltham, Massachusetts.

56. *The Daily Atlas*, Boston, April 5, 1853.

57. *Taunton Gazette*, October 2, 1853.

58. Reprinted in the *Taunton Gazette*, November 2, 1853.

59. *The Daily Atlas*, Boston, September 9, 1854.

60. *The American Whig*, September 28, 1854.

61. *Taunton Gazette*, December 2, 1854.

62. *Ibid.*

63. *Boston Courier*, November 13, 1854.

64. *Boston Evening Transcript*, November 7, 1854.

65. *Taunton Whig*, November 30, 1854.

66. *Taunton Gazette*, December 2, 1854.

67. 5 Gray 78, Supreme Judicial Court of Massachusetts, 1855.

68. Bennett, p. 53.

69. *Providence Post*, December 18, 1854.
70. *Taunton Gazette*, December 19, 1854.
71. Bristol County Court, MA, 1854.
72. U.S. District Court, District of Massachusetts, Case No. 918, 1868.
73. Bristol County Court, MA, 1854, and U.S. District Court, District of Massachusetts, Case No. 918, 1868.
74. U.S. District Court, District of Massachusetts, Case No. 918, 1868.
75. Bristol County, MA, Registry of Deeds, Grantor and Grantee Indices.

Chapter 5

1. Michael F. Holt, *The Rise and Fall of the American Whig Party: Jacksonian Politics and the Onset of the Civil War* (New York: Oxford University Press, 1999), p. 27.
2. 23rd Congress, 1st Session, House of Representatives Document 253, March 31, 1834.
3. McGrane, p. 70.
4. *The Daily Atlas*, Boston, March 10, 1853.
5. *Taunton Daily Gazette*, March 10, 1853.
6. *Springfield Republican*, May 5, 1853.
7. *Springfield Republican*, May 30, 1853.
8. Frothingham, Louis Adams, *A Brief History of the Constitution and Government of Massachusetts, with a Chapter on Legislative Procedure* (Cambridge: Harvard University, 1916).
9. *Official Report of the Debates and Proceedings in the State Convention Assembled May 4th, 1853 to Revise and Amend the Constitution of the Commonwealth of Massachusetts* (Boston: White & Potter, 1853).
10. *Boston Courier*, April 17, 1854.
11. *Taunton Gazette*, November 16, 1853.
12. *Acts and Resolves Passed By the General Court of Massachusetts in the Year 1854* (Boston: William White, 1854), p. 2.
13. *Boston Courier*, April 17, 1854.
14. *Acts and Resolves 1854*, p. 417 ff.
15. *Ibid.*, Chapter 38.
16. *Ibid.*, Chapter 61.
17. *The Daily Atlas*, Boston, February 22, 1854.
18. *The Daily Atlas*, Boston, January 26, 1854.
19. *Acts and Resolves 1854*, Ch. 225 and 266.

20. *Ibid.*, Ch. 3 and 378.
21. *Boston Courier*, April 10, 1854.
22. *Acts and Resolves 1854*, Chapter 226.
23. Guilford Transportation/Pan Am Railways website, http://panamrailways.com/Maps/Map.pdf.
24. *Acts and Resolves 1854*, Chapter 435.
25. *The Daily Atlas*, Boston, June 26, 1854.
26. Debra McArthur, *The Kansas-Nebraska Act and "Bleeding Kansas" in American History* (Berkeley Heights, NJ: Enslow, 2003).
27. *The Daily Atlas*, Boston, February 18, 1854.
28. *National Aegis*, Cambridge, Massachusetts, April 5, 1854.
29. Albert J. Von Frank, *The Trials of Anthony Burns: Freedom and Slavery in Emerson's Boston* (Cambridge: Harvard University Press, 1998).
30. *The Daily Atlas*, Boston, June 27, 1854.
31. *The Daily Atlas*, Boston, June 26, 1854.
32. *The Daily Atlas*, Boston, June 30, 1854.
33. *The Daily Atlas*, Boston, July 21, 1854.
34. *The Daily Atlas*, Boston, August 17, 1854.
35. *National Aegis*, Cambridge, Massachusetts, August 23, 1854.
36. *The Pittsfield Sun*, August 24, 1854.

Chapter 6

1. John R. Mulkern, *The Know-Nothing Party in Massachusetts: The Rise and Fall of a People's Movement* (Boston: Northeastern University Press, 1990), pp. 61–86.
2. *The Daily Atlas*, Boston, January 8, 1855.
3. Paul Simon, *Lincoln's Preparation for Greatness: The Illinois Legislative Years* (Urbana: University of Illinois Press, 1971), p. 224.
4. This is implied from the fact that he ran as a Whig-Know-Nothing candidate in the fall elections. Only members of twigs could run as Know-Nothing candidates, Mulkern, p. 62. See note 6, below.
5. *Massachusetts Spy*, Worcester, September 6, 1854.

6. *The Daily Atlas*, Boston, September 8, 1854.

7. Biographical Directory of the United States Congress, http://bioguide.congress. gov.

8. Francis Curtis, *The Republican Party: A History of its Fifty Years' Existence and a Record of its Measures and Leaders* (New York: G.P. Putnam's Sons, 1904), p. 207.

9. Mulkern, pp. 74–75.

10. *The Taunton Democrat*, November 17, 1854.

11. Mulkern, p. 75.

12. *The Daily Atlas*, Boston, February 1, 1855.

13. *Acts and Resolves Passed By the General Court of Massachusetts in the Year 1855* (Boston: William White, 1855), p. 494.

14. *The Barre Patriot*, Barre, Massachusetts, January 5, 1855.

15. Mulkern, p. 88.

16. *The Daily Atlas*, Boston, January 4, 1855.

17. *Acts and Resolves, 1855*, p. 993.

18. *Ibid.*

19. *Acts and Resolves, 1855*, Ch. 28, and Article XVIII.

20. *The Daily Atlas*, Boston, January 9, 1855.

21. *The Daily Atlas*, Boston, January 27, 1855.

22. *The Daily Atlas*, Boston, January 29, 1855.

23. *The Daily Atlas*, Boston, February 21, 1855.

24. *Acts and Resolves, 1855*, Ch. 124.

25. Letter, David Wilmot to Simon Cameron, 24 October 1857, Cameron Papers, Library of Congress, quoted in Mark Voss-Hubbard, *Beyond Party*, (Baltimore: Johns Hopkins University Press, 2002), p. 161.

26. *The Daily Atlas*, Boston, February 21, 1855.

27. *The Daily Atlas*, Boston, February 23 and 24, 1855.

28. *Acts and Resolves, 1855*, Ch. 489.

29. *Acts and Resolves, 1855*, p. 1009.

30. *The Daily Atlas*, Boston, May 22, 1855.

31. *Acts and Resolves, 1855*, pp. 946 and 975.

32. *The Daily Atlas*, Boston, March 24, 1855.

33. *The Daily Atlas*, Boston, March 28–30, 1855.

34. *Boston Evening Transcript*, April 20, 1855.

35. *The Daily Atlas*, Boston, April 21, 1855.

36. *The Daily Atlas*, Boston, April 27, 1855.

37. Robert L. Hampel, *Temperance and Prohibition in Massachusetts, 1813–1852* (Ann Arbor: UMI Research Press, 1982), p. 147.

38. *Ibid.*, pp. 11–24.

39. *Ibid.*, pp. 61–78.

40. *Ibid.*, pp. 147–178.

41. *The Daily Atlas*, Boston, March 9, 1855.

42. *Acts and Resolves*, 1855, Ch. 215.

43. *The Daily Atlas*, Boston, April 16, 1855.

44. Jack S. Blocker, *American Temperance Movements: Cycles of Reform* (Boston: Twayne, 1989), p. 58.

45. *Acts and Resolves, 1855*, p. 494.

Chapter 7

1. Cecil Eby, *"That Disgraceful Affair": The Black Hawk War* (New York: Norton: 1973), pp. 106–109 and 268–269.

2. W.H. Carpenter, and T.S. Arthur, *The History of Illinois from Its Earliest Settlement to the Present Time* (Philadelphia: Lippincott, Grambo, 1854), pp. 181–212.

3. *Lake Shore & Michigan Southern Railway System and Representative Employees* (Buffalo: Biographical Publishing Company, 1900), p. 36.

4. *Taunton Daily Gazette*, September 30, 1855.

5. H.W. Beckwith, *History of Iroquois County* (Chicago: H.H. Hill, 1880), p. 289.

6. *Ibid.*, p. 288.

7. Marna E. Peterson, *The Village of Loda: 1854–1976* (Cedar Falls, IA: privately published, 1875), p. 5.

8. Iroquois County, Illinois, Registry of Deeds, Book 1, page 689.

9. Iroquois County, Illinois, Registry of Deeds, Book 1, page 688.

10. Ronald C. White, *A. Lincoln* (New York: Random House, 2009), p. 216.

11. *Ibid.*, p. 229.

12. Official biography, Illinois State Library.

13. *Middleport Press*, August, 1856, quoted in Peterson, p. 6.

14. Wilbur Sauer and Shirley Johnson, *A Ticket to the Best* (Paxton, IL: Ford County Historical Society, 1989), pp. 1–7.

15. Beckwith.

16. *The Iroquois Republican*, February 17, 1859.

17. Sauer, pp. 1–7.

18. U.S. Census Bureau.

Chapter 8

1. *The Iroquois Republican*, April 1, 1858.

2. Simon, pp. 252–256.

3. United States Constitution, Article 1, Section 3, Paragraph 1.

4. Robert Walter Johannsen, *Stephen A. Douglas* (New York: Oxford University Press, 1973).

5. Mark M. Krug, "Lyman Trumbull and the Real Issues in the Lincoln-Douglas Debates," *Journal of the Illinois State Historical Society*, Vol. 57, No. 4 (Winter 1964), pp. 380–396.

6. Robert W. Johannsen, ed., *The Lincoln-Douglas Debates of 1858* (New York: Oxford University Press), 1965.

7. *Collected Works of Abraham Lincoln*, vol. 2 (Brunswick, NJ: Rutgers University Press, 1953), p. 476.

8. *The Iroquois Republican*, October 14, 1858.

9. *Ibid.*

10. McArthur, p 81.

11. *Springfield Republican*, October 1, 1858.

12. D.W. Lusk, *Politics and Politicians: A Succinct History of the Politics of Illinois from 1856 to 1884* (Springfield, IL: D.W. Lusk, 1884), pp. 42–44.

13. *Journal of the House of Representatives of the Twenty-First General Assembly of the State of Illinois* (Springfield, IL: Bailhache & Baker, 1859), p. 4.

14. *Chicago Times*, January 13, 1859.

15. *Journal of the House of Representatives of the Twenty-First General Assembly of the State of Illinois*, pp. 20–29.

16. *Chicago Times*, January 13, 1859.

17. *Journal of the House of Representatives of the Twenty-First General Assembly of the State of Illinois*, p. 32.

18. See Chapter 9.

19. *The Iroquois Republican*, January 21, 1859.

20. *Journal of the House of Representatives of the Twenty-First General Assembly of the State of Illinois*, p. 432.

21. *The Iroquois Republican*, February 17, 1859.

22. Hood vs. Hood, Kane County, IL Circuit Court, May Term, 1861, case #7771.

23. Anna M. Hood vs. James M. Hood, Bristol County Circuit Court, MA, October Term, 1865.

24. U.S. Census, 1860.

25. Adam Goodheart, *1861: The Civil War Awakening* (New York: Alfred Knopf, 2011), p. 35.

26. *Ibid.*, p. 34.

27. Peterson, p. 12.

28. Marriage certificate, J.M. Hood and S. Botsford, May 24, 1861.

29. Anna M. Hood vs. James M. Hood, Bristol County Circuit Court, MA, October Term, 1865.

30. Hood vs. Hood, Kane County, IL Circuit Court, May Term, 1861, case #7771.

31. Obituary, Sarah A. Brown, Joiner Historical Room, Sycamore Library, Sycamore, Illinois.

32. Donald L. Jacobus and Otis M. Botsford, *An American Family* (privately published, 1933), p. 57.

33. Goodheart, pp. 350–351.

34. J.N. Reece, *Report of the Adjutant General of the State of Illinois*, rev. ed. (Springfield, IL: Phillips Bros., 1900), Vol. 8, p. 222.

35. *Sycamore True Republican*, March 23, 1895.

36. O.T. Willard Scrapbook, Joiner Historical Room, Sycamore Public Library, Sycamore, Illinois.

Chapter 9

1. Letter, J.F. Farnsworth et al. to A. Lincoln, January 1854, Letters of Application and Recommendations During the Administration of Abraham Lincoln and Andrew Jackson, 1861–1869, M650, NARA.

2. Lusk, pp. 519–520.

3. Letter, J.F. Farnsworth et al. to A. Lincoln, January 1854.

4. Eldon Griffin, *Clippers and Consuls:*

American Consular and Commercial Relations with Eastern Asia, 1845–1860 (Wilmington, DE: Scholarly Resources, 1972), p. 104.

5. *Sycamore True Republican*, reprinted April 13, 1895.

6. *Ibid.*

7. U.S. Senate Journal, April 21, 1864.

8. Senate Executive Document 107, 34th Congress, 1st Session, Part III, *Consular Returns*, 1855, p. 653.

9. Robert White Stevens, *On the Stowage of Ships and Their Cargoes* (London: Longmans, Green, Reader & Dyer, 1871), p. 399.

10. David P. Werlich, *Peru: A Short History* (Carbondale: Southern Illinois University Press, 1978), p. 99.

11. *United States Consul's Manual*, p. 400.

12. U.S. Senate Journal, May 18, 1864 and January 16, 1865.

13. F.W. Seward to G.W. Virgin, October 1864, Instructions to the U.S. Consul at Bangkok, Siam, 1857–1912, RG 85, T403, NARA.

14. List of U.S. Consular Officers, RG 84, MS87, NARA.

15. J.M. Hood, Despatch No. 1, Despatches from U.S. Consuls.

16. *Sycamore True Republican*, April 16, 1870.

17. *United States Consul's Manual*, Sec. 306, p. 126.

18. Letter, J.M. Hood to J.F. Farnsworth, Letters of Application.

19. Letter, R.E. Tucker to J.F. Farnsworth, Letters of Application.

20. F.W. Seward to J.M. Hood, Despatch No. 7, Instructions to the U.S. Consul, op. cit.

21. J.M. Hood, Despatches No. 2, 3, & 4, Despatches from U.S. Consuls.

22. J.M. Hood, Despatch No. 4, Despatches from U.S. Consuls.

23. F.W. Seward to J.M. Hood, Despatch No. 10, Instructions to the U.S. Consul.

24. J.M. Hood, Despatches No. 5 & 6, Despatches from U.S. Consuls.

25. J.M. Hood, Despatches No. 5, 8, & 10, Despatches from U.S. Consuls.

26. J.M. Hood, Despatch No.9, Despatches from U.S. Consuls.

27. Letter, F. Mauran to H.B. Anthony, Letters of Application.

28. Endorsement of H.B. Anthony, Letters of Application.

29. J.M. Hood, Despatch No.10, Despatches from U.S. Consuls.

30. J.M. Hood, Despatch No.9, Despatches from U.S. Consuls.

31. *Papers Relating to Foreign Affairs Accompanying the Annual Message of the President to the First Session of the Thirty-Eighth Congress* (Washington, D.C.: Government Printing Office, 1864).

32. Lagrange, pp. 99–100.

33. The Maritime History Virtual Archives, http://www.bruzelius.info/Nautica/Nautica.html.

34. Crothers, p. xviii.

35. Bradley, p. 118.

36. *Ibid.*, p. 95.

37. This trial and its consequences, including accusations that Captain Hood had predetermined the outcome of the trial after meeting Burdon, are discussed in detail in Chapter 11.

38. *New York Times*, January 7, 1865.

39. See Chapter 11.

40. *New York Times*, April 9, 1865.

41. *New York Times*, August 30, 1865.

42. Anna M. Hood vs. James M. Hood, Bristol County Circuit Court, October Term, 1865.

43. *New York Times*, September 21, 1865.

44. List of U.S. Consular Officers, RG 84, MS87, NARA.

45. Bradley, p. 20.

46. Article reprinted in the *Sycamore True Republican*, December 20, 1905; *Bangkok Recorder*, September 1865; and diary of Dr. Dan Beach Bradley, RG 30/5, Oberlin College Archives.

47. Reprinted in the *Sycamore True Republican*, December 20, 1905.

Chapter 10

1. Diary of Dr. Dan Beach Bradley, RG 30/5, Oberlin College Archives.

2. Noah A. McDonald, *A Missionary in Siam*, orig. pub. 1871 (Bangkok: White Lotus, 1999), p. 15.

3. J.M. Hood, Despatch No. 11, Despatches from U.S. Consuls.

4. Bradley, p. 140.

5. J.M. Hood, Inventory accompanying Despatch No. 11, Despatches from U.S. Consuls.

6. Griffin, p. 47.

7. Bradley, p. 95.

8. *Ibid.*, pp. 96–97.

9. *Ibid.*, pp. 51–56.

10. *Ibid.*, p. 96.

11. Bradley diary.

12. David K. Wyatt, *Thailand: A Short History* (New Haven: Yale University Press, 1984), p. 63.

13. McDonald, p. 52.

14. Bradley diary.

15. Bradley, p. 110.

16. J.M. Hood, Despatch No. 13, Despatches from U.S. Consuls.

17. *United States Consul's Manual*, Sec. 30, p. 16.

18. J.M. Hood, Despatch No. 13, Despatches from U.S. Consuls.

19. J.M. Hood, Despatch No. 59, Despatches from U.S. Consuls.

20. J.M. Hood, Despatch No. 12, Despatches from U.S. Consuls.

21. Moffat.

22. Robert R. Davis, Jr., "Diplomatic Plumage: American Court Dress in the Early National Period," *American Quarterly*, Vol. 20, No. 2, Part 1 (Summer 1968), pp. 164–179.

23. *Ibid.*

24. Bradley diary.

25. J.M. Hood, Despatch No. 12, Despatches from U.S. Consuls.

26. Bradbury, p. 8.

27. J.M. Hood, Attachment to Despatch No. 12, Despatches from U.S. Consuls.

28. Bradley diary.

29. J.M. Hood, Despatch No. 12, Despatches from U.S. Consuls.

30. Thomson.

31. Kenneth P. Landon, "Thailand's Quarrel with France in Perspective," *The Far Eastern Quarterly*, Vol. 1, No. 1 (November 1941), pp. 25–42.

32. J.M. Hood, Despatch No. 15, Despatches from U.S. Consuls.

33. J.M. Hood, Despatch No. 16, Despatches from U.S. Consuls.

34. J.M. Hood, Despatch No. 14, Despatches from U.S. Consuls.

35. J.M. Hood, Report accompanying Despatch No. 24, Despatches from U.S. Consuls.

36. *United States Consul's Manual*, pp. 3–17.

37. J.M. Hood, Report accompanying Despatch No. 24, Despatches from U.S. Consuls.

38. J.M. Hood, Despatch No. 18, Despatches from U.S. Consuls.

39. *Ibid.*

40. Letter, J.M. Hood to H.B. Anthony, Letters of Application.

41. Despatch, Fifth Auditor, U.S. Treasury Department to J.M. Hood, April 6, 1866.

Chapter 11

1. Bradley, p. 55.

2. Edwin T. Freedley, *Leading Pursuits and Leading Men: A Treatise on the Principal Trades and Manufactures of the United States* (Philadelphia: Edward Young, 1856), p. 290.

3. Unless otherwise noted, all quotes in this chapter are taken from J.M. Hood, Despatch No. 31, and the transcript of the record of the trial that was attached to it, Despatches from U.S. Consuls.

4. *United States Consul's Manual*, Sec. 136, p. 59, and Sec. 198–200, pp. 84–86.

5. *Bangkok Recorder*, December 14, 1865.

6. Bradley diary.

7. Bradley, p. 123.

8. Bradley diary.

9. J.M. Hood, Despatch No. 31, Despatches from U.S. Consuls.

Chapter 12

1. China Williams, *Thailand* (Oakland: Lonely Planet, 2009), p. 473.

2. John M. Thompson, *Buddhism* (Westport, CT: Greenwood Press, 2006), p. 148.

3. J.M. Hood, Despatch No. 22, Despatches from U.S. Consuls.

4. *Ibid.*

5. J.M. Hood, Report accompanying Despatch No. 24, Despatches From U.S. Consuls, op. cit.

6. *Ibid.*

7. The Sina bodi, literally "great courtiers," were the officers of the royal court (McDonald, p. 17).

8. J.M. Hood, Report accompanying Despatch No. 24, Despatches from U.S. Consuls.

9. *Ibid.*

10. Bradley diary.

11. J.M. Hood, letter to King Mongkut, Despatches from U.S. Consuls.

12. J.M. Hood, Report accompanying Despatch No. 24, Despatches from U.S. Consuls.

13. *Ibid.*

14. J.M. Hood, Despatch No. 25, Despatches from U.S. Consuls.

15. Bradley, pp. 70–73 and 75–79.

16. J.M. Hood, attachment D to Despatch No. 30, Despatches from U.S. Consuls.

17. J.M. Hood, attachment A to Despatch No. 30, Despatches from U.S. Consuls.

18. J.M. Hood, Despatch No. 33, Despatches from U.S. Consuls.

19. J.M. Hood, attachment A to Despatch No. 32, Despatches from U.S. Consuls.

20. J.M. Hood, Despatch No. 34, Despatches from U.S. Consuls.

21. Letter, D.B. Bradley to King Mongkut, April 9, 1866, Oberlin College Archives.

22. *Ibid.*

23. J.M. Hood, Despatch No. 40, Despatches from U.S. Consuls.

24. *Ibid.*

25. *Ibid.*

26. *Ibid.*

27. J.M. Hood, Despatch No. 49, Despatches from U.S. Consuls.

28. J.M. Hood, Despatch No. 39, Despatches from U.S. Consuls.

29. F.W. Seward, Despatch No. 22, Instructions to the U.S. Consul, op. cit.

30. J.M. Hood, Despatch No. 41, Despatches from U.S. Consuls.

31. S. Visconti, attachment to J.M. Hood, Despatch No. 41, Despatches from U.S. Consuls.

32. J.M. Hood, Despatch No. 45, Despatches from U.S. Consuls.

33. Bradley diary.

34. J.M. Hood, Despatch No. 46, Despatches from U.S. Consuls.

35. J.M. Hood, Despatch No. 47, Despatches from U.S. Consuls.

36. J.M. Hood, Despatch No. 48, Despatches from U.S. Consuls.

Chapter 13

1. Lawrence P. Briggs, "Aubaret and the Treaty of July 15, 1867 Between France and Siam," *The Far Eastern Quarterly*, Vol. 6, No. 2 (Feb. 1947), pp. 122–138.

2. *Bangkok Recorder*, May 1, 1866.

3. *Bangkok Recorder*, May 16, 1866.

4. *Bangkok Recorder*, June 1, 1866.

5. Unless otherwise noted, all quotes in this chapter attributed to D.B. Bradley are from his diary.

6. J.M. Hood, attachment D to Despatch No. 30, Despatches from U.S. Consuls.

7. Thomson.

8. J.M. Hood, Despatch No. 30, Despatches from U.S. Consuls.

9. Bradley diary.

10. Letter, D.B. Bradley to King Mongkut, April 9, 1866, Oberlin College Archives.

11. Guanzhong Luo, *Romance of the Three Kingdoms*, trans. C.H. Brewitt-Taylor (Rutland, VT: C. E. Tuttle, 1959).

12. Thanapol Limapichart, *The Prescription of Good Books*, Ph.D. Thesis, University of Wisconsin, 2008, p. 56.

13. J.M. Hood, Despatch No. 38, Despatches from U.S. Consuls.

14. Letter, D.B. Bradley to King Mongkut, August 7, 1866, Oberlin College Archives.

15. Bradley diary.

16. J.M. Hood, Despatch No. 41, Despatches from U.S. Consuls.

17. *Bangkok Recorder*, December 20, 1866.

18. *Bangkok Recorder*, January 16, 1867.

19. U.S. Naval History and Heritage Command.

20. Bradley diary.

21. *Ibid.*

22. The trial is described in an attachment to J.M. Hood, Despatch No. 52.

23. King James Bible, Romans 89: 33–35.

24. L.P. Briggs, "The Aubaret Versus Bradley Case at Bangkok, 1866–1867," *Far Eastern Quarterly*, VI (1947), 262–281.

25. A. Leonowens, *The English Governess at the Court of Siam* (London: Trubner & Co., 1870), p. 285.

Chapter 14

1. F.W. Seward, Despatch No. 26, Instructions to the U.S. Consul.

2. J.M. Hood, Despatch No. 49, Despatches from U.S. Consuls.

3. Bradley diary.

4. *Ibid.*

5. J.M. Hood, Despatch No. 55, Despatches from U.S. Consuls.

6. *United States Consul's Manual*, Sec.635, p. 260.

7. J.M. Hood, Despatch No. 59, Despatches from U.S. Consuls.

8. Letter, W. Dean et al. to Department of State, attachment to J.M. Hood, Despatch No. 59, Despatches from U.S. Consuls.

9. *United States Consul's Manual*, Ch. 10, p. 111.

10. Letter, N.A. McDonald to Department of State, attachment to J.M. Hood, Despatch No. 59, Despatches from U.S. Consuls.

11. Bradley diary.

12. Bradley diary.

13. Leonowens, A., op. cit., p. 285.

14. Bradley diary.

15. J.M. Hood, Despatch No. 61, Despatches from U.S. Consuls.

16. Letter, J. Campbell to the Department of State, attachment to J.M. Hood, Despatch No. 61, Despatches from U.S. Consuls.

17. J.M. Hood, Despatch No. 66, Despatches from U.S. Consuls.

18. J.M. Hood, Despatch No. 72, Despatches from U.S. Consuls.

19. Bradley diary.

20. King James Bible, Psalm 37: 1.

21. Bradley, pp. 146–147.

22. Bradley diary.

23. *Ibid.*

24. F.W. Seward, Despatch No. 40, Instructions to the U.S. Consul.

25. J.M. Hood, Despatch No. 73, Despatches from U.S. Consuls.

Chapter 15

1. Bradley diary.

2. *Daily Evening Bulletin*, San Francisco, March 7, 1868.

3. Crothers, p. xvii

4. *Daily Evening Bulletin*, San Francisco, March 7, 1868.

5. U.S. District Court, District of Massachusetts, Case No. 918, 1868.

6. Albert B. Paine, *Mark Twain's Letters* (New York: Harper & Brothers, 1917), p. 152.

7. This is derived from the shipping news as reported in the *Daily Evening Bulletin*, San Francisco. Given the Hoods' arrival date in San Francisco and their departure date from Aspinwall, Panama (see note 9), the *Sacramento* is the only ship they could have sailed on.

8. John H. Kemble, *The Panama Route, 1848–1869* (Berkeley: University of California Press, 1943), p. 244.

9. Passenger list, *S.S. Henry Chauncey*, April 28, 1868.

10. Kemble, p. 230.

11. Passenger list, *S.S. Henry Chauncey.*

12. U.S. District Court, District of Massachusetts, Case No. 918, 1868. All of the information relating to this bankruptcy is taken from the court papers for this case, obtained from NARA.

13. *Ibid.*

14. Letter, J.M. Hood to the Department of State, July 16, 1868.

15. Letters, J.M. Hood to the Department of State, December 16, 1868 and March 23, 1869.

16. Letter, J.M. Hood to the Department of State, July 16, 1868.

17. F.W. Seward, Despatch to N.A. McDonald, Instructions to the U.S. Consul.

18. Letter, D.B. Bradley to W.H. Seward, December 18, 1868.

19. Letter, J.M. Hood to the Department of State, December 16, 1868.

20. *Journal of the House of Representatives of the United States, 1868–1869*, Monday, December 14, 1868.

21. Letter, G. Graham to W.H. Seward, December 1868.

22. Letter, J.H. Chandler to W.H. Seward, December 1868.

23. Moffat, pp. 169–181.

24. Wyatt, pp. 191–192.

25. Letter, J.M. Hood to E.B. Washburne, March 4, 1869, in Letters of Resignation and Declination of Federal Office, 1789–1895, Record Group 59, NARA.

26. *Sycamore True Republican*, December 15, 1869.

27. *Sycamore True Republican*, February 26, 1870.

28. *Sycamore True Republican*, May 24, 1871, obituary of J.M. Hood.

29. *Sycamore True Republican*, April 27, 1870.

30. History of the Marsh Harvester Company, Northern Illinois University Digital Library, http://dig.lib.niu.edu/dekalb/hist-marsh.html.

31. *Sycamore True Republican*, November 16, 1870.

32. DeKalb County Registry of Deeds, Book 50, pp. 438, 400 and 442.

33. *Sycamore True Republican*, November 16, 1870.

34. O.T. Willard Scrapbook, Joiner Historical Room, Sycamore Public Library, Sycamore, Illinois.

35. *Sycamore True Republican*, March 9, 1870.

36. *Sycamore True Republican*, March 16, 1870.

37. *Sycamore True Republican*, July 13, 1870.

38. *Sycamore True Republican*, August 31, 1870.

39. *Sycamore True Republican*, March 9, 1870.

40. *Sycamore True Republican*, February 23, 1870.

41. *Sycamore True Republican*, August 17, 1870.

42. *Sycamore True Republican*, October 8, 1870.

43. Howe and Matthews, p. 401.

44. Bradbury, p. 95.

45. *Sycamore True Republican*, June 15, 1870.

46. *Sycamore True Republican*, August 31, 1870.

47. Nancy M. Beasley and S.J. Bigolin, *Sycamore: A Walk Through History* (Sycamore, IL: The Ten-Bit Committee, 1983), p. 27.

48. *Sycamore True Republican*, February 26, 1870.

49. Reece, Vol. 1, p. 179.

50. *Sycamore True Republican*, March 9, 1870.

51. *Sycamore True Republican*, July 27, 1870.

52. *Sycamore True Republican*, May 24, 1871.

53. *Ibid.*

Chapter 16

1. Will Book 1, page 139, Joiner History Room, Sycamore Library, Sycamore, IL.

2. U.S. Census, Sycamore, IL, 1870.

3. DeKalb County Registry of Deeds, Book 141, p. 52.

4. DeKalb County Registry of Deeds, Book 52, p. 129.

5. *Sycamore True Republican*, May 4 and May 8, 1872.

6. Reece, Vol. 5, p. 665.

7. *Sycamore True Republican*, August 31, 1887.

8. Obituary, Sarah A. Brown, Joiner Historical Room, Sycamore Library, Sycamore, Illinois.

9. Hood vs. Hood, Bristol County Superior Court, October Term 1872.

10. Gravestone, Anna Moison, Center Street Cemetery, Dighton, MA.

Bibliography

Books

Arnold, James N. *Vital Record of Rhode Island, First Series*. Providence, RI: Narragansett Historical Publishing Company, 1896.

Bauer, K. Jack. *Surfboats and Horse Marines: U.S. Naval Operations in the Mexican War, 1846–1848*. Annapolis, MD: United States Naval Institute, 1969.

Beasley, Nancy M., and S.J. Bigolin. *Sycamore: A Walk Through History*. Sycamore, IL: The Ten-Bit Committee, 1983.

Beckwith, H.W. *History of Iroquois County*. Chicago: H.H. Hill, 1880.

Beers & Co. *Representative Men and Old Families of Southeastern Massachusetts*. Chicago: J.H. Beers, 1912.

Bennett, Edward H. *Fire Insurance Cases*. New York: Hurd and Houghton, 1874.

Blocker, Jack S. *American Temperance Movements: Cycles of Reform*. Boston: Twayne, 1989.

Blunt, Joseph, *The Shipmaster's Assistant and Commercial Digest*. New York: E. & G.W. Blunt, 1837.

Bosson, Mary Jane (Jennie) Hood. *John Hood of Lynn, Massachusetts and Some of His Descendants*. Salem, MA: Essex Institute, 1909.

Bradbury, James E. *Seafarers of Somerset*. Somerset, MA: privately published, 1996.

Bradley, William L. *Siam Then*. Pasadena: William Carey Library, 1981.

Carpenter, W.H., and T.S. Arthur. *The History of Illinois from Its Earliest Settlement to the Present Time*. Philadelphia: Lippincott, Grambo, 1854.

Clark, Arthur H. *The Clipper Ship Era*. New York: G.P. Putnam's Sons, 1920.

Crothers, William L. *The American Built Clipper Ship: 1850–1856*. Camden, ME: International Marine, 1996.

Curtis, Francis. *The Republican Party: A History of its Fifty Years' Existence and a Record of its Measures and Leaders*. New York: G.P. Putnam's Sons, 1904.

Cutler, Carl. *Greyhounds of the Sea*. New York: G.P. Putnam's Sons, 1930.

Eby, Cecil. *"That Disgraceful Affair": The Black Hawk War*. New York: Norton, 1973.

Fiore, Jordan. *Abraham Lincoln Visits The Old Colony*. Taunton, MA: The Old Colony Historical Society, 1978.

Freedley, Edwin T. *Leading Pursuits and Leading Men: A Treatise on the Principal Trades and Manufactures of the United States*. Philadelphia: Edward Young, 1856.

Frothingham, Louis Adams. *A Brief History of the Constitution and Government of Massachusetts, with a Chapter on Legislative Procedure*. Cambridge: Harvard University, 1916.

Goodheart, Adam. *1861: The Civil War*

Awakening. New York: Alfred Knopf, 2011.

Griffin, Eldon. *Clippers and Consuls: American Consular and Commercial Relations with Eastern Asia, 1845–1860.* Wilmington, DE: Scholarly Resources, 1972.

Grifiths, J.W. *Treatise on Marine and Naval Architecture,* New York: D. Appleton and Company, 1854.

Griffiths, John W. *The Ship-Builder's Manual and Nautical Referee.* New York: J.W. Griffiths, 1853.

Hampel, Robert L., *Temperance and Prohibition in Massachusetts, 1813–1852.* Ann Arbor: UMI Research Press, 1982.

Hanna, William. *Abraham Among the Yankees.* Taunton, MA: The Old Colony Historical Society, 1983.

Hart, William A. *History of the Town of Somerset.* Somerset, MA: Town of Somerset, 1940.

Holt, Michael F. *The Rise and Fall of the American Whig Party: Jacksonian Politics and the Onset of the Civil War.* New York: Oxford University Press, 1999.

Howe, George. *Mount Hope: A New England Chronicle.* New York: Viking Press, 1959.

Howe, Octavious T., and Frederick C. Matthews. *American Clipper Ships: 1833–1858.* New York: Argosy Antiquarian, 1967.

Hurd, D. Hamilton. *History of Bristol County, Massachusetts.* Philadelphia: J.W. Lewis, 1883.

Jacobus, Donald L., and Otis M. Botsford. *An American Family.* Privately published, 1933.

Johannsen, Robert W., ed. *The Lincoln-Douglas Debates of 1858.* New York, Oxford University Press, 1965.

Johannsen, Robert Walter. *Stephen A. Douglas.* New York: Oxford University Press, 1973.

Kemble, John H. *The Panama Route, 1848–1869.* Berkeley: University of California Press, 1943.

Kennedy, Edward F. *The Crockers of*

Taunton. Taunton, MA: The Old Colony Historical Society, 1988.

Lagrange, Helen, and Jacques Lagrange. *Clipper Ships of America and Great Britain: 1833–1869.* New York: G. P. Putnam's Sons, 1936.

Lake Shore & Michigan Southern Railway System and Representative Employees. Buffalo: Biographical Publishing Company, 1900.

Landon, Margaret. *Anna and the King of Siam.* New York: John Day, 1944.

Leonowens, Anna. *The English Governess at the Court of Siam.* London: Trubner & Co., 1870.

Limapichart, Thanapol. *The Prescription of Good Books.* Ph.D. Thesis, University of Wisconsin, 2008.

Lincoln, Abraham. *Collected Works of Abraham Lincoln.* New Brunswick, NJ: Rutgers University Press, 1953.

Luo, Guanzhong. *Romance of the Three Kingdoms.* Trans. C. H. Brewitt-Taylor. Rutland, VT: C. E. Tuttle, 1959.

Lusk, D.W. *Politics and Politicians: A Succinct History of the Politics of Illinois from 1856 to 1884.* Springfield, IL: D.W. Lusk, 1884.

Luther, Leslie. *The Luther Family in America.* Moravia, NY: privately printed, 1976.

MacGregor, David. *The Tea Clippers.* London: Conway Maritime Press, 1983.

Massachusetts, Office of the Secretary of the Commonwealth. *Massachusetts Soldiers and Sailors in the Revolution.* Boston: Wright and Potter Printing Co., State Printers, 1896–1908.

McAdam, Roger W. *Salts of the Sound.* New York: Stephen Daye Press, 1957.

McArthur, Debra. *The Kansas-Nebraska Act and "Bleeding Kansas" in American History.* Berkeley Heights, NJ: Enslow, 2003.

McDonald, Noah A. *A Missionary in Siam.* 1871. Bangkok: White Lotus, 1999.

McGrane, Reginald C. *The Panic of 1837: Some Financial Problems of the Jack-*

sonian Era. New York: Russell & Russell, 1965.

Moffat, Abbott Low. *Mongkut, the King of Siam*. Ithaca: Cornell University Press, 1961.

Morgan, John S. *Robert Fulton*. New York: Mason/Charter, 1977.

Mulkern, John R. *The Know-Nothing Party in Massachusetts: The Rise and Fall of a People's Movement*. Boston: Northeastern University Press, 1990.

Paine, Albert B. *Mark Twain's Letters*. New York: Harper & Brothers, 1917.

Paine, Ralph D. *The Old Merchant Marine, A Chronicle of American Ships and Sailors*. New Haven: Yale University Press, 1919.

Peterson, Marna E. *The Village of Loda: 1854–1976*. Cedar Falls, IA: privately published, 1875.

Poor, Henry V. *History of the Railroads and Canals of the United States of America*. New York: John H. Schultz, 1860.

Ranlett, Charles Everett. *Master Mariner of Maine*. Portland, ME: The Southworth-Anthoensen Press, 1942.

Reece, J.N. *Report of the Adjutant General of the State of Illinois*, rev. ed. Springfield, IL: Phillips Bros., 1900.

Sauer, Wilbur, and Shirley Johnson. *A Ticket to the Best*. Paxton, IL: Ford County Historical Society, 1989.

Simon, Paul. *Lincoln's Preparation for Greatness: The Illinois Legislative Years*. Urbana: University of Illinois Press, 1971.

Smith, Justin H. *The War with Mexico*. New York: MacMillan, 1919.

Sprague, William F. *Barnstaple and Yarmouth Sea Captains and Ship Owners*. Boston: privately printed, 1913.

Stevens, Robert White. *On the Stowage of Ships and Their Cargoes*. London: Longmans, Green, Reader & Dyer, 1871.

Thompson, John M. *Buddhism*. Westport, CT: Greenwood Press, 2006.

Von Frank, Albert J. *The Trials of Anthony Burns: Freedom and Slavery in Emerson's Boston*. Cambridge: Harvard University Press, 1998.

Voss-Hubbard, Mark. *Beyond Party: Cultures of Antipartisanship in Northern Politics Before the Civil War*. Baltimore: Johns Hopkins University Press, 2002.

Werlich, David P. *Peru: A Short History*. Carbondale: Southern Illinois University Press, 1978.

White, Ronald C. *A. Lincoln*. New York: Random House, 2009.

Williams, China, *Thailand*. Oakland: Lonely Planet, 2009.

Woodman, Richard. *The History of the Ship*. New York: Lyons Press, 1997.

Wyatt, David K. *Thailand: A Short History*. New Haven: Yale University Press, 1984.

Articles

Briggs, Lawrence P. "Aubaret and the Treaty of July 15, 1867 Between France and Siam." *The Far Eastern Quarterly*, Vol. 6, No. 2 (Feb. 1947), pp. 122–138.

_____. "The Aubaret Versus Bradley Case at Bangkok, 1866–1867." *Far Eastern Quarterly*, VI (1947), 262–281.

Davis, Jr., Robert R. "Diplomatic Plumage: American Court Dress in the Early National Period." *American Quarterly*, Vol. 20, No. 2, Part 1 (Summer 1968), pp. 164–179.

Hickey, Donald R. "American Trade Restrictions during the War of 1812." *The Journal of American History*, Vol. 68, No. 3 (Dec. 1981), pp. 517–538.

Krug, Mark M. "Lyman Trumbull and the Real Issues in the Lincoln-Douglas Debates." *Journal of the Illinois State Historical Society*, Vol. 57, No. 4 (Winter 1964).

Landon, Kenneth P. "Thailand's Quarrel with France in Perspective." *Far Eastern Quarterly*, Vol. 1, No. 1 (November 1941).

Salvucci, Linda K. "Atlantic Intersections: Early American Commerce and the

Rise of the Spanish West Indies." *The Business History Review*, Vol. 79, No. 4 (Winter 2005), pp. 781–809.

Thomson, R. Stanley. "The Diplomacy of Imperialism: France and Spain in Cochin China, 1858–63." *The Journal of Modern History*, Vol. 12, No. 3 (Sep. 1940), pp. 334–356.

Manuscripts

Bradley, Dr. Dan Beach. Diary, RG 30/5, Oberlin College Archives.

_____. Letters, RG 30/5, Oberlin College Archives.

Despatches from U.S. Consuls in Bangkok, Siam 1856–1906, RG 84, M448, NARA.

Instructions to the U.S. Consul at Bangkok, Siam, 1857–1912, RG 85, T403, NARA.

Letters of Application and Recommendations During the Administration of Abraham Lincoln and Andrew Jackson, 1861–1869, M650, NARA.

Letters of Resignation and Declination of Federal Office, 1789–1895, Record Group 59, NARA.

O.T. Willard Scrapbook, Joiner Historical Room, Sycamore Public Library, Sycamore, Illinois.

Passenger list, S.S. *Henry Chauncey*, April 28, 1868.

Passenger manifest of the Brig *James*, May 10, 1823.

Records of the Fall River Customs District, RG 36, NARA, Waltham, Massachusetts.

Revolutionary War Pension Application, Mary Peck, widow of Peleg Peck, RG 21, NARA, Waltham, Massachusetts.

Ship manifests, Fall River Customs District, RG 36, NARA, Waltham, Massachusetts.

Newspapers

The Albion, New York
American Whig, Taunton, Massachusetts
Argus, Melbourne, Australia
Baltimore Patriot
Bangkok Recorder
The Barre Patriot, Barre, Massachusetts
Boston Commercial Gazette
Boston Courier
Boston Evening Transcript
Chicago Times
Columbian Centinel, Boston
The Daily Atlas, Boston
Daily Evening Bulletin, San Francisco
Gazette, Edenton, North Carolina
Hunt's Merchants' Magazine and Commercial Review, New York
The Iroquois Republican, Middleport, Illinois
Massachusetts Spy, Worcester
Milwaukee Sentinel
National Aegis, Cambridge, Massachusetts
New Bedford Mercury, New Bedford, Massachusetts
New York Times
Newport Mercury, Newport, Rhode Island
Ohio Statesman, Columbus
Pensacola Democrat, Pensacola, Florida
The Pittsfield Sun, Pittsfield, Massachusetts
Providence Gazette, Providence, Rhode Island
Providence Patriot, Providence, Rhode Island
Providence Post, Providence, Rhode Island
Rhode-Island American and Providence Gazette, Providence, Rhode Island
Springfield Republican, Springfield, Massachusetts
The Sun, Baltimore
Sycamore True Republican, Sycamore, Illinois
Taunton Gazette, Taunton, Massachusetts
Taunton Whig, Taunton, Massachusetts
The Taunton Democrat, Taunton, Massachusetts
The Times, London
Times-Picayune, New Orleans

Government Documents

Acts and Resolves Passed By the General Court of Massachusetts in the Year 1854. Boston: William White, 1854.

Acts and Resolves Passed By the General Court of Massachusetts in the Year 1855. Boston: William White, 1855.

Bristol County, Massachusetts, Registry of Deeds, Records.

Bristol County Circuit Court, Massachusetts, Records.

Bristol County Superior Court, Massachusetts, Records.

Cutter History File, Coast Guard Historian's Office, USCG HQ.

DeKalb County, Illinois, Registry of Deeds, Records.

DeKalb County, Illinois, Will Books, Sycamore Library, Sycamore, Illinois.

Iroquois County, Illinois, Registry of Deeds, Records.

Journal of the House of Representatives of the Twenty-First General Assembly of the State of Illinois (Springfield, Illinois: Bailhache & Baker, 1859).

Kane County, Illinois, Circuit Court, Records.

Lightship History File, Coast Guard Historian's Office, USCG HQ.

List of U.S. Consular Officers, RG 84, MS87, NARA.

Military Sea Transportation and Shipping Control, Bureau of Naval Personnel, Navpers 10829-A, Washington, D.C., 1954.

Official Report of the Debates and Proceedings in the State Convention Assembled May 4th, 1853 to Revise and Amend the Constitution of the Commonwealth of Massachusetts (Boston: White & Potter, 1853).

Papers Relating to Foreign Affairs Accompanying the Annual Message of the President to the First Session of the Thirty-Eighth Congress (Washington, D.C.: Government Printing Office, 1864).

Ship Registers of Dighton-Fall River 1783–1938, The National Archives Project, NARA, 1939.

Somerset, Massachusetts, Town Records.

Supreme Judicial Court of Massachusetts, Records.

Treaty Between the United States and the First and Second Kings of Siam, 1856.

U.S. Census Records, NARA.

U.S. District Court, District of Rhode Island, Records.

U.S. District Court, District of Massachusetts, Records.

United States Constitution.

United States Consul's Manual, 2nd Edition, Washington, DC: Hudson Taylor, 1863.

Vital Records of Swansea Massachusetts to 1850, transcribed by H.L. Peter Rounds, 1992.

Websites

Biographical Directory of the United States Congress, http://bioguide.congress.gov.

Guilford Transportation/Pan Am Railways website, http://panamrailways.com/Maps/Map.pdf.

History of the Marsh Harvester Company, Northern Illinois University Digital Library, http://dig.lib.niu.edu/dekalb/hist-marsh.html.

Library of Congress, Journals of Congress, http://memory.loc.gov/ammem/amlaw/lwjrnl.html.

Measuring Worth, http:/www.measuringworth.com.

The Maritime History Virtual Archives, http://www.bruzelius.info/Nautica/Nautica.html.

U.S. Naval History and Heritage Command, http://www.history.navy.mil/.

Index

233

French-Siamese treaties 130, 162–163
fugitive slaves 85

Gardner, Henry 79–81
Goldsborough, John 173–174, 177–178
Governor Morton 46, 60, 204
Graham, George 150, 200
Greenfield 44, 46, 60
Griffiths, John Willis 47
Gurvey, Michael 178, 193
Gyre, Francisco D. & Co. 27

Harris, Townsend 6, 121
S.S. *Henry Chauncy* 197
Herndon, William 94
Higgins, William 184, 192
Hood, Alfred H. 59, 196
Hood, Anna Moison 25, 27, 104, 118, 209–210
Hood, Elisha 92, 106
Hood, George B. 25, 27, 34, 54, 62
Hood, James Madison 6, 66, 106, 202; ancestry 15; arrival in Bangkok 5; audience with King Mongkut 126–130; bankruptcies 26–27, 58–59, 197–198; Baptist Church 18, 201; birth 13; consular appointment 108–111; consular finances 131–132, 135–136; death 207; divorce 105; fires 41–42, 55–58, 110; house in Sycamore 205; Illinois legislature campaign 100–101; leave of absence 192, 195, 198–199; marriage to Anna Moison 25; marriage to Sarah Botsford 105; private relief bill 200; resignation 201; separation from Anna Moison 104; threatened by Capt. Jones 53; travel home 196–197; travel to Siam 113–119
Hood, James Madison, Jr. 26, 28
Hood, John 13, 17, 62
Hood, Mary Ann Bowers 13, 32
Hood, Noble 16–19
Hood, Noble, Jr. 18
Hood, Sarah Botsford 8, 105–106, 208–209
Hood, William Perry 34, 55, 56–58, 93
Hoosac Tunnel 67
Horation Ames 54
Hornet 115
House, Samuel 178

Illinois Central Railroad 92, 95, 102, 105
Illinois Legislature 102–104
Independence 25
Insurance Company Regulations 67–68, 82–84
Isaac Hicks 26

J.C. Dobbin (cutter) 50, 60
J.C. Jewett & Co. 115
Jackmel Packet 153–154
Jackson, Andrew 62
James C. Campbell (cutter) 50, 60
Jefferson Davis (cutter) 50, 60
Johnson, Andrew 24, 117
Jones, Ezekiel 53

Kansas-Nebraska Act 69–72, 100
Kimball, William 82
King Fisher 196
Know-Nothing Party 77; Massachusetts convention 79
Knox, Thomas 8, 171
Kralahom Sri Suriyawongse 169, 200
Krom Luang Womsa 157

Lady Adams 54
Lamache, M. 163
Lamar Insurance Company 201
Lazarus, Aaron 27
Lecompton Bill 101
Leonowens, Anna 8, 169, 175–177, 181, 190
Lincoln, Abraham 109; assassination 6, 117; Black Hawk War 90; Douglas debates 100; and Know-Nothings 77; in Massachusetts 36–38; presidential nomination 105; Republican Party 94; Senate race 99–103 105
Loda, Illinois 90–93, 105
Lovejoy, Owen 94, 108
Luther, George B. 32
Luther, John Hood 202, 207
Luther, William 114
LV-3, *Shovelful Shoal* 50, 53, 60
LV-7, *Minot's Ledge* 53, 60
LV-11 54, 60
LV-13, *Succonnessett Shoal* 50, 53, 60
LV-16, *Sandy Hook* 50, 60
LV-E, *Rattlesnake* 53, 60
Lydia 31

Madison, James 61
Main Law 87–89
Marble, George A. 24
Marble, Joseph 54, 197
Marsh, Mary Thomas 150
Marsh Harvester Company 202
Mary and Susan 60
Massachusetts Constitutional Convention 63–64
Massachusetts Great and General Court 64–70, 79–89
Matanzas, Cuba 18, 19